What Works in Probation and Youth Justice

LOAN

What Works in Probation and Youth Justice

Developing evidence-based practice

edited by

Ros Burnett and Colin Roberts

WILLAN
PUBLISHING

Published by

Willan Publishing
Culmcott House
Mill Street, Uffculme
Cullompton, Devon
EX15 3AT, UK
Tel: +44(0)1884 840337
Fax: +44(0)1884 840251
e-mail: info@willanpublishing.co.uk

Published simultaneously in the USA and Canada by

Willan Publishing
c/o ISBS, 920 NE 58th Ave, Suite 300
Portland, Oregon 97213-3644, USA
Tel: +001(0)503 287 3093
Fax: +001(0)503 280 8832
e-mail: info@isbs.com
website: www.isbs.com

First published 2004

ISBN 1-84392-059-X (paperback)

British Library Cataloguing-in-Publication Data
A catalogue record for this book is available from the British Library

Project management by Deer Park Productions, Tavistock
Typeset by GCS, Leighton Buzzard, Beds
Printed and bound by T.J. International, Padstow, Cornwall

Contents

Foreword by Roger Hood   vii
List of abbreviations   ix
Notes on the contributors   xiii

1   The emergence and importance of evidence-based
practice in probation and youth justice   1
Ros Burnett and Colin Roberts

2   Evidence-based practice in the National Probation Service   14
Christine Knott

3   Towards effective practice in the Youth Justice System   29
Cedric Fullwood and Helen Powell

4   Assessment tools in probation: their development and
potential   46
Simon Merrington

5   Is *Asset* really an asset? Assessment of young offenders
in practice   70
Kerry Baker

6   Exploring effective educational interventions for young
people who offend   88
Geoff Hayward, Martin Stephenson and Maggie Blyth

7   Probation interventions to address basic skills and
    employment needs   109
    Ilona Haslewood-Pócsik and Gráinne McMahon

8   Offending behaviour programmes: emerging evidence
    and implications for practice   134
    Colin Roberts

9   Intensive supervision and surveillance programmes for
    young offenders: the evidence base so far   159
    Robin Moore

10 One-to-one ways of promoting desistance: in search of an
    evidence base   180
    Ros Burnett

11 Using community service to encourage inclusive
    citizenship: evidence from the CS pathfinder   198
    Sue Rex and Loraine Gelsthorpe

12 Opportunity, motivation and change: some findings from
    research on resettlement   217
    Peter Raynor

13 Pursuing evidence-based inspection   234
    Rod Morgan

Index   253

Foreword

Roger Hood
Emeritus Professor of Criminology, former Director of the Centre for Criminological Research, University of Oxford

Two highly successful colloquia, bringing together researchers, practitioners and policy makers, were held by the Probation Studies Unit of the Centre for Criminological Research in 1996 and 1998 and the Proceedings were published by the Centre.[1] A third colloquium for a small number of invited participants was held at St Catherine's College, Oxford in July 2003. In what was a stimulating and informative meeting, the papers from this third colloquium were the basis for chapters in this collection edited, appropriately enough, by the former and current head of the Unit. The purpose was to bring to notice the contributions made by the PSU, as well as those who have collaborated with it in the probation and youth justice services and at other universities, to the development of what has become known as the 'what works agenda'. Like so many of the other contributions made over the years by the Oxford Centre, the aim, as the editors emphasise in their introduction, has been to try to establish a reliable and valid evidential basis for the development of penal practices.

The chapters presented here show both how much has been achieved and why so much thinking and research still remains to be done. There has been a danger that the question 'What works?' has been too rapidly transformed into a prescription under the pressures to show that a difference can be made. The contributions to this volume sound just the

---

[1]Burnett, R. (ed.) (1997) *The Probation Service: Responding to Change.* Probation Studies Unit Report No. 3; Faulkner, D. and Gibbs, A. (eds) (1998) *New Politics, New Probation?* Probation Studies Unit Report No. 6, Oxford: Centre for Criminological Research.

right mixture of cautious optimism and healthy scepticism. As penal history has taught us over and over again, there are no panacea, no magic bullets that will solve the problems associated with crime and recidivism. Yet the more we understand these problems the more capable we shall be to respond to them with justice, humanity and rationally based argument.

Department of Sociology
University of Hong Kong
May 2004

List of abbreviations

ABE	Adult Basic Education (Canada)
ACE	Assessment, Case Management and Evaluation
ACOP	Association of Chief Officers of Probation
ACR	Automatic Conditional Release
ACTO	Advisory Council on the Treatment of Offenders
ASBO	Anti-Social Behaviour Order
ASRO	Addressing Substance Related Offending
CCF	Cognitive Centre Foundation
CCO	Community Corrections Officer (Australia)
CDRP	Crime and Disorder Reduction Partnership
CPO	Community Punishment Order
CPRO	Community Punishment and Rehabilitation Order
CRAMS	Case Recording and Management System
CRO	Community Rehabilitation Order
CS	Community Service
CSAP	Correctional Services Accreditation Panel
DAT	Drug Action Team
DCR	Discretionary Conditional Release
DfEE	Department for Education and Employment
DHSS	Department of Health and Social Security
DTO	Detention and Training Order
ECP	Enhanced Community Punishment
EFQM	European Foundation for Quality Model
eOASys	Electronic Offender Assessment System
EPQA	Effective Practice and Quality Assurance
ESI	Effective Supervision Inspection

ESRC	Economic and Social Research Council
ETE	Education, Training and Employment
ETS	Enhanced Thinking Skills
FEFC	Further Education Funding Council
FOR	'Focus on Resettlement'
GED	[6.23] (USA) General Educational Development (USA)
HDC	Home Detention Curfew
HMIP	Her Majesty's Inspectorate of Probation
HMIPP	Her Majesty's Inspectorate of Prison and Probation
HO	Home Office
HR	Human Resources
ICCP	Intensive Change and Control Programme
IMPACT	Intensive Matched Probation and After-Care Treatment
INSET	In-service Training
IP	Intensive Probation
ISSP	Intensive Supervision and Surveillance Programme
IT	Intermediate Treatment
LASCH	Local Authority Secure Children's Home
LEA	Local Education Authority
LGA	Local Government Association
LSI-R	Level of Service Inventory – Revised
MAPPA	Multi-Agency Public Protection Arrangement
NACRO	National Association for the Care and Resettlement of Offenders
NOMS	National Offender Management Service
NPD	National Probation Directorate
NPS	National Probation Service
NVQ	National Vocational Qualification
OASys	Offender Assessment System
OCN	Open College Network
OGRS	Offender Group Reconviction Scale
OI	Offender Index
OPSR	Office of Public Services Reform
PASRO	Prison Addressing Substance Related Offending
PNC	Police National Computer
PO	Probation Officer
PREP	Post-Release Employment Project (USA)
PSA	Public Service Agreement
PSM	Pro-social Modelling
PSO	Probation Service Officer
PSR	Pre-sentence Report

PSU	Probation Studies Unit (Centre for Criminological Research, Oxford University)
PYO	Persistent Young Offender
R&R	Reasoning and Rehabilitation
RCT	Randomised Control Trial
RDSD	Research, Development and Statistics Directorate (Home Office)
ROC	Receiver Operating Characteristic
SDA	Service Delivery Agreement
SKOPE	Skills, Knowledge and Organisational Performance
SNOP	Statement of National Operations and Purpose
SSR	Specific Sentence Reports
STC	Secure Training Centre
STOP	Straight Thinking on Probation
WDYT	'What Do YOU Think?' (self-assessment)
YJB	Youth Justice Board
YOI	Young Offender Institution
YOT	Youth Offending Team

Notes on the contributors

Kerry Baker (MA/DipSW) joined the Centre for Criminological Research and Probation Studies Unit in 1997 and has been closely involved in the design, testing and validation of Asset for the Youth Justice Board since its initial development in 1999. She is currently engaged in ongoing research on *Asset* including an evaluation of its ability to measure change in offenders' lives and the extension of structured risk assessment methods for use with young people at the 'pre-crime' stage.

Maggie Blyth (MA, PGCE) is Head of Practice at the Youth Justice Board. She was the founding YOT Manager of the Oxfordshire Youth Offending Team and previously worked in the Inner London Probation Service and Oxfordshire Probation Service. She managed the National Literacy and Numeracy Strategy for the Youth Justice Board alongside the development of the new Youth Justice National Qualifications Framework, setting standards of effective practice in staff training.

Ros Burnett (DPhil) is a Research Fellow in Criminology at the University of Oxford Centre for Criminological Research and Deputy Head of its Probation Studies Unit. She has a DPhil in social psychology (University of Oxford) and has previous employment experience as a probation officer and a relationship counsellor. Her publications include books and articles on interpersonal relationships, probation practice, youth justice and desistance from crime.

Cedric Fullwood (CBE, MA) was Chief Probation Officer from 1982 to 1998 of Greater Manchester Probation Service, which was the co-host with Hereford and Worcester Probation Service for the What Works Conferences from 1989 to 1998. He has been a Member of the Youth Justice Board since its inception in 1998 and prior to that was a member of the government's Task Force on Youth Justice. He chaired the Penal Affairs Consortium from 2000 to 2003 and has been the chair of Cheshire Probation Board since 2002.

Loraine Gelsthorpe (MPhil, PhD) is a Senior University Lecturer at the Institute of Criminology, University of Cambridge and a Fellow at Pembroke College. Her involvement in the evaluation of the Community Service Pathfinder projects reflects broad interests in the development, nature and operation of community penalties and youth justice. She has taken particular interest in race and gender issues in the conception and delivery of penalties and has published extensively in this and related areas.

Ilona Haslewood-Pócsik (PhD) qualified as a lawyer and lectured in criminal law at Szeged University, Hungary, for five years. Her doctoral thesis (awarded by the University of Leeds) examined the emergence of the public protection agenda and its implications for the Probation Service in England and Wales. She joined the Probation Studies Unit of the Centre for Criminological Research in 1998 since when she has undertaken a number of studies centred around the evaluation of probation practice.

Geoff Hayward (DPhil) is a Lecturer in Education Studies at the University of Oxford and an Associate Director of the ESRC Research Centre on Skills, Knowledge and Organisational Performance (SKOPE). His research interests revolve around vocational education and training, education–work transitions and issues of social inclusion.

Christine Knott (CBE, MA) has an MA in psychology and physiology from Somerville College, Oxford. She trained as a probation officer at University College, Cardiff. She was instrumental in introducing the first Reasoning and Rehabilitation programme in the UK and in commissioning research and Crime Pics to evaluate the work. In 1994, she moved to Greater Manchester as a Deputy Chief and was then promoted to Chief Officer in 1998. In 2003, she was awarded a CBE for her work in Probation, with special reference to her contribution to What Works.

Gráinne McMahon (MSSc) joined the Centre for Criminological Research in August 2000. She worked on the Home Office Basic Skills Pathfinder evaluation project until September 2002 and is currently undertaking research with the Youth Justice Board to determine the most effective means of ensuring that young people in the youth justice system are fully engaged in education, training or employment.

Simon Merrington (MA, MSc) has been an Associate Member of the Probation Studies Unit at the Centre for Criminological Research since 2001. He is a freelance researcher based in Cambridge working in the area of probation and youth justice, with a special interest in assessment and evaluation. Until 1996 he was Research and Information Officer with Cambridgeshire Probation Service.

Robin Moore (MA, PhD) is a Research Officer at the Centre for Criminological Research and Probation Studies Unit. His doctoral thesis (Birmingham University) was on the subject of court fines and he is now the lead researcher on the national evaluation of the ISSP project.

Rod Morgan (PhD) was Her Majesty's Chief Inspector of Probation for England and Wales from 2001 to March 2004 and is now the Chair of the Youth Justice Board. He was previously Professor of Criminal Justice in the Faculty of Law, University of Bristol and remains Professor Emeritus there. He is the author of many books and articles on aspects of criminal justice (including being co-editor of *The Oxford Handbook of Criminology*, 3rd edn, OUP, 2002) and he is an advisor to the Council of Europe and Amnesty International regarding custodial conditions and processes.

Helen Powell (MA) is responsible for managing the Youth Justice Board's research programme. She has worked at the YJB for four years, and previously worked with the States of Jersey police developing a crime strategy for the island. She has a BA (Hons) in Social Science and an MA in Criminology and is currently completing a PhD looking at the effectiveness of crime prevention measures with young people at risk of offending and reoffending.

Peter Raynor (PhD) is Professor of Applied Social Studies in the School of Social Sciences, University of Wales, Swansea. He is a former probation officer and has been involved in probation research for the last 26 years, including studies of probation programmes, pre-sentence reports, risk and need assessment, drug projects, through-care and resettlement, and most recently Black and Asian offenders on probation.

His most recent book is *Understanding Community Penalties* (Open University Press, 2002, with Maurice Vanstone).

Sue Rex (LLB, PhD) is a Senior Research Associate at the Institute of Criminology, University of Cambridge, whose key research interests lie in the areas of sentencing principles and the supervision of offenders in the community. She currently holds a post-doctoral fellowship with the Economic and Social Research Council to conduct a research programme to develop community penalties in theory and practice, an area in which she teaches and presents widely to students and practitioners.

Colin Roberts (MA) is a Fellow of Green College, University Lecturer in Probation Studies and Head of the Probation Studies Unit. He is also a member of the Accreditation Panel of Correctional Services in England and Wales. He has been a leading figure in the development of evidence-based practice in the probation service and, more recently, in youth justice. He has an international reputation as a consultant and expert in this field.

Martin Stephenson (PhD) is Director of Social Inclusion at the Nottingham Trent University. He was previously a board member of the Youth Justice Board and Chief Executive of INCLUDE, a national charity working with children and young people excluded from mainstream education. He was also a senior policy adviser in the DfES leading on the establishment of the National Connexions Service, and has specialist knowledge of prison service education and resettlement and integration policy.

On behalf of the Probation Studies Unit at the Centre for
Criminological Research
we dedicate this volume to the memory of our friend
and staunch supporter
Sir Graham Smith
former Chief Probation Officer of the Inner London Probation
Service and distinguished HM Chief Inspector of Probation

Ros Burnett and Colin Roberts
University of Oxford
May 2004

Chapter 1

The emergence and importance of evidence-based practice in probation and youth justice

Ros Burnett and Colin Roberts

Over thirty years ago, in their classic textbook on criminological issues, Roger Hood and Richard Sparks (1970: 71) observed that, while research into the effectiveness of treatments to prevent recidivism was 'still limited and very rudimentary', the stage was set for considerably more research to extend the knowledge-base over the next few years. The advances made in research methodology at that time were certainly adequate to achieve that task. Yet, in the decades that followed, there were many countervailing influences that limited the amount of research done. Chief among these was the credence given to the precipitous conclusion that 'nothing works', following an early review of research findings (Martinson 1974), thereby shifting research attention away from the question of effectiveness. Changes in legislation and related variations to the official purposes of criminal justice services also intervened, thereby redirecting the research enterprise onto other lines of enquiry. In particular, the rise of the 'just deserts' paradigm led to the development of 'punishments in the community' based on pro-portionate retributive principles, against which questions of the com-parative effectiveness of 'treatments' became irrelevant.

Whether or not probation was an effective means of reducing recidivism, in any case, has not always been central to the work of the Probation Service. At various times in its history more emphasis has been placed on providing help. The specified mission of probation officers for a sustained period of the service's history was to 'advise, assist and befriend' offenders. Later on, concerns that the treatment model was ineffective and led to injustices through disproportionate periods of supervision gave rise to the 'non-treatment paradigm'

(Bottoms and McWilliams 1979), which reframed probation work as a collaboration between the worker and the offender aimed at providing help with problems defined by the offender. In youth justice, the main responsibility prior to the reforms following the Crime and Disorder Act 1998, was to look after the welfare of children and young people who had come into conflict with the law.

When, for the first time, the Probation Service was given an official Statement of National Operations and Purpose (SNOP) (Home Office 1984), it marked the beginning of a sustained period of review and readjustment in which the service was required to be more accountable and to provide evidence of its effectiveness. Questions about the value and achievements of the service came from both outside and within. A report by the Audit Commission (1990) called into question the cost-effectiveness of the service. In his address to the 1991 conference of the Association of Chief Officers of Probation (ACOP), Cedric Fullwood (1992) challenged probation managers to open up the variety of approaches in probation to evaluative scrutiny. Yet studies of the reoffending rates following community and custodial penalties have generally shown very little difference between the outcomes, even after taking into account differences in the types of offenders and their criminal histories (Lloyd et al. 1994). Even the most committed and ardent supporters of the probation service had little by way of concrete evidence to support their advocacy.

It was not until the mid-1990s that the advance in accumulating evidence of effective practice, as had been envisaged by Hood and Sparks, was 'back on course'. Following the 'nothing works' era and the corresponding shift in the ethos and purpose of probation away from rehabilitation towards surveillance and control (Garland 1997), optimism in the effectiveness of community interventions was re-kindled, initially among probation service managers. The factors that lay behind this were: the emergence of some encouraging reviews of research, particularly through the use of the new technique of meta-analysis leading to findings that contradicted previous negative evidence of effectiveness; and the modernisation agenda and new public management, with its emphasis on providing hard evidence of 'value for money' and efficient use of resources (Raynor and Vanstone 2002). Several influential reviews which employed meta-analysis showed that some interventions have had a small but statistically significant effect (e.g. Andrews et al. 1990; McGuire 1995). Such research also indicated the importance of process and implementation in achieving positive outcomes (for example, programmes must be appropriately targeted and systematically delivered) and provided the basis for the formulation of effective practice principles and criteria.

In the UK, the renewed commitment to rehabilitative work with offenders was reflected in an annual series of What Works conferences beginning in 1991 which were initiated by two probation services, as well as a series of ACOP conferences. Although most of the research that inspired the What Works movement originated in Canada and North America, there were isolated, well-designed studies in England and Wales (see, in particular, Roberts 1992; Raynor and Vanstone 1997) that attracted attention as rare examples of evidence in this country that some interventions might be associated, at least in the short term, with lower reconviction rates than was the case for comparison groups.

A collaborative study between Warwickshire Probation Service and the Probation Studies Unit at the University of Oxford (Roberts et al. 1996) demonstrated the feasibility of a systematic assessment procedures (known as ACE) that was linked to case-management and integral evaluation by practitioners. Under the leadership of Graham (later Sir Graham) Smith, the Probation Inspectorate commissioned a comprehensive survey of probation practice which found that systematic evaluations, of sufficient rigour to provide convincing evidence of effectiveness, had only been undertaken in four of the 267 programmes (Underdown 1998). The incoming New Labour government in 1997, in conformity to its commitment to evidence-based public policy, launched the *Effective Practice Initiative* (Home Office 1998). The *Crime Reduction Programme* invested in a series of 'pathfinders' to identify best practice and methods for reducing offending and protecting the public, and seminal reviews of the What Works literature by academics and Home Office researchers (see McGuire 1995; Vennard et al. 1997; Goldblatt and Lewis 1998) were widely read. The Home Office also published *Evidence Based Practice: A Guide to Effective Practice* to provide practical assistance and guidance to practitioners (Chapman and Hough 1998), as well as a What Works strategy document (Home Office 2000).

One of the main messages of the What Works meta-analytical reviews was that cognitive-behavioural approaches were generally associated with lower reconviction rates in comparison with the reconviction rates related to other methods. Not surprisingly, therefore, both the Prison Service and the National Probation Service have invested considerably in the development and implementation of cognitive-behavioural approaches (see Social Exclusion Unit 2002). Critics have argued that the wide-scale implementation of such programmes was too swift and exclusive, and that a focus on changing reasoning and thinking patterns should be matched by a focus on environmental and social factors linked to offending (Merrington and Stanley 2000; Mair 2004). Such judgements are now less valid because the National Probation Service has continued to expand its pathfinder programme and the curriculum has included, for example, basic skills, employment, community punishment and 'approved premises' (formerly, probation and bail hostels). Indeed, while evidence of effectiveness remains patchy, the service deserves credit for taking part in a significant enterprise, and it is appropriate to acknowledge the considerable advances that have been made:

> From being unable in 1997 to point to more than a handful of evaluated effective initiatives, the probation service has been transformed within a few years into an organisation able to offer quality-controlled programmes throughout England and Wales, in what is believed to be the largest initiative in evidence-based corrections to be undertaken anywhere in the world. (Raynor and Vanstone 2002: 95)

Like the Probation Service, the youth justice service has been overhauled, resulting in an intensified focus on its role in preventing offending by young people and in reducing recidivism. A corresponding period of challenge and change in the youth justice service occurred in the 1990s, when the Audit Commission's (1996) review *Misspent Youth* and subsequent government policy documents led to the Crime and Disorder Act 1998 and a radically reformed Youth Justice System. One of the central tenets running through the reconstituted youth justice is that the effectiveness of interventions must be monitored and evaluated.

Sharing progress in probation and youth justice

A glance through the literature on probation work and youth justice services suggests that the two domains, especially from a managerial perspective, often seem to coexist separately despite their parallel endeavours in establishing policies and practices that are based on rigorous research and evaluation. Just as the Prison Service and Probation Service are now poised to be integrated (Carter 2004; Home Office 2004), there is a need for youth justice services to be appropriately linked with evidence-based services for adult offenders. Indeed, this is recognised in the strategy document for the National Probation Service, *A New Choreography*, which referred to its role in providing services for young people, either directly or in partnership, and stated its intentions to 'strengthen the relationship with the Youth Justice Board and apply the lessons from the evidence-based practice to young adult offenders' (NPS 2001). Both services obviously need to work together in providing continuity of service for young people on the cusp of the age divide and as they progress from the age group served by youth justice to the older age bracket when they become the responsibility of the Probation Service.

There may be much for the National Offender Management Service (NOMS) to learn from the Youth Justice System in current developments to strengthen and merge the Probation and Prison Services. While the latter two services have made exemplary progress in their implementation of evidence-based interventions, it is the reformed youth justice system that has led the way in providing inter-agency services (Burnett and Appleton 2004) and in developing restorative justice approaches (Crawford and Newburn 2003).

A major aim of this volume has therefore been to bring together perspectives on developments in both probation and youth justice. The chapters are based on papers that were presented at a colloquium, *Towards Evidence-Based Practice in Probation and Youth Justice,* held from 31 July to 1 August 2003 at St Catherine's College, Oxford. The colloquium was the latest in a series of activities and events arranged by the Probation Studies Unit (PSU) of the Centre for Criminological Research at the University of Oxford. The PSU was set up in 1996 with the main goal of carrying out research into the effectiveness of different practices and probation's role within the criminal justice system. The Unit has worked closely with senior members and policy staff of the Probation Service and the Youth Justice Board (YJB), as well as with Probation Areas and Youth Offending Teams, in the introduction and evaluation of evidence-based practice. It has collaborated with other departments in the University of Oxford (notably Education; Psychiatry; Economics and Statistics) and has worked in conjunction with researchers in other universities, including the Institute of Criminology at Cambridge and the University of Wales (Swansea), in carrying out its programme of work. The colloquium and its outcome in this volume provide an opportunity to share the findings from some of that body of work.

In some cases, therefore, the chapters refer to 'work in progress', or to the findings of completed projects that have not been officially released. The projects discussed are associated with significant changes and exciting developments in probation and youth justice and it is important that the lessons and insights drawn from them are shared with all parties in the evidence-based community. A complaint made by some practice managers attending the conference and referred to by Christine Knott in her chapter is that it generally takes too long for research findings to be communicated to those who are affected by it. We agree with this assessment. Admittedly, some of the responsibility for delays lies in the research process which is necessarily extended by stages of data collection and analysis and the allowance of sufficient time for interventions to have an effect and for change to be observed. But long delays, sometimes unfathomable, can also occur between the time when research reports are submitted to funding organisations and the time when findings are released. The collaboration of Home Office and YJB officials in this volume effectively serves as an endorsement of the view that it is sometimes useful to share preliminary findings rather than suspending all feedback until the final outcomes are known. We welcome the opportunity, through the medium of this volume, to disseminate this body of work to open up the findings and their implications for wider debate.

We have organised the contributions to this volume, where possible, into pairs of chapters. One in each pair deals with an issue largely related to probation services while the other pertains more to youth justice services. Of course, and as our purpose requires, there is often some overlap. The first pair of chapters presents an overview of progress in implementing effective practice agendas in each service from the perspective of managers in both services.

The key developments in the Probation Service, transforming it into an evidence-based service, are traced by Christine Knott in her chapter. The Underdown report (Underdown 1998), referred to above, opened eyes within the service to the inadequacy of internal evaluation practices and the paucity of evidence available to substantiate claims of effectiveness, and led to the introduction of the *Effective Practice Initiative*. As Knott indicates, the amalgamation of hitherto disjointed local services into a single National Probation Service in 2001 served as a turning point because it facilitated a coordinated approach. She identifies the various building blocks and continuing initiatives that are required to increase the effectiveness of practice, and provides insight into the scale of change and challenges involved for members of the probation service, and the problematic issues still to be resolved. Some of these difficulties, she suggests, may be partly attributed to the rapid pace at which pathfinder programmes have had to be adopted and implemented.

Cedric Fullwood and Helen Powell outline the YJB's strategy for developing effective practice to reduce reoffending by young people. The extent of the YJB's commitment to research and evidence-based practice is made clear in the range of achievements they describe. The Board has promoted the use of electronic information systems and collects data from Youth Offending Teams (YOTs) on a quarterly basis so as to build up a database on children and young people and interventions. When the YOTs were first formed in 2000, the YJB funded an extensive programme of development and evaluation to identify effective interventions and best practice. These initiatives were supported by training provision, national standards, a series of guidance notes and quality assurance procedures including a performance target system. The YJB has not placed the same emphasis on accredited programmes as the NPS, but instead has adopted a broader framework to reflect a multi-modal approach. The most recent Audit Commission Report, *Youth Justice 2004*, concludes that 'the new system is a considerable improvement on the old one' (2004: 12), but it also identifies areas where 'more could be done' and in its recommendations refers to the importance of examining the effectiveness of new interventions, particularly those for persistent young offenders.

A vital element of evidence-based practice has been the development and accepted usage of systematic assessment tools as is charted in the next pair of chapters. Simon Merrington explains the evolution and use of assessment tools in probation, and Kerry Baker describes the development of the assessment tool for youth justice. This tool, *Asset*, was designed, pre-tested and validated by Kerry Baker and Colin Roberts, and followed the earlier developmental work done in the PSU on ACE. Both review the implications of these tools for many aspects of service delivery and improvement, including appropriate targeting of services, prediction of risk, measurement and review of progress, case management decisions and collection of data on effectiveness.

The extent to which the Home Office crime reduction programme invested in cognitive behavioural programmes – a policy which has been questioned both from within its ranks (Gorman 2001) and outside (Merrington and Stanley 2000; Ellis and Winstone 2002; Mair 2004) – is evident in Colin Roberts's detailed review of programmes in prisons and in adult probation services and their evaluation. The early positive results from the first prison evaluation have not been subsequently replicated and the latest studies show no substantial benefits from offending behaviour programmes alone. In the retrospective and prospective studies of the Think First programme (the most commonly used programme in probation) evidence of high levels of attrition have severely limited the chances of the programme having a significant impact on reconviction rates. Evidence in the prospective study shows the equal importance of good case management, meeting the social needs of offenders (e.g. employment, accommodation, drug treatment) and engaging their motivation.

One of the distinctive aspects of the YJB's approach drawn out by Fullwood and Powell was its early investment in intensive community interventions for more persistent offenders or those who have committed offences of a more serious nature. The Intensive Supervision and Surveillance Programme (ISSP) has been the subject, appropriately enough, of an intensive and detailed evaluation covering 41 areas. The Probation Service is now piloting a similar programme for adults, the Intensive Change and Control Programme (ICCP). In Chapter 9, Robin Moore surveys previous research into and evaluations of intensive approaches and explains the approach that has been taken in evaluating ISSP in the major research programme currently underway in the Oxford PSU.

Education, Training and Employment (ETE) is another area of intervention in which substantial inroads are being made in both probation and youth justice. Geoff Hayward, Martin Stephenson and Maggie Blyth (Chapter 6) provide a challenging discussion of the evidence basis for the YJB's vision of integrated educational provision and youth justice services. In a complementary chapter discussing the development of basic skills interventions in the probation service, Ilona Haslewood-Pócsik and Gráinne McMahon (Chapter 7) bring together the accounts of progress in the *Basic Skills Pathfinder* and in the *Employment Pathfinder.* Both of these programmes, financed by the Home Office Crime Reduction Programme, were impeded by the perennial problems of attrition (offenders do not attend or do not complete programmes) and 'delivery failure' (while the interventions may be valid, they fail because they were not delivered as intended). While the results have been disappointing it is valuable to share these experiences which exemplify problems that need to be tackled in order to make best use of resources whatever the nature of the intervention.

As pointed out by Christine Knott, the What Works Strategy in 2000 emphasised the importance of 'case management' in addition to group work programmes – a development that she welcomes. From her inside perspective in the probation service, Knott acknowledges a crisis of confidence among probation officers but anticipates that this will be resolved as the case management role comes increasingly to include a renewed focus on casework skills. It is this area of practice that is the focus of Ros Burnett's discussion of one-to-one work with offenders (Chapter 10). Like many other contributors to this volume Burnett addresses the importance of the relationship between offenders and those who work with them to assist their desistance from crime. She identifies interpersonal processes as the common element underpinning voluntary befriending or mentoring work and skilled motivational interviewing but argues that more research is needed to investigate how these processes lead to changes in behaviour.

Sue Rex and Loraine Gelsthorpe (Chapter 11) discuss the constructive thinking behind the *Community Service Pathfinder* (Rex et al. 2004). Although community service was renamed as 'punishment', its inclusion in the Crime Reduction Programme reflected an emphasis on its rehabilitative potential rather than punitive aspects, and, likewise, the evaluation of its implementation and effectiveness has focused on it as an opportunity for offenders to learn responsible behaviour, to gain skills and to make a contribution to society. Key elements of the projects were the use by supervisors of pro-social modelling and offenders' acquisition of employment skills. With reference to plans for Enhanced Community Punishment they conclude that the best potential of community service lies in these reintegrative aspects, especially if sentencers and programme developers have regard, in their decision-making, to cultural and social diversity.

Peter Raynor (Chapter 12) discusses the findings and implications of another of the Probation Service Pathfinder projects, the Resettlement Pathfinder, aimed at evaluating services for short-sentence prisoners who are not subject to statutory supervision following their release – that is, ex-prisoners who at one time would, as a matter of course, been offered 'voluntary after-care' by the Probation Service. There were variations in the approaches of the seven projects evaluated, allowing a comparative research design. In an intriguing analysis of different approaches to resettlement and their relationship to alternative implicit theories of desistance from crime, Professor Raynor found that 'probation-led' projects, which were more focused on developing motivation and problem-solving skills, produced consistently better results than the 'voluntary-organisation-led' projects, which focused on 'welfare' problems. Raynor suggests that the latter services reflect an 'opportunity deficit' model, that sees offenders as victims of their deprived circumstances and therefore concentrate on providing resources and opportunities. In contrast, the probation-led projects are informed by an 'offender's responsibility' model that sees offenders as capable of desisting from crime and able to choose between alternative responses to their circumstances. The implication is that resettlement services, and community interventions more generally, will be most effective when they provide both opportunities to change (their) offenders' life courses and programmes to address thinking and motivation.

An underlying assumption of the present volume – and indeed of evidence-based practice – is that there should be close integration between the research agenda and the development and monitoring of what is now to be called 'offender management services'. Inspection of services is also implicated in this interrelationship. In an analysis of what is involved in evidence-based inspection, Rod Morgan (Chapter 13) refers to a 'symbiotic relationship between what an inspectorate does and the performance management capacity of the service it inspects'. In his capacity as the Chief Inspector of Probation when writing his chapter, though soon to be Chairman of the Youth Justice Board, Professor Morgan provides an illuminating account of what evidence-based inspection should entail.

Where next? The challenges and limits of evidence-based practice

Measuring their progress by the performance indicators that have been set for them, both the NPS and the YJB have cause for some satisfaction in the progress that they have made. The What Works movement in the UK has provided many countries, including the new democracies in Eastern Europe, with the impetus to make similar transformations to their own services (van Kalmthout et al. 2003). Yet the need for additional research to support the development of evidence-based practice must also be acknowledged.

Leading experts in the field of correctional interventions have cautioned that, although clear trends have emerged from meta-analytical reviews, summaries of findings and effective practice principles should not be confused with an assumption that we have definitive answers to the question: 'what works?' While much progress has been made, there is a requirement for further methodologically well-founded studies to investigate the effects of specific types of pro-grammes for different categories of offenders in varying contexts and stages (Lösel 2001; McGuire 2002). Indeed, similar proposals were made by Roger Hood nearly 40 years ago when he wrote that 'research must be a continuous process of evaluation and re-evaluation' to take account of changes in the form and use of sanctions, and to investigate the interaction effects between types of treatment and types of offenders (Hood 1967).

The development of evidence-based practice in probation and youth justice should build on the experience and achievements in this field. Nutley and Davies have identified the following as being among the strengths of evaluation research in criminal justice, worth noting by other public services (1999: 52–3):

- an established research culture in criminology which uses a plurality of approaches;

- an interest in theory and a desire to understand the causal linkages;

- a commitment on the part of many staff to evaluate the effectiveness of their practice;

- the encouragement of discussion and provision of advice by professional bodies such as the Association of the Chief Officers of Probation.

Nutley and Davies also noted the danger of interpreting evidence-based practice as implementing a set of principles rather than as a continuing interrelationship between research and practice. Those who have been critical of the wholesale and quick-fire way in which both the NPS and the YJB have rolled out programmes across services, prior to the availability of more definitive research findings, will find some reassurance in the prudent approach advocated in *Managing Offenders – Reducing Crime* (Carter 2004). This influential report distinguishes short-term goals from medium-term goals, recommending that expensive decisions should be deferred until further evidence is available. Clearly this should not be read as a prompt for inaction or a return to the unsystematic eclecticism that was prevalent in practice even as recently as the mid-1990s (Burnett 1996). However, it does underline the fact that we are not at the end of the journey in the quest to find out what works in achieving the goals and targets that have been set for Probation, Prison and Youth Justice Services. The question mark after What Works is now usually omitted, but many of the answers remain to be investigated. While there is now a rapid accumulation of understanding and knowledge in this field, choosing and implementing interventions in a changing social and political landscape will have to be the subject of continual enquiry.

References

Andrews, D.A., Zinger, I., Hoge, R.D. et al. (1990) 'Does correctional treatment work? A clinically relevant and psychologically informed meta-analysis', *Criminology*, 28, 369–404.

Audit Commission (1996) *Misspent Youth: Young People and Crime*. London: Audit Commission.

Audit Commission (2004) *Youth Justice 2004*. London: Audit Commission.

Bottoms, A.E. and McWilliams, W. (1979) 'A non-treatment paradigm for probation practice', *British Journal of Social Work*, 9, 159–202.

Burnett, R. (1996) *Fitting Supervision to Offenders: Assessment and Allocation in the Probation Service*, Home Office Research Study 153. London: Home Office Research and Statistics Directorate.

Burnett, R. and Appleton, C. (2004) 'Joined-up services to tackle youth crime: a case study in England', *British Journal of Criminology*, 44 (1), 34–54.

Carter, P. (2004) *Managing Offenders, Reducing Crime* (The Carter Report). London: Home Office. Available at: www.homeoffice.gov.uk/new.asp.

Chapman, T. and Hough, M. (1998) *Evidence-Based Practice: A Guide to Effective Practice*. London: Home Office.

Crawford, A. and Newburn, T. (2003) *Youth Offending and Restorative Justice*. Cullompton: Willan.

Ellis, T. and Winstone, J. (2002) 'The policy impact of a survey of programme evaluations in England and Wales', in J. McGuire (ed.), *Offender Rehabilitation and Treatment: Effective Programmes and Policies to Reduce Re-offending*. Chichester: Wiley.

Garland, D. (1997) 'Probation and the reconfiguration of crime control', in R. Burnett (ed.), *The Probation Service: Responding to Change*. Oxford: Centre for Criminological Research, pp. 2–10.

Gorman, K. (2001) 'Cognitive behaviouralism and the Holy Grail: the quest for a universal means of managing offender risk', *Probation Journal*, 48 (1), 3–9.

Home Office (1984) *Probation Service in England and Wales: Statement of National Objectives and Priorities*. London: Home Office.

Home Office (1998) *Effective Practice Initiative: National Implementation Plan for the Supervision of Offenders*, Probation Circular 35/1998. London: HMSO.

Home Office (2000) *What Works Strategy for the Probation Service*, Probation Circular 60/2000. London: Home Office.

Home Office (2004) *Reducing Crime, Changing Lives: The Government's Plans for Transforming the Management of Offenders*. London: Home Office. Available at: www.homeoffice.gov.uk/new.asp.

Hood, R. (1967) 'Research on the effectiveness of punishments and treatments', in Council of Europe, *Collected Studies in Criminological Research*, Vol. 1. Strasbourg: Council of Europe Press.

Hood, R. and Sparks, R. (1970) *Key Issues in Criminology*. London: Weidenfeld & Nicolson.

Lloyd, C., Mair, G. and Hough, M. (1994) *Explaining Reconviction Rates: a Critical Analysis*, Home Office Research Study 136. London: HMSO.

Lösel, F. (2001) 'Evaluating the effectiveness of correctional treatment: a review and synthesis of meta-evaluations', in G.A. Bernfeld, D.P. Farrington and A.W. Leschied (eds.), *Offender Rehabilitation in Practice: Implementing and Evaluating Effective Programs*. Chichester: John Wiley & Sons.

McGuire, J. (ed.) (1995) *What Works: Reducing Re-offending: Guidelines from Research and Practice*. Chichester: Wiley.

McGuire, J. (2002), 'Integrating findings from research reviews', in J. McGuire (ed.), *Offender Rehabilitation and Treatment: Effective Programmes and Policies to Reduce Re-offending*. Chichester: Wiley.

Mair, G. (2004) 'The origins of What Works in England and Wales: a house built on sand?', in G. Mair (ed.), *What Matters in Probation*. Cullompton: Willan.

Martinson, R. (1974) 'What works? Questions and answers about prison reform', *The Public Interest*, 35, 22–54.

Merrington, S. and Stanley, S. (2000) 'Doubts about the what works initiative', *Probation Journal*, 47 (4) 272–5.

National Probation Directorate (2001) *A New Choreography: An Integrated Strategy for the National Probation Service for England and Wales*. London: Home Office.

Nutley, S.M. and Davies, H.T.O. (1999) 'The fall and rise of evidence in criminal justice', *Public Money and Management*, January–March, 47–54.

Raynor, P. and Vanstone, M. (1997) *Straight Thinking on Probation (STOP): The Mid-Glamorgan Experiment*, Probation Studies Unit Report 4. Oxford: Centre for Criminological Research.

Raynor, P. and Vanstone, M. (2002) *Understanding Community Penalties: Probation, Policy and Social Change*. Buckingham: Open University Press.

Rex, S., Gelsthorpe, L., Roberts, C. and Jordan, P. (2004) *What's Promising in Community Service: Implementation of 7 Pathfinder Projects*, Home Office Findings 231. London: Home Office.

Roberts, C. (1992) 'What works: using social work methods to reduce reoffending in serious and persistent offenders', *Proceedings of the ACOP Conference, York 1991*. Wakefield: ACOP.

Roberts, C. (1996) 'Effective practice and service delivery', in J. McGuire (ed.), *What Works: Reducing Reoffending*. Chichester: Wiley, pp. 221–36.

Roberts, C., Burnett, R., Kirby, A. and Hamill, H. (1996) *A System for Evaluating Probation Practice: A Method Devised and Piloted by the Oxford Probation Studies Unit and Warwickshire Probation Service*, Probation Studies Unit Report 1. Oxford: Centre for Criminological Research.

Social Exclusion Unit (2002) *Reducing Re-offending by Ex-prisoners*. London: Social Exclusion Unit.

van Kalmthout, A., Roberts, J. and Vinding, S. (eds) (2003) *Probation and Probation Service in the EU Accession Countries*. Utrecht, The Netherlands: Wolf Legal Publishers.

Vennard, J., Sugg, D. and Hedderman, C. (1997) *Changing Offenders' Attitudes and Behaviour: What Works?*, Home Office Research Study 171. London: Home Office.

Underdown, A. (1998) *Strategies for Effective Supervision: Report of the HMIP What Works Project*. London: Home Office.

Chapter 2

Evidence-based practice in the National Probation Service

Christine Knott

The National Probation Service for England and Wales was created by statute in April 2001. The legislation brought together the previously independent 54 Probation Areas to a form a National Probation Service with 42 Probation Areas. For the first time, in probation history, there was the opportunity for coordinated national strategies at both policy and operational level. At the same time, the new service was set the challenging target of achieving a 5 per cent reduction in reoffending for those under its supervision by the year 2005. Prior to April 2001, there had been a number of strategic initiatives in relation to What Works, or 'Effective Practice', led by the late Sir Graham Smith in his time as Chief Inspector of Probation.

This was set against a background of evidence which showed that the Probation Service had made no impact on reoffending rates for the last twenty years. Despite a range of different initiatives, reoffending rates had remained at about 56 per cent. The Probation Service was not alone in this; a similar picture exists for the Prison Service.

The Effective Practice Initiative

Sir Graham Smith commissioned a survey to assess the extent of effective practice initiatives across the Probation Services for England and Wales and to review 'What Works' developments (Underdown 1998). The survey, known as 'The Underdown Report' after its author, found that there were 210 different programmes running in 54 Probation Areas, mostly developed by practitioners, and that only eleven were able to show any evidence of effectiveness. That is not to say that the remaining 199 were ineffective, but that the overwhelming majority had not been evaluated and therefore it was impossible to reach any conclusion as to their value in reducing reoffending. Availability of programmes across the whole of England and Wales was inconsistent and patchy; in some areas offenders were having to wait a long time for programmes and in others programmes were not available at all. In effect, the Probation Service was unwittingly operating a system of 'justice by geography'. This was unacceptable to Sir Graham Smith and was certainly a situation which needed to be rectified by the new National Probation Service.

This led to the launch of the Effective Practice Initiative. This was first set out in June 1998 in a Probation Circular (Home Office 1998), which set some standards and expectations. All offenders were to be supervised according to effective practice principles which had been set out in Andrew Underdown's report (see Table 2.1).

Pathfinder projects were to be set up in Probation Areas that already had some experience of working to effective practice principles. Three programmes were designated as pathfinders: a programme for sex offenders, a programme for women offenders and what is now known as Think First, a generic cognitive skills programme. The Home Office was to set up a Joint Accreditation Panel with Sir Duncan Nichol as the Chair. This panel would oversee and accredit the development of effective practice programmes for both prisons and probation. The panel would ensure that programmes met international standards and were evaluated for their impact on further offending. The circular also announced the development of a joint assessment tool, evidence based, that would be used by both the Probation and the Prison Services in England and Wales. This was to be known as OASys (Offender

Table 2.1 Effective practice principles

- Practice based on evidence
- Use design methods
- Commit to learn and develop practice
- Work for quality and consistency
- Commit to evaluate
- Use cognitive and behavioural perspectives
- Engage offenders in a change process
- Develop personal and social responsibility
- Work for community integration
- Emphasise staff's personal impact

Assessment System) and would ensure that offenders were assessed according to the same criteria, irrespective of where they lived or who was their probation officer.

In July 1999, there was a further announcement that the Home Office Probation Unit had been successful in obtaining funding from the Crime Reduction Programme to develop pathfinder programmes for a range of different offenders. This was to include, among others, general offending behaviour programmes, programmes for domestic violence offenders, sex offenders and substance misuse. In addition, Community Service, now known as Community Punishment, was to develop a pathfinder to integrate effective practice principles (Enhanced Community Punishment or ECP). There were also to be pathfinders for short-term prisoners and basic skills. The evaluations of some of these pathfinders are published elsewhere in this book.

The What Works Strategy 2000

While attempts had been made to develop the effective practice initiative in a strategic way, this had never been communicated as such. It was clear that there was a need for a more holistic strategic approach which would ensure that *all* aspects of the Effective Practice Principles were integrated into probation practice and to restate that the emphasis was not just on group work programmes. Probation Circular 60/2000 (Home Office 2000) was issued which set the scene for a raft of other developments (see Figure 2.1).

Case management	Offending behaviour	Accredited Community Punishment
• Supervision planning • Structured assessment • Targeting • Motivation • Reinforcement • Application • Compliance • Enforcement • Surveillance • Evaluation	•Cognitive skills foundation •Offence or risk specific **Associated personal factors** •Substance misuse •Mental health •Relationship problems **Reintegration factors** •Accommodation •Basic skills •Employment •Budgeting/debt counselling	•Pro-social modelling •Targeted placements to reinforce programme learning •Accredited skill development

Figure 2.1 The What Works strategy for the Probation Service.

This included an emphasis on case management, which has proved to be an essential component of any successful work with offenders (Kemshall and Canton 2002) and accredited programmes, offending behaviour programmes, some offence-specific, some offending-specific, e.g. substance misuse. The strategy reinforced the role of social reintegration, perhaps now better known as 'social inclusion', in reducing reoffending and identified the development of initiatives to improve the basic skills and employability of offenders. Finally there was a role for Community Punishment and further advice on the Enhanced Community Punishment programme.

The creation of the National Probation Service was already underway by the time this circular was issued and there was much emphasis on the need to continue to demonstrate improvements in effectiveness, while at the same time the centre and Probation Services, some more than others, were subject to massive structural change. In London alone, five previously independent probation services were being merged into one single Probation Area to cover the whole of Greater London. This new area is now responsible for some 20 per cent of the work of the National Probation Service as a whole.

Progress to date

OASys

The development of OASys, the Offender Assessment System, has been a critical component of the What Works agenda. Prior to its introduction, there were a variety of different assessment tools in use, some very effective, others less so (Raynor et al. 2000), but there was no accepted consistency of assessment, particularly when assessing risk of harm and risk of reoffending. The intention was that OASys would be used across all Probation Areas and prisons in England and Wales. At the time of writing (January 2004), all Probation Areas are using OASys and it has been introduced into many prisons. OASys is a comprehensive assessment tool which covers risk of reconviction, risk of harm and criminogenic needs. It also triggers in-depth assessments where they are necessary. The assessment leads into the supervision or sentence plan which is then reviewed on a regular basis. OASys is a very thorough assessment tool and is therefore time consuming. The time factor has been an area of concern for some probation staff, but feedback suggests that most probation staff see it as an effective and useful assessment tool.

Only some Probation Areas are currently using an electronic version of OASys and when this is fully available, expected in 2004, it will enable the automatic collection and aggregation of data about the reasons why people offend and the levels of risk that they present to the public. The recording of dynamic risk factors will also allow for the assessment of change during the course of a community or custodial sentence. This will provide additional evidence for the effectiveness or otherwise of work that is undertaken with offenders, on an individual level where offenders can see their own improvements and on an aggregate level where workers and their organisations can have an overview of progress.

Cognitive behavioural programmes

By the middle of 2003, 13 offending behaviour programmes had been accredited by the Joint Accreditation Panel. These have included general offending behaviour programmes such as Think First, substance misuse programmes such as Addressing Substance Related Offending (ASRO) and its equivalent for prisons Prison Addressing Substance Related Offending (PASRO), a women's acquisitive crime programme, sex offender programmes, violent offender programmes and drink-driver programmes. The portfolio is set to grow with hate crime and domestic violence offender programmes already in the pipeline. The choice of programmes in any one Probation Area is subject to local determination, so there is still the danger of 'justice by geography'. This is often dependent on offender need. Smaller Probation Areas may struggle with only small numbers of offenders who would fit certain criteria, for example sex offenders, resulting in lengthy waiting times for offenders to start a group work programme. In larger areas, the throughput may be significant, but the demand may exceed capacity and resources and therefore waiting times may accrue. There are unacceptably high levels of attrition from the making of a community order to the completion of an accredited programme and there is a real need for much more information to understand and then improve on this situation.

Currently there is little integration between prison and probation programmes, although in Greater Manchester there has been some experimentation with running the substance misuse programmes (ASRO and PASRO) 'through the prison gate', the intention being that offenders complete some modules while in custody and the rest in the community. Under current legislation, with only offenders subject to custodial sentences of over 12 months being released on licence, most of the medium-risk offenders who would meet the suitability requirements for these programmes do not get referred because their licences are too short. Running programmes 'through the gate' would mean that far more offenders could be referred. The recent Correctional Services Review (Carter 2004) proposes a much more integrated approach to delivery of all interventions, irrespective of whether the offender is in custody or the community, and it is to be hoped that there will be the scope for further developments in this work in the months to come.

Social reintegration and partnerships

The What Works agenda has always included a heavy emphasis on social reintegration as an essential component of the supervision of offenders. The cognitive skills programme will help the offenders to improve their thinking skills, but this is of little use if they remain homeless or lack a basic level of education necessary to put that new thinking into practice. Stephen Farrall's (2002) research identified that offenders performed better on supervision, when there was an improvement in what he called their 'social capital', thereby improving their ability to become a useful member of society. This therefore needed to be the next stage of the evidence-based practice initiative. This included a range of practical interventions.

Basic skills

There is a mass of evidence to suggest that most offenders have very limited basic skills. Many have dropped out of the education system, often because of their own unruly behaviour. They lack the reading and writing ability to complete an average application form and are therefore unlikely to ever get access to anything other than the manual labour market. The drive to improve the basic skills of all offenders has led to partnerships with the Learning and Skills Councils at local and national level, with £30 million being made available for offender education in 2003/04. Now both Probation and the Learning and Skills Council have targets to improve the basic skills levels of offenders, and in Greater Manchester offenders have shown themselves capable of passing GCSEs much to everyone's delight.

Employment

There is a close correlation between reducing reoffending and employment (see for example, Downes 1998; and Chapter 7, this volume). Here the picture has been similar to that of basic skills, only in this instance the agency with responsibility is Job Centre Plus. At a national level, Job Centre Plus has been set targets to improve the employability of 'hard to reach' groups. The Probation Service has been able to provide ready access to such groups and in many Probation Areas, including my own (Greater Manchester), Job Centre Plus has been able to locate staff in Probation offices, which has proved to be very effective in increasing referrals and helping offenders into work.

Drug treatment

There is a very close link between drug use and offending. Indeed I would argue that, for all but the very rich, it is impossible to maintain a drug habit and not offend, whether that be by dealing themselves, prostitution or burglary and shoplifting. At a local level, Probation Areas have entered into partnerships with local DATs (Drug Action Teams) to ensure that offenders who misuse drugs have access to treatment. Again the availability and types of treatment vary across the country, with some DATs able to offer access to treatment within 24 hours for all who need it, and some can only offer this for at-risk groups, e.g. released prisoners, whereas for other DATs this remains an aspiration. The Drug Treatment and Testing Order is now available across the country and early results from the pilot areas demonstrated some significant success in reducing drug use and reoffending (Turnbull et al. 2000). Treatment funding is provided to the DATs and Probation Areas work closely with DAT coordinators to identify needs and jointly commission treatment.

Accommodation

This is a key area which is an essential part of social reintegration. It does not take much imagination to realise how difficult it is to lead an offence-free life if you are homeless or living in inadequate accommodation. Again, the Probation Service has needed to enter into partnerships with local people, supporting initiatives to ensure that offenders are also recognised as a 'needy' group. This is not always a popular message and it is understandable that offenders appear to be an undeserving group. However, the report of the Social Exclusion Unit (2002) has recognised the need to have an effective accommodation strategy for offenders. In addition, the Probation Service operates a number of probation hostels, now known as 'approved premises', which provide accommodation and supervision for offenders, often at risk and recently released from lengthy prison sentences. The effective practice initiative includes a pathfinder regime for approved premises, based on the principles of 'pro-social modelling' (National Probation Service 2002). A hostel in Greater Manchester is one of the pathfinders for this and staff are very positive about the initiative and looking forward to seeing the impact of their work.

Victims and public protection

Victims remain at the heart of every aspect of probation practice, but nowhere is it more important or more critical than our work with dangerous and high-risk offenders. Whatever the public view may be, there are only a few prisoners in the system for whom 'life' means life. Most will be released at some time during their sentences, often on very long licences, enabling the Probation Service to monitor their behaviour and impose sanctions should there be any indication of a breakdown (Appleton and Roberts 2003). The Multi-Agency Public Protection Panels, established by statute in 2001 and jointly managed by Probation and the police are key to ensuring that every high-risk offender released from prison has a risk management plan which will secure the best possible chance of offender rehabilitation and public protection. Victims have the opportunity to register their concerns and these feature strongly in the risk management plan. Nationally, the Probation Service provides over 35,000 reports to the parole board every year, reporting on the likelihood of risk and including any victim issues and known concerns.

Restorative justice is becoming a growing feature of the adult criminal justice system, having already been well established for juveniles. There are a number of pilots across the country, but we are still well behind our European partners in this initiative. The Carter Report recognises its value and it is likely to feature even more in the future.

Community punishment

This is the last of the main building blocks of effective practice and is being rolled out in every Probation Area in 2003/04, with performance bonus targets being set for 2004/05. Now known as Enhanced Community Punishment or ECP, this includes four main components:

- pro-social modelling
- placement quality standard
- guided skills learning
- integrated case management.

Gill McIvor's (1990) research, as far back as 1989, demonstrated that the more meaningful the community punishment order was to the offender, the more likely the order was to reduce reoffending. ECP incorporates the need to do unpaid work in the community with the opportunity to acquire basic skills along the way. For many offenders, the health and safety certificate they get presented with very early in their community punishment order is often the only certificate they have ever received. Sue Rex and Loraine Gelsthorpe report elsewhere in this volume on the impact of ECP on offender citizenship which has emerged from the evaluation of the ECP pathfinders.

Changing culture, changing practice

The change programme for the Probation Service has been on a massive scale, particularly as it has run alongside the creation of the National Probation Service, the amalgamation of many Probation Areas as well as changes in criminal law. The level and pace of change has proved challenging for many existing staff, whereas others have seized the opportunity to develop skills and expertise that might not otherwise have been available to them. Evidence-based practice has opened up the Probation Service to different skills and expertise. Roles such as 'treatment manager' and 'programme manager' are no longer the sole domain of the probation officer. We only have to look at the Drug Treatment and Testing Order and the mix of staff involved, from Probation, the Health Service and Education, to see the extent of the multi-agency and partnership work that is developing. Assessment centres have been introduced for all programme tutors and ECP supervisors, and while this was at first threatening for existing staff, it is now an accepted method of selection for those who are to impart cognitive and behavioural skills to offenders. The extent of the training programme has been such that Probation Areas have been forced to choose between running programmes and training staff. Accredited trainers have been at a premium and our ability to roll out programmes and go to scale has been limited by availability of trainers.

The introduction of OASys, in both probation and prisons, has led to a revision of the skills necessary to undertake assessment; many have appreciated the refresher training and recognise the value of OASys as an assessment tool. Their reservations are about the time taken to complete the assessment and what they perceive as inadequate workload allowance while the learning is taking place. The end result though will be a comprehensive assessment tool, used by trained and competent staff, capable of being shared across the boundary of prison and probation practice, and capable of measuring progress under supervision, whether in custody or in the community.

In the midst of all this change, with the benefits and the focus on the level three or PSO level of staff, the probation officers themselves have suffered a crisis of confidence. They have seen their probation service officer (PSO) colleagues develop new skills and expertise, while perceiving their own skills in assessment and offender supervision being undermined or undervalued. However, this is not to last. Most of the research studies into effective practice reported in the present book recognise the importance of case management in order to ensure completion and maximise the effectiveness of the intervention. In laypersons' language, the more the supervisor is interested, inquisitive and supportive of the intervention, the more likely it is to succeed. Personally, I prefer the term casework, rather than case management. My fear is that case management is interpreted as something that is 'hands off' whereas what is clearly required is 'hands on'. The supervising officer is not only the referrer and the enforcer; he or she is the motivator, the reinforcer and the person who holds onto the longer-term aims of social reintegration and reducing reoffending. In short, casework needs to be an integral part of the supervision plan and not a detached event. It is to be hoped that this renewed focus on the role of the caseworker will re-empower the role of the probation officer, but at the same time, will begin to develop our knowledge base of what constitutes effective casework.

The end result of the changes outlined here, for most staff, will be a committed and confident workforce, with a clearer understanding of their skills, qualifications and their ability to market their skills. Indeed the challenge for the service now is to retain the staff that it has trained and developed, and it is to be hoped that the discussions on pay and rewards taking place in 2004 will improve retention of key groups of staff who might otherwise have had little in the way of a career path in the old Probation Service.

Performance management framework

Effective practice cannot exist without an effective performance management framework, and the setting of targets has been a critical part of the initiative. Many in the service, myself included, have found the targets challenging, particularly in a framework of very tight resources, but the targets themselves have been critical in going to scale and taking the work forward. In my own Probation Area, our performance management framework and information systems have developed to the extent that we can now confidently predict the numbers of completers of accredited programmes from the numbers of orders that are made. We can therefore focus our efforts on the main points of influence rather than rely on retrospective data which is too late to change. Performance is monitored at a local and national level and fed back to areas so that they can track their own performance and benchmark change against the performance of other similar areas. The same is necessary at a local team level although the frequency of monitoring, at least in the early stages of the roll-out, needs to be more often than monthly. Our performance framework has been greatly enhanced by the availability of local evaluation, helping to inform our understanding of the factors which affect attrition and completion.

Attrition and completion rates remain the challenge for the National Probation Service. Our monitoring data tells us that too many offenders never start their interventions and, of those who do, too many do not complete. While we may guess at the reasons for this, there is very little evidence to explain this or assist in developing strategies to reduce such high levels of wastage. We have yet to develop an authoritative link between our quality audits and completions. It will be important to know what will improve completions. Is it quality of delivery, motivation, assessment or targeting, or simply programme availability? There is clearly a need for more research into why some offenders complete and others do not, and the lessons learned need to be translated quickly into practice if we are to realise the full benefits of the initiative.

There have been national drives to improve performance, including various activities, from conferences where there is the opportunity to benchmark and disseminate good practice, to the establishment of performance improvement action teams, using the excellence model of the European Foundation for Quality Model (EFQM). These are multi-grade teams which focus on the specific area for improvement and use their collective expertise to develop systems and processes to improve performance.

The performance across areas continues to vary, although the differences are not as stark as they used to be. Regional What Works groups and the appointments of regional What Works managers have helped areas to identify best practice and understand the lessons that can be transferred to their own organisation.

There is still much that can be done. Research and evaluations are very slow to be published. Valuable information is disseminated through conferences, but this method only imparts knowledge to the 'chosen few' and is rarely followed up with a more comprehensive communication. The practioners who are undertaking the work do not have access to the outcomes of research in a format that they can use or digest.

There are vast databases of pre and post psychometric testing and other related information, but these are rarely interrogated to improve our understanding of what really is working. Local research and evaluation is often very helpful in improving management decisions and local targeting, but it is always hampered by the impossibility of obtaining reconviction data to provide a comparative indicator of success. In short, the initiative has been, properly, heavily loaded on the operational side, but it is now time to pay more attention to some of the background issues which still need to be resolved.

Improvement initiatives

There have been a number of national improvement initiatives identified, although some are slow to produce any findings. These include: attrition, case management, engagement and motivation, pro-social modelling, training review, targeting review, psychometric test review and issues about infrastructure. I have commented elsewhere in this chapter on the importance of a 'hands-on' approach to case management. There is work underway to create a single model for case management for both prisons and probation and the very recent announcement of the National Offender Management Service (Home Office 2004) will reinforce the importance of this work. There is a possibility though that it will also mystify an area of work that has been an integral part of probation practice, almost since the beginning of the police court missionaries. Case management must include the need to secure the appropriate interventions for offenders, but it must also include enthusing, motivating and supporting offenders through these interventions (see also the chapter by Ros Burnett, this volume). The Carter Report (Carter 2004) proposes local and regional offender managers who will have the role of commissioning interventions. Care will need to be taken to ensure that, at the delivery end of this new organisation, there is close integration between the case supervisor and the programme providers. If there is not, the best intentions of case management will not be realised.

Learning from experience

We can be encouraged by looking back to see how far we have come in a few short years. We have moved from 54 autonomous, independent, creative organisations, but with a poor track record on implementation and evaluation, to a National Probation Service. Many of our business processes have been re-engineered, and we have learnt that during such a level of change it is important to pay attention to detail. However, we must continue to be sure that we are paying attention to the right detail, supported by evidence which all can understand, to avoid the perception of becoming over-bureaucratised and over-controlling.

We have learned to control creativity, moving from organisations that were overrun with creativity but thin on sustained improvement, to an organisation which channels creativity through an accreditation process. However, we must learn to reharness the creativity of our local practitioners, not only in the way that they deliver the interventions, but also remembering that many of the original ideas were developed from the experience of practice and not from the office of the researcher. Much closer integration between research and practice and the idea of the 'inquisitive practitioner' are concepts that we cannot afford to lose.

We have learnt to start from Pathfinders, benefiting from the lessons of implementation in a controlled environment and then going to scale, and I think this model has served us well. The pace of change has been rapid, too fast, clearly driven by political imperatives, but it is arguable that had we started with a slower pace, we may have been able to avoid the high levels of attrition that we are currently experiencing and still delivered on the required reductions in reoffending.

In looking back to learn from mistakes in the past, we should not allow that to distract us from the real achievements we have made. Leaving aside the structural issues, in 1998 we were unable to demonstrate any impact on reoffending in anything other than one or two isolated projects. There was little in the way of quality control or consistency in the range of probation programmes that were available, and there was limited evidence of a willingness or an ability to learn from the experiences of others. In 2003, we have consistent assessment, an identifiable product range, with core programmes available in every Probation Area and emerging signs of effectiveness in reducing re-offending. My own experience of visiting offenders at the end of their programmes is compelling.

Has it worked?

The important measure – and the one which the government will judge us on overall – is the reconviction rate. The two-year actual reconviction rate compared to that predicted for offenders convicted in 1999 has been reduced as follows:

- by 3.1 per cent for probation service interventions overall;
- by 4.9 per cent for Community Punishment Orders;
- by 4.9 per cent for Orders with Programme Conditions.

These figures show that we have been able to make a difference. Moreover, if evidence-based practice is working we should see further improvement in these figures in the years to come. Cases that were supervised in 1999 were at the very early days of the roll-out of accredited programmes; cases supervised in 2003 should show much better results if the programmes are having an impact on reoffending.

Future developments

Those of us who practice in criminal justice are all too familiar with living in an ever-changing world. The Carter Report proposes major structural changes for the future, including a merger of the prison and probation services. The Criminal Justice Act 2003 provides some operational challenges and a single generic sentence which could provide a real opportunity to integrate learning on accredited programmes with a further programme of interventions which would allow for practical application of the skills learned in a supportive environment. The custody-plus sentence has been widely welcomed as filling a very obvious gap for short-term prisoners. The challenge will be for the prison and probation services to provide planned interventions for offenders who currently get little from either. Integrated case management and intervention will be key to this new sentence impacting on reoffending for what is known to be a high-risk group.

There is no doubt that the implications of these structural and operational changes will be enormously challenging to both managers and practitioners over the next few years, particularly as we need to continue to maintain reductions in reconviction for those under our supervision. That said, we have a great deal of success on which to build and a tremendous wealth of talent and skill within the Probation Service, together with a real commitment and drive to see improved services to offenders that ultimately create a safer and better society. We are in good shape, and we have the wherewithal to do even better.

References

Appleton, C. and Roberts, C. (2003) *The Resettlement of Discretionary Life-sentenced Offenders: Report to the Home Office.* Oxford: Centre for Criminological Research.

Carter, P. (2004) *Managing Offenders, Reducing Crime: A New Approach.* London: Home Office Strategy Unit.

Downes, D. (1998) 'The role of employment and training in reducing recidivism', *European Offender Employment Forum, Bulletin No. 6.*

Farrall, S. (2002) *Rethinking What Works with Offenders: Probation, Social Context and Desistance from Crime.* Cullompton: Willan Publishing.

Home Office (1998) *Effective Practice Initiative: National Implementation Plan for the Supervision of Offenders.* Probation Circular 35/1998. London: HMSO.

Home Office (2000) *What Works Strategy for the Probation Service*, Probation Circular 60/2000. London: Home Office.

Home Office (2004) *Reducing Crime, Changing Lives: The Government's Plans for Transforming the Management of Offenders.* London: Home Office.

Kemshall, H. and Canton, R. (2002) *The Effective Management of Programme Attrition.* Leicester: Community and Criminal Justice Unit, De Montfort University.

McIvor, G. (1990) *Sanctions for Serious or Persistent Offenders.* Stirling: Social Work Centre.

McIvor, G. (1995) 'Practitioner evaluation in probation', in J. McGuire (ed.), *What Works: Reducing Reoffending: Guidelines from Research and Practice.* Chichester: Wiley.

National Probation Service (2002) *Hostels Pathfinder: Update on Developments,* Probation Circular 20/2002. London: Home Office.

Raynor, P., Kynch, J., Roberts, C. and Merrington, S. (2000) *Risk and Need Assessment in the Probation Services: An Evaluation.* Home Office Research Study, 211, London: Home Office Research, Development and Statistics Directorate.

Social Exclusion Unit (2002) *Reducing Reoffending by Ex-prisoners.* London: Social Exclusion Unit.

Turnbull, P.J., McSweeney, T., Webster, R., Edmunds, M. and Hough, M. (2000) *Drug Treatment and Testing Orders: Final Evaluation Report.* Home Office Research Study 212. London: Home Office Research, Development and Statistics Directorate.

Underdown, A. (1998) *Strategies for Effective Supervision: Report of the HMIP What Works Project.* London: Home Office.

Chapter 3

Towards effective practice in the Youth Justice System

Cedric Fullwood and Helen Powell

The government, in a companion to its Green Paper *Every Child Matters* (2003), restated its commitment 'to tackle effectively the problems caused by, and the needs of, those young people who do become involved in crime – 200,000 of them are dealt with by the youth justice system each year' (Home Office 2003: 3). The report refers to the substantial improvements made over the past few years. At the heart of these improvements is the Youth Justice Board.

This chapter will first provide an overview of the Crime and Disorder Act 1998 reforms, including the establishment of the Youth Justice Board (YJB), set within the historical political context of youth justice. The background, context and strategy the YJB has developed to achieve effective practice in working with children and young people in the community and secure estate are also discussed. The chapter explains the YJB's work to date in establishing an evidence base of effective practice through its research programme and its Effective Practice and Quality Assurance (EPQA) Strategy, and the differences and similarities of this approach with that being taken by the National Probation Service in collaboration with the Prison Service. The chapter explores the development of the *Key Elements of Effective Practice* as our major training strategy and its essential interrelationship with research. The chapter concludes with the identification of key next steps to be taken in future development of evidence-based practice in youth justice.

The authors believe that the youth justice reforms will be successful in achieving the fundamental aim of reducing offending if the effective practice agenda outlined is sustained over the years to come. In keeping with the theme of this book, the aim of this chapter is to provide an account, from the YJB perspective, of the development of effective practice in youth justice.

The emergence of a new youth justice system

Efforts to deal with children and young people committing offences or deemed 'at risk' of offending go back to the nineteenth century when governments of the day and penal reformers wrestled with the grave problem of children and young people in adult prisons. Throughout the twentieth century almost every decade has witnessed legislative and policy attempts to tackle what became known as juvenile delinquency. Borstals, Home Office approved schools, detention centres, attendance centres and probation homes were penal and residential responses to these efforts. Probation orders, supervision and care orders and intermediate treatment schemes were examples of what became known as community interventions. They emphasised the care side of the 'care and control' debate and they stressed the welfare of the child (a policy that stretched from the 1933 Children and Young Persons Act to the 1989 Children Act). Prevention was emphasised and even in the 1960s and 1970s the merits of non-intervention (young delinquents would grow out of their offending) were propagated.

The Audit Commission's seminal report *Misspent Youth* (1996) was followed, when the Labour government came into office in 1997, with a Task Force on Youth Justice (Home Office 1997a) and a White Paper entitled *No More Excuses* (Home Office 1997b). Proposals made by the White Paper were implemented through the Crime and Disorder Act 1998. The Act required all agencies working within the youth justice system to work towards achieving the statutory aim of preventing offending by children and young people.

In taking these objectives forward, the Act implemented a number of reforms to the youth justice system, all of which came into force nationally between April and June 2000. One of the most notable changes made by the Act was the replacement of the old cautioning system with reprimands and final warnings. Young people can receive only one of each before being formally charged, signalling the end of repeat cautioning. In addition final warnings include intervention aimed at addressing the factors associated with offending behaviour. A range of court orders were introduced including Child Safety Orders, Anti-Social Behaviour Orders, Parenting Orders, Action Plan Orders, Reparation Orders and the Detention and Training Order (DTO). The reforms of the system adopted the recommendation made by *Misspent*

Youth with the introduction of more intervention-based orders. The range of orders implemented sought to reinforce parental responsibilities, to require more young offenders to make reparation to their victims, and to address offending behaviour and areas of identified need and risks.

The Crime and Disorder Act 1998 also placed a statutory requirement on local authorities to establish Youth Offending Teams (YOTs). The Act stated that the police, social services, probation, education and health must be represented in these multi-agency teams. Such a multi-agency approach to dealing with young offenders was deemed an effective way of responding to youth crime locally and nationally. Fullwood (2001) provides an account of these changes, documenting the process of implementation.

To ensure changes made by the 1998 Act were successfully implemented and maintained, the government created a national body, the Youth Justice Board for England and Wales (YJB), to advise ministers on setting standards for service delivery and to monitor performance. The function of the YJB, established as a non-executive non-departmental public body, is to monitor the operation of the youth justice system; to identify, disseminate and promote good practice; and to provide advice to the Home Secretary. It also became responsible for purchasing places for young offenders in secure establishments, and for ensuring that those contracted by the YJB to provide such places comply with the requirements.

The YJB's work to date has witnessed the emergence of four specific policy and practice developments. These can be summarised as follows. First, the prevention agenda was developed at the heart of the YJB's legislative and service strategy. Second, an approach to tackling persistent young offending was introduced through the development of highly intensive and structured interventions known as Intensive Supervision and Surveillance Programmes (ISSP). Third, measures were taken to improve the quality of experience for young people in the secure estate, particularly in relation to education. And fourth, strategies for effective practice and quality assurance were introduced. The development of the YJB's effective practice strategy and implications of this work on the youth justice system are discussed in the remainder of this chapter.

Development of effective practice strategy

The YJB has identified effective practice as a key element in developing and improving youth justice services. It is committed to identifying and promoting effective practice across the whole youth justice system, both within YOTs and the secure estate, to ensure that work with young people is based on evaluated practice and research evidence. With initially limited information available on what is effective in addressing youth crime the YJB has sought, from its conception, to identify and gather evidence of effectiveness.

The YJB's evaluation strategy

The first notable attempt by the YJB to gather such evidence was through the development fund. With a budget of £80 million the fund sought to develop and sustain a range of initiatives over three years aimed at preventing and reducing offending. Funding, distributed by the YJB, was allocated to local areas through a bidding process. It was awarded to services that demonstrated the need for particular interventions together with the mechanisms of how such programmes would operate. The YJB provided tapered funding to local YOTs and voluntary organisations over three years to develop a range of initiatives. These included cognitive behaviour; restorative justice; substance misuse; education, training and employment; parenting; interventions supporting final warnings; and generic preventative services.

Projects, as part of their funding, were required to appoint a local evaluator whose role was to monitor and evaluate the progress of the programme. Alongside this, the YJB appointed national evaluators to oversee and provide guidance to the local evaluation. The national teams were required to develop evaluation plans and provide monitoring tools where necessary to assist in the collation of information on the work of the programme. Information submitted from local evaluators to the national teams was aggregated, reporting on the inputs, outputs and outcomes of programmes with the overall aim to identify promising approaches in working with young offenders and young people at risk of offending.

Local and national evaluators collected data on the way in which programmes were implemented, the involvement of local agencies, the operation and management of the programme, and the throughput and impact of the various initiatives. The evaluations, despite time and methodological limitations, revealed promising approaches in working with young offenders. The initial outcomes of many programmes being implemented showed reductions in antisocial and offending behaviour, and improvements in educational attainment. Restorative Justice and

Parenting Programmes also reported parental and victim satisfaction from those in receipt of such interventions.

In a recent article documenting the YJB's strategy for the evaluation of restorative justice programmes and the conclusions drawn, Wilcox (2003) questions the extent to which the national evaluation was able to evidence effectiveness – a concern raised by all the national evaluators in their reports. However, the national evaluations identified important findings regarding programme delivery, and drew out lessons that have been used to inform and strengthen the effective practice research base. In the main these initiatives were community-based and therefore provided no evidence of programme effectiveness in the secure estate. The YJB accepts that this gap in knowledge exists and is seeking to address this through its current research programme.

A strategy for effective practice and quality assurance

The YJB has developed an Effective Practice and Quality Assurance (EPQA) strategy aimed at improving practice across the whole of the youth justice system based on emerging evidence of what is effective in working with young people. It is designed to address factors associated with the offending behaviour of a wide range of young people dealt with by the youth justice system. It also seeks to establish processes for improving the quality of practice. The strategy promotes guidance that focuses on the assessment process through to the content of orders, services and interventions, aimed at ensuring that the needs of young people are addressed effectively. The YJB has acknowledged that a broad approach is needed, when working with young people, to ensure the range of complex needs that exist are addressed.

There are three main aims of the EPQA strategy:

- to articulate effective practice guidance to practitioners, managers and strategic partners;
- to monitor, assure the quality of and externally review the application of the guidance on the ground;
- to establish processes to improve over time the quality of practice on the ground.

The YJB acknowledges that it is essential that effective practice is implemented across the working practice of both the secure estate and

YOTs. The YJB is intent that the strategy does not identify ways of replacing systems but more the means by which they can operate effectively. It is essential that this emphasis on improving practice and performance is the focus not only of managers and strategic partners but practitioners as well.

The strategy is built on the foundation provided by *Asset*, a structured assessment profile that assesses the risk factors and needs of all young offenders coming into contact with the YJS (see the chapter by Baker for a discussion of the development of *Asset*). The tool assists practitioners in identifying the needs of young people and, thereby, in shaping the services they receive.

The premise behind the YJB's strategy is not dissimilar to that which underpins the approach of the Prison Service and National Probation Directorate (NPD). All three services seek to engage and motivate offenders through the provision of programmes (particularly offending behaviour programmes) and acknowledge the necessity of having fully trained and competent staff. There are, however, clear differences in the approaches taken. The main focal point for the Probation Service, and for the Prison Service, has been the introduction and development of accredited offending behaviour programmes. Youth Justice is a broader service than 'correctional services' as currently defined by prison and probation services. The approach of the YJB differs in that it does not see accredited programmes alone as being the answer, but as just one of the many elements required to ensure an effective multi-modal method of working.

The EPQA strategy, therefore, offers a different strategic approach to that used by the NPD and Prison Service but one that is necessitated by the following:

- the breadth of areas of practice that the YJB is aiming to influence;
- the multi-agency approach to youth justice;
- the different style of work required for children compared to adults;
- the devolved local nature of youth justice;
- the importance of a flexible approach to secure family engagement.

One initial difference in the approach taken by the YJB was the launch in 2001 of the Intensive Supervision and Surveillance Programmes (ISSP) (see Moore's chapter, this volume) as an option for dealing with the most persistent young offenders. The programme was designed to provide a strict and closely supervised regime that can be used where a custodial or secure remand or custodial sentence might otherwise be an option. The aims of ISSP are: to reduce the frequency and seriousness of offending in the target group; to tackle the underlying needs of offenders which give rise to offending, with particular emphasis on education and training; and to provide reassurance to communities through close surveillance backed up by rigorous enforcement. As such, ISSP is less an offending behaviour programme, more a framework within which a mix of interventions and surveillance is provided to tackle the individual risks and needs of young persons who persistently or seriously offend.

The piloting of ISSP over a two-year period (the programme is being rolled out nationally during 2004) has been the subject of a rigorous evaluation (Moore et al. forthcoming), the findings of which will contribute to the evidence-base for effective practice. Based on the same premise as ISSP, the National Probation Service is now developing Intensive Control and Change Programmes (ICCP) for 18–20 year olds. As with ISSP, ICCP seeks to provide rigorous community-based interventions that embody key effective practice principles.

Implementing effective practice

The YJB's effective practice strategy is characterised by the following:

- a corporate target to reduce offending by young offenders by 5 per cent by 2006 compared to the 2000 baseline;
- interrelated strategies for effectiveness, research and human resources;
- the development of a more coordinated performance management system;
- a network of regional managers and national implementers.

To ensure each of these characteristics is effectively taken forward the YJB has in support of these points established a performance target system. Thirteen targets for YOTs and eight targets for the secure estate in 2003/04 have been developed, all of which set out key components of interventions required to reduce reoffending. To assist in improving practice and meeting these targets the YJB have appointed regional managers to offer support and guidance.

Guidance

To take the EPQA strategy forward the YJB has identified what it sees are key areas of effective practice needed to inform and strengthen the work of managers and practitioners in the youth justice system. A series of guidance papers entitled *Key Elements of Effective Practice* covering the main components of youth justice work have been developed and disseminated across the secure estate and YOTs. They cover all aspects of the youth justice system from the assessment process to the content of orders, services and interventions to ensure that all young people who are assessed receive effective services. By November 2003 15 *Key Elements of Effective Practice* were published:

- Assessment, planning interventions and supervision
- Education, training and employment
- Final warning interventions
- Mentoring
- Offending behaviour programmes
- Parenting
- Remand management
- Restorative justice
- Swift administration of justice
- Young people who sexually abuse
- Targeted neighbourhood prevention programmes
- Substance misuse
- Resettlement
- Intensive supervision and surveillance programmes
- Mental health.

Each of these papers is written by an expert in their field and is supported by a source document that contains references, bibliography and examples of effective practice. They are grounded on existing practice and have been informed by the evaluation of programmes running in the youth justice system since April 2000. Each has been designed as a simple, easy-to-use manual that can be adopted by anyone working with young offenders in both the community and secure estate. They describe the features of effective youth justice services, allowing delivery to be shaped by need and local context, while also supporting consistency of delivery across youth justice services.

Each guidance note is structured to have specific sections for three main users: (1) practitioners (working directly with young people in a professional or voluntary capacity); (2) managers in the community and secure estate; and (3) strategic partnerships who guide the work of the youth justice system and allocate resources. They apply both to the work of volunteers and paid practitioners in YOTs as well as within the secure estate.

It has proved more difficult to find a way of implementing effective practice in the secure estate. The Prison Service has agreed to pilot a new sentence planning tool in two young offender institutions in 2003/04. This tool will provide the basis for implementing the *Key Elements of Effective Practice* that are most relevant to the secure estate: Education, training and employment; Assessment, planning interventions and supervision; Offending behaviour programmes; and Resettlement. Work is also underway to pilot the EPQA process in Local Authority Secure Children's Homes (LASCHs) during 2003/04. Similar discussions are also underway with Secure Training Centres (STCs).

The use of *Asset* alongside the effective practice guidance increases the ability of practitioners and others to effectively address the risks and needs of all young offenders in the youth justice system. Each guidance note includes a sample of key indicators of quality used to self-assess, audit and develop effective services. These are the foundations of a simple quality assurance system that the YJB wishes to see implemented in all youth justice services. The guidance notes are promoted through practitioners' and managers' events held across the country, allowing the opportunity for concerns to be addressed and issues of applicability to be discussed.

Training

The Effective Practice and Quality Assurance Process also supports the identification of staff learning and development needs. The YJB has developed a National Qualifications Framework, including several qualifications aimed at providing youth justice services with a range of tools (such as targeted in-service training) in effective practice, to ensure their staff are equipped to deliver the services described in the *Key Elements of Effective Practice*. This framework for qualifications builds on the series of guidance papers by enabling the development needs of staff to be identified effectively across youth justice services and by providing training opportunities specifically designed to support practitioners in the delivery of the services described in these documents. In conjunction with work in community YOT settings, the YJB influences training provision in the juvenile secure estate through service level agreements which exist between Young Offender Institutions (YOIs), LASCHs and STCs and the Prison Service. The Prison Service is currently redesigning its induction training for prison officers in three pilot sites. This will ensure that prison officers are well informed of the necessary requirements to ensure services are run effectively and efficiently as well as introducing a specific juvenile- focused induction training.

The design of the National Qualifications Framework is being completed in partnership with a consortium of higher education institutions and government departments and in consultation with youth justice practitioners and managers. Through this partnership, a series of learning pathways for youth justice practitioners has been developed which will provide staff with the skills to meet the challenges of delivering the services described in the *Key Elements of Effective Practice*.

The Professional Certificate in Effective Practice (Youth Justice) is the most significant of the qualifications being developed by the YJB for the majority of practitioners currently working in the youth justice system. The Professional Certificate is aimed at all practitioners. It contains three modules, takes nine months, while working, to complete and is gained through a higher education institution. This is to be the core professional qualification in youth justice. The YJB is committed to ensuring that 80 per cent of youth justice practitioners achieve the Professional Certificate or equivalent by 2006.

Other courses being developed alongside the Professional Certificate include Advanced Modern Apprenticeships (Modern Apprenticeship in Wales) to provide young and unqualified staff with a route into youth justice work. There is an Effective Practice In-service Training (INSET) pack covering each of the *Key Elements of Effective Practice*. INSET will support staff induction as well as refreshing the knowledge of experienced practitioners in specialist fields and provides a targeted solution to address any learning needs identified in the quality assurance process (see below). A post-qualifying programme is also under development.

Quality assurance

To ensure that the guidance notes are put into practice and an adequate standard is achieved, the YJB has published a *Quality Assurance Framework* to complement the *Key Elements of Effective Practice*. It contains details of the quality assurance process that the Youth Justice Board wishes services to put in place. The aim is for managers to sample and monitor the performance of their services against the requirements of each of the *Key Elements of Effective Practice*. This evidence should then be used to identify strengths and develop an improvement plan to address any weaknesses. The quality assurance process is structured around eight core areas which reflect all aspects of the service (for example, assessment, service delivery, service development and monitoring and evaluation). The evidence gathered as part of this process will enable the YJB to develop and share evidence of effective practice. As new research evidence becomes available, or as legislation or national standards change, the YJB will revise and reissue these documents to reflect what has been learnt or changed in the youth justice system. It is envisaged that they will be updated every two to three years. In reviewing the guidance required to continually improve service delivery the YJB has identified five key priorities to take forward in 2003/04. These are: final warnings; education, training and employment; assessment and completion of *Asset*; reducing the demand for custody; and parenting.

The *Key Elements of Effective Practice* intend to inform and shape the work in the youth justice field. As practice, research and experience develop within YOTs and across the secure estate, the guidance will be amended to increase the effectiveness of the youth justice system. Guidance will be updated to take account of additional findings on effectiveness and to allow for local contexts and circumstances. This approach allows for a powerful knowledge-base to develop. Through this and further research, it is likely that over time the development of some programmes similar to those that are currently accredited in the Probation and Prison Services will be established.

The research base

The YJB is committed to informing the research base of what works in youth crime. The YJB's research strategy is reviewed annually with the purpose of strengthening the effective practice evidence base. The current expectations and priorities of the strategy, as set out in the YJB research strategy paper (Powell and Finegan 2003), include:

- assessment of the effectiveness of interventions;
- improving our understanding of causes of crime;
- attaining comprehensive knowledge of all findings on youth offending;
- identifying gaps in the research knowledge-base;
- connecting with the research and evidence-based community;
- communicating research to managers and practitioners.

Considerable progress has been made in relation to each of these points. The YJB has published numerous studies including *Young People and Street Crime* (FitzGerald et al. 2003), *Patterns of Sentencing* (NACRO 2002), *Positive Parenting* (Ghate and Ramella 2002), *Assessment of the Detention and Training Order* (Hazel et al. 2002), and *Validity and Reliability of ASSET*

(Baker et al. 2003). Copies of all reports published are available to download from the YJB's website.

The YJB research unit has also developed good links with the research and practice community, which is essential in ensuring that a robust and detailed knowledge base of what works is compiled. Also, strong working relationships exist between the YJB and the Home Office Research Development and Statistics Directorate (RDSD). Research methodologies adopted by the YJB in research undertaken are agreed in consultation with the RDSD and other relevant organisations such as university departments to ensure findings are valid and reliable for dissemination.

With much of the research undertaken ranging from prevention to custody, the YJB has developed a detailed knowledge base on why young people offend; the youth justice system's response to young people who offend; outcomes of new reforms implemented under the 1998 Act; the operation and effectiveness of services locally (both in custody and the community); and factors associated with the likelihood of reoffending. The considerable evidence already generated by much of the research commissioned has strengthened the YJB's knowledge of all findings on youth offending. In addition to this the YJB holds extensive aggregate data on young people in contact with YOTs, provided through quarterly and annual data returns from the teams.

Updating and refining the evidence base

It is both necessary and essential that the *Key Elements of Effective Practice* are based on a robust evidence base. McIvor (1995) and Roberts et al. (1996), among others, have noted the crucial contribution which systematic evaluative research can make to effective practice in working with offenders and have called for a 'culture of evaluation' to be developed in agencies; something the YJB is working hard to encourage. The *Key Elements of Effective Practice* to date have been informed by the YJB's research strategy and research undertaken by other government departments and academic and voluntary organisations. Constant updating and strengthening of the research base has been acknowledged by the YJB as a necessity to informing the *Key Elements of Effective Practice*. The effective practice agenda is reflected in the identification of future research priorities, as set out in the YJB's research strategy. Without the continual process of enquiry and updating of knowledge from local and national research the YJB cannot be assured that the most robust effective practice approaches are informing practitioners' working practice.

The YJB is also keen to provide examples of effective practice and promising approaches that are essential to ensure the guidance is fully effective for implementation. Practitioners and managers will understandably be more amenable to adopting the guidance in their work if they can see it has been 'tried and tested', and if there is a growing evidence-base of what works best with whom. The first wave of *Key Elements of Effective Practice* has been informed by the YJB's current research base. Not only will this base be continually strengthened through the YJB's research strategy but also in the local monitoring and evaluation of the use of the guidance.

To assist local areas in monitoring their performance against the effective practice key indicators of quality, the YJB will encourage the use of a standard evaluation model containing the core details required to allow for regional and national evaluation and research. This will identify local innovation in effective practice as well as ensuring that local monitoring and evaluation is consistent across a wider sample base. Standardisation will allow for more robust findings to be gathered, representative of those in the youth justice system.

For the 'what works' question to be addressed there is a need for more high-level and large-scale quantitative research to be undertaken. Much of the research conducted on behalf of the YJB to date has provided examples of promising approaches and has served as a starting point on which the guidance can be based. However, the availability of robust evidence on what effectively prevents youth crime remains limited. In seeking to address this, future research to be commissioned by the YJB is to include more longitudinal studies, including comparative analysis, self-reporting and robust reconviction studies. Findings generated from these studies will provide reliable and valid indicators of effectiveness in working with young offenders. All of these findings will inform subsequent revisions of the *Key Elements of Effective Practice* which will, in turn, strengthen evidence-based practice.

High-quality detailed information is needed to enhance the knowledge of what is effective, and assist the monitoring of the operation and performance of the youth justice system. Firm conclusions of what works with young offenders are still limited but current developments are adding to the knowledge base. New developments and innovations need to be evaluated fully in order for useful lessons to be learned. By improving its understanding of the causes of crime the YJB is much better placed to inform practitioners and policy-makers of effective means of preventing youth offending. It is imperative to assimilate evidence and implications from research undertaken. Emerging findings from research undertaken to date are being disseminated both locally and centrally, with the purpose of informing policy and working practice.

To achieve all this, the research that is commissioned needs to be detailed and wide ranging, and inclusive of effective practice evidence on all aspects of the youth justice system. The YJB strategy is shaped by the knowledge that services and interventions work best if based on well-grounded research.

The necessity of updating and extending the knowledge base is crucial to continuous performance improvement. The production of the *Key Elements of Effective Practice* indicated large gaps in research and evaluation. YJB resources are targeted at research that complements both individual *Key Elements of Effective Practice* and issues that are thematic. For example, the impact of assessment on the shape of interventions is important for offending behaviour, mental health, education and final warning, if not all aspects of services provided within the youth justice system. The flow chart in Figure 3.1 demonstrates how research and evaluation inform youth justice practice which in turn contributes to the evidence base.

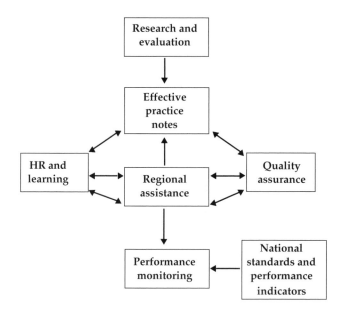

Figure 3.1   Reciprocal feedback between research and practice.

Next steps

It is essential that the *Key Elements of Effective Practice* become embedded in the working practice of YOTs and the secure estate. The audit of activity encouraged by the guidance notes should become integral to the work of practitioners, managers and strategic partners, developing a base of effective practice which meets young people's risks and needs effectively.

The future developments of the YJB's effective practice and research strategy will need to consider and reflect the changes arising from the 'Youth Justice – The Next Steps' companion document, implemented through the Criminal Justice Act 2003 and the Anti-Social Behaviour Bill. Research commissioned by the YJB will need to consider issues such as the implementation of a generic community sentence, pre-court diversion developments and strengthening of parental involvement. Continuing to evaluate the effectiveness of such developments is the key to ensuring a robust evidence base exists on which practitioners can establish and influence their working practice.

Practitioners from all backgrounds need to have a common knowledge base of effective practice. This process is being enhanced in a number of ways. Not only is the provision of *Key Elements of Effective Practice* (based on research evidence) informing their knowledge but training is also being developed whereby practitioners can gain pro-fessional certificates in effective practice. All this activity is seeking to ensure that services target the right young people and address their risks and needs effectively, greatly reducing the likelihood of further offending.

The day-to-day working practice of practitioners, managers and others is expected to be improved by the provision of a clear focus on the essentials of effective services. An important role will be played by the YJB's regional managers who are working with YOTs and secure establishments to ensure performance is in line with the effective practice guidance, performance targets are met and national standards and guidelines are adhered to. In assuring the quality of work by practitioners, managers and strategic partnerships, the regional managers will seek to assist local areas in enhancing their service delivery. In all, it is hoped, this will encourage a multi-agency approach to the local development of effective practice, informing the activities and plans of statutory organisations as well as voluntary agencies and community members.

It is essential for all of the work discussed in this chapter to be underpinned by high-quality and sustained communication. Clarity on who the 'practice' is supposed to be 'effective' for is essential. The YJB has identified politicians and policy advisors, courts, communities and victims, children, young people and their carers as being key to the dissemination of effective practice. A major focus for the YJB's future communication activity will be to ensure that all managers and practitioners in the youth justice system are briefed on effective practice and human resource development. Regional practitioner events and work with sentencers all seek to effectively convey the implications of the YJB's effective practice work with the aim of improving services.

The desired outcome from all this is the broad-based nature of the YJB's approach, which gives wholeness that is meaningful to the complexity of young people's troubled lives.

References

Audit Commission (1996) *Misspent Youth: Young People and Crime.* London: Audit Commission.

Baker, K., Jones, S., Roberts, C. and Merrington, S. (2002) *Validity and Reliability of ASSET.* London: Youth Justice Board.

FitzGerald, M., Stockdale, J. and Hale, C. (2003) *Young People and Street Crime: Research into Young People's Involvement in Street Crime.* London: YJB.

Fullwood, C. (2001) 'Youth justice – a Board perspective', *Probation Journal,* 48 (2), 135–8.

Ghate, D. and Ramella, M. (2002) *Positive Parenting: The National Evaluation of the YJB's Parenting Programme.* London: YJB.

Hazel, N., Hagell, A., Liddle, M., Archer D., Grimshaw, R. and King, J. (2002) *Assessment of the Detention and Training Order and Its Impact on the Secure Estate across England and Wales.* London: YJB.

Home Office (1997a) *A New National and Local Focus on Youth Crime: A Consultation Paper.* London: HMSO.

Home Office (1997b) *No More Excuses: A New Approach to Tackling Youth Crime.* London: HMSO.

Home Office (2003) *Youth Justice – The Next Steps: Companion Document to Every Child Matters.* London: Stationery Office.

McGuire, J. (ed.) (1995) *What Works: Reducing Reoffending: Guidelines from Research and Practice.* Chichester: Wiley.

McIvor, G. (1995) 'Practitioner evaluation in probation', in J. McGuire (ed.), *What Works: Reducing Reoffending: Guidelines from Research and Practice.* Chichester: Wiley.

Moore, R., Gray, E., Roberts, C., Merrington, S., Waters, I., Fernandez, R., Hayward, G. and Rogers, R.D. (forthcoming) *National Evaluation of the*

Intensive Supervision and Surveillance Programme: Final Evaluation Report to the Youth Justice Board. London: YJB.

NACRO (2002) *Patterns of Sentencing: Differential Sentencing Across England and Wales*. London: YJB.

Powell, H. and Finegan, B. (2003) 'The YJB Research Strategy'. Unpublished.

Roberts, C., Burnett, R., Kirby, A. and Hamill, H., (1996) *A System For Evaluating Probation Practice*, Probation Studies Unit Report 1. Oxford: Centre for Criminological Research.

Wilcox, A. (2003) 'Evidence-based youth justice? Some valuable lessons from an evaluation for the Youth Justice Board', *Youth Justice*, 3 (1), 19–33.

Chapter 4

Assessment tools in probation: their development and potential

Simon Merrington

This chapter looks at risk and need assessment tools in the Probation Service of England and Wales. It reviews their evolution and their value for improving practice, from both a technical and a user perspective. This is set against a background of the emergence of What Works and evidence-based practice.

Historical development of risk and need assessment

Probation practice in the mid-1990s

Several surveys of assessment practice in the early-to-mid 1990s were done, for example by MacDonald (1993) and Burnett (1996). This was a period when the Home Office was more concerned about national minimum standards than about the content of practice. Burnett's survey looked at assessment, supervision planning and casework in ten probation services. She found that officers had considerable autonomy in how they assessed offenders, decided what to recommend in pre-sentence reports (PSRs), and what they then did during the course of an order. Their assessments were mainly concerned with the current offence and the reasons underlying it. There was little use of structured assessment methods except for specific offences or interventions (e.g. sex offender groups or intensive probation centres), and formal assessment tools were limited to specific problems (e.g. in relation to dyslexia). There were no examples of comprehensive assessment systems for use at PSR or supervision planning stage. Burnett (1996: 69) concluded that:

A more systematic assessment of offending-related needs will enhance the accuracy and status of probation assessments, will foster optimum use of in-house and partnership specialists, and would facilitate integrated evaluation of the effectiveness of community supervision.

MacDonald's earlier research looked in detail at assessment practice in a single probation team. She used case records to determine the officers' assessments of what factors were associated with offending in each case. Despite the fact that officers' caseloads appeared similar (e.g. on offence type), there was a marked difference in their perceptions of factors associated with offending. Some viewed offending as influenced by a range of social, behavioural and cognitive factors, others selecting only a small number of social factors. Overall, behavioural and cognitive factors tended to be underplayed. These variations in assessment were also reflected in the range of interventions used. Although counselling was popular with all officers, the use of behavioural methods, alcohol education, family work and hostels were limited to a minority. McDonald concluded that a more consistent and professional approach to assessment was needed.

What Works

During the same period the What Works movement was gathering pace in the UK, especially by means of annual conferences at which researchers and practitioners exchanged ideas on the principles of evidence-led practice. James McGuire's influential book (McGuire 1995) summarised the most important findings to date on what was effective in reducing reoffending, and in particular a number of What Works 'principles'. The most relevant for assessment were that:

- criminogenic needs should be distinguished from non-criminogenic ones, and focused on as targets for intervention if the goal is to reduce offending (the so-called need principle); and

- service levels should be matched to an offender's risk of reoffending, with higher-risk individuals receiving more intensive services (the risk principle).

In the same book, Roberts argued for more comprehensive assessment, covering criminogenic needs such as social circumstances, health/ mental disorder, addictions and educational ability (Roberts 1995).

Definition of the risk and need assessment tool

The bringing together of risk and need assessments is a recent idea. Managing risk to the public has become an important way of conceptualising probation work over the last ten years (see, for example, Kemshall 1996), but the term 'risk' has been used in two ways: to mean probability of any reoffending; and, more specifically, the danger of an offence causing harm to specific victims. While both are important, the What Works research has paid more attention to the former, and consequently risk of reoffending has played a more important part in the construction and validation of risk/need assessment tools.

Bonta (1996) has described the evolution of risk/need assessment tools in three phases:

1. What he calls 'first-generation tools' describe the traditional interview and assessment process used by probation officers. These are based on professional and subjective judgement involving unspecified criteria and decision rules which are difficult to replicate.

2. 'Second-generation tools' use actuarial models to predict reoffending risk based on 'static' factors such as age and criminal history. The best known of these in the UK is the Offender Group Reconviction Scale (OGRS), which predicts a probability of reconviction over a two-year period. This is useful not only for assessment, but also in evaluating programmes by comparing actual and predicted outcomes for a group of offenders.

3. 'Third-generation tools' combine 'static' and 'dynamic' risk factors into a single integrated instrument. Dynamic risk factors, such as alcohol and drug misuse, can change over time, and are the same thing as the criminogenic needs described above under the 'need principle'.

Only third-generation tools can truly be called risk/need assessment tools because they combine three functions (Sutton and Davies 1997), namely to:

1. estimate a risk of reconviction for an offender based on static and dynamic risk factors;

2. produce a profile of where to target interventions to achieve greatest impact on recidivism;

3. measure changes in risk and need during a period of supervision.

Development of LSI-R and introduction to the UK

The first risk/need assessment tool meeting the above criteria was developed in Canada. Now called the Level of Service Inventory – Revised (LSI-R), it was designed in the early 1980s by two 'correctional psychologists' (Andrews and Bonta 1995). Its purpose was to assist practitioners to select offenders who required more intensive supervision because of higher risk levels. It was designed for use by probation officers and within institutions, and the content was influenced by three primary sources: the recidivism literature, the professional opinions of probation officers and a broad social learning perspective on offending.

The development of LSI-R was backed up by an impressive series of validation studies, most of which were carried out by Bonta and Andrews in Canada during the 1980s (see Andrews and Bonta 1995: 31). LSI-R total scores were found to be predictive not only of reconviction, but also self-reported offending, parole outcome, breaches of prison rules and breaches of supervision requirements. Furthermore a meta-analysis of reconviction prediction tools by Gendreau (Gendreau et al. 1995) found that LSI-R was the most useful measure to predict recidivism when compared to other measures such as the Salient Factor Score Scale and the Wisconsin system.

Starting in 1996, LSI-R was introduced under licence in the UK by the Cognitive Centre Foundation (CCF) (Raynor et al. 2000). As an assessment tool it complemented the cognitive-behavioural programmes being developed and marketed for use by the CCF. It proved attractive as a compact, practical and robust tool which had been validated as a risk predictor. On the minus side, there were some language problems due to its Canadian origins and some concerns about its validity in the UK. By 1999 LSI-R was in use by 20 probation services and some prisons. The Cognitive Centre maintained a training and support role which included summarising and disseminating LSI-R profile data.

Development and introduction of ACE

Development of ACE began in 1993 when Warwickshire Probation Committee decided to undertake an evaluation of the effectiveness of its supervision of offenders in the community (Roberts et al. 1996). This resulted in a three-year contract with Oxford University Centre for Criminological Research, where the project was led by Colin Roberts and Ros Burnett. The project was broader than the scope of LSI-R, and included developing methods to evaluate one-to-one supervision and groupwork programmes. Even the one-to-one aspect included a range of tools for supervision planning and review, and self-assessment by offenders, as well as the core ACE form for use by staff. This multiple focus is captured in the ACE title (Assessment, Case management and Evaluation).

ACE went through a long gestation period and was developed jointly by researchers and practitioners. Raynor et al. (2000: 6) describe the process:

> … the researchers undertook a literature survey of research findings on criminal careers, the characteristics of persistent offenders, the limited research on desistance factors … At the same time they convened a number of workshops to ascertain from the assigned probation practitioners what they considered, from their experience of working directly with offenders, were the best ways to systematically assess offenders, to document their characteristics and their social needs, and to measure changes in individual offenders.

The core assessment was based very much on the criminogenic needs being identified by emerging What Works research, as was the revised version of LSI-R which appeared at about the same time. However, unlike LSI-R, no static factors were added to ACE. Instead, it was designed to be used alongside OGRS.

The success of the pilot study led on to operational adoption of the ACE system by Warwickshire staff, and adoption by other probation services under agreement with Oxford and Warwickshire. Oxford provided a similar training and support role to that provided by the Cognitive Centre Foundation. Other services were allowed to make amendments to the ACE forms to reflect local concerns, whereas with LSI-R the copyright version could not be changed. This flexibility created some difficulties for the collation of ACE profiles across a number of services. By 1999 ACE was in use by 25 services and some prisons.

Development and introduction of OASys

In 1998 the Home Office approved a research project to validate LSI-R and ACE in a UK probation setting. By then there was acceptance that all services should adopt an assessment system, and a reconviction study was needed to test the predictive validity of both scales.

The expectation among ACE/LSI-R users was that one or either, or both, would be chosen for national use. However, in 1999 the Home

Office decided to develop its own assessment system, building on the lessons already learned (Home Office 1999). Work on this started immediately, in other words before the results of the validation study were known. A consequence of this was that, going on the experience of LSI-R and ACE, there was likely to be a three-year delay before a new tool could be developed, piloted and validated.

OASys was developed as part of a national What Works strategy through which central government took responsibility for developing standardised intervention programmes and the assessment process to drive them. It was consciously based on the What Works principles of risk and need. The development of OASys was undertaken by an in-house team at the Home Office, led by Danny Clark. It started with a thorough literature review, and took account of existing tools such as LSI-R and ACE. Like ACE, OASys was conceived as a set of tools including a core assessment by staff, an offender self-assessment, supervision planning and review forms. In other words, it specified to a large extent the format for case management. Taken as a whole, OASys is more similar to ACE than it is to LSI-R.

Piloting of OASys extended over two years and ran to three versions. Feedback was sought from practitioners at each pilot stage and a number of user groups were convened who gave detailed feedback and discussed planned changes. However, there have been no formal user surveys to date. The final version is being rolled out nationally to probation areas and prisons over 2002/04. Due to its length and complexity, an electronic version (eOASys) was also developed. Notwithstanding its value, this has held back the roll-out timetable. The launch of OASys was accompanied by a large national training programme for all staff, involving individual accreditation and the production of comprehensive user manuals. Overall, the development of OASys has been impressive, although slow.

Conclusions on the development of assessment tools

The importance and structuring of assessment in probation has come a long way in the last ten years. It has moved from the informal and piecemeal approach observed by McDonald and Burnett to the comprehensive and mandatory process required by OASys. This has come about because of two main factors: the What Works movement, and the creation of a national probation service in 2001 which has used What Works to drive reform. In the next section we will consider the benefits that these assessment tools have brought.

Validity and value of assessment tools

Value as need assessments

User surveys show that the main value practitioners see in these tools is that they improve assessment of criminogenic needs (Aye Maung and Hammond 2000; Gibbs 1999). They are seen as more thorough, consistent and focused on relevant areas, give structure to the assessment interview and assist engagement with the offender. On the other hand, the main criticisms are that they can be time-consuming, repetitive, difficult to fill in, have irrelevant questions and practitioners can feel deskilled. To some extent these are an unavoidable consequence of having a comprehensive, rather than selective, approach to assessment.

How comprehensive is the coverage they provide? Table 4.1 compares the main (scored) areas of criminogenic need covered by LSI-R, ACE and OASys. It shows the family resemblance of all three, but also one or two differences. As mentioned previously, ACE does not have a static criminal history score, preferring instead to use OGRS. OASys on the

Table 4.1 A comparison of criminogenic need areas (scored topics only)

LSI-R	ACE	OASys
Criminal history		Offence/offending history
Education	Education/training/	Education/training/
Employment	employment	employability
Financial	Finances	Financial management/ income
Family/marital	Family/personal relationships	Relationships
Accommodation	Accommodation/ neighbourhood	Accommodation
Leisure/recreation Companions	Lifestyle/associates	Lifestyle/associates
Alcohol/drugs	Substance abuse	Drug and alcohol misuse
Emotional/personal	Physical/mental health	Emotional well-being
Attitudes/orientation	Attitudes Motivation	Attitudes
	Personal skills Individual characteristics	Thinking and behaviour

other hand includes an analysis of the current offence, which goes beyond need assessment and is helpful for PSR preparation. The other surprising difference is that LSI-R does not cover 'thinking and behaviour' – surprising because its authors must have been aware of the importance of this topic in the What Works literature.

Within these domains, though, depth of coverage varies greatly. At one extreme, LSI-R consists of 54 closed questions and covers two sides of paper. It is estimated to take 45 minutes to complete. At the other extreme, the full version of OASys consists of 73 scored questions, plus unscored closed questions and open questions, covering 18 pages. It takes between two and three hours to complete. ACE falls somewhere between the two.

Are these need assessments equally valid and reliable? Inter-rater reliability is the aspect most frequently examined, normally by arranging assessments by two different people and comparing the results. This has been done for LSI-R, OASys and *Asset*. An LSI-R test, for example, showed close agreement (within three points) in 80 per cent of a sample of 35 cases (Raynor et al. 2000). The other aspect of reliability that has been examined is 'disclosure effects', where assessments done at different times may yield different results because of the subject's greater willingness to disclose problems. Testing of LSI-R and ACE showed a tendency for assessments done at start of supervision to yield higher scores than those done at pre-sentence stage (Raynor et al. 2000). This could be due to a disclosure effect.

There has been less attention to validity in this country. In Canada, though, LSI-R was tested at the development stage, and the results are quoted in the manual (Andrews and Bonta 1995). For example, concurrent validity was examined by comparing domain scores with results obtained from other, validated scales measuring things such as family conflict. The other tools have not been validated in this way. Table 4.2 compares some need profiles produced by LSI-R, ACE and OASys. Any comparison is fraught with dangers: the domains do not correspond exactly, the scoring systems vary and the samples are different. Nevertheless, one is tempted to speculate about what it may mean for the validity of the instruments.

There is general agreement that lifestyle and peers are a major risk factor in all samples. Also drugs are a problem consistently identified in about a third of cases. Several other factors like relationship and accommodation problems and emotional well-being also show consistency. But other topics have a very uneven distribution. For instance, employment and financial problems appear to be much more serious for the LSI-R sample. This could be due to measurement error, but since about half

Table 4.2 A comparison of criminogenic need profiles (percentage of cases having a significant problem)*

Need area (based on OASys)	LSI-R (N = 805)	ACE (N = 10,866)	OASys (N = 1,376)
Offence/offending history	40%	n/a	Current offence 19% Criminal history 39%
Education/training/employability	Education 43% Employment 71%	29%	Education/training 22% Employability 28%
Financial management/income	62%	31%	23%
Relationships	31%	27%	25%
Accommodation	22%	16%	25%
Lifestyle/associates	Companions 43% Leisure 59%	36%	33%
Drug and alcohol misuse	37%	Alcohol 38% Drugs 32%	Alcohol 22% Drugs 29%
Emotional well-being	18%	Emotional 23% Physical 4%	19%
Attitudes	20%	Attitudes 22% Motivation 17%	41%
Thinking and behaviour	n/a	Personal skills 22% Individual characteristics 17%	Thinking/behaviour 52% Interpersonal problems 15%

*Measured as % of maximum score (LSI-R), fairly/very offending-related (ACE), and above cut-off point (OASys).

of this sample are from South Wales, known for its problems of long-term structural unemployment, it is possible that the difference is a real one. The other areas of discrepancy are attitudes and thinking/behaviour. Here it appears that OASys is over-recording. Since one would not expect these problems to be regionally biased, the discrepancies may be more due to measurement error – for instance because there is less agreement about how these concepts are defined. Another possible explanation is that the OASys sample is more recent, reflecting a period when staff have been heavily exposed to What Works messages on thinking skills. Further research would be useful into the validity of these scales as need assessments, for instance looking at whether there is more between-scale variance than within-scale variance.

Aye Maung and Hammond's user survey showed that that the shortest scale, LSI-R, was more valued for its use in risk assessment, whereas the longer tool, ACE, was more valued for supervision planning. ACE users appreciated the value of having comment boxes in each section for recording evidence and aspects that need addressing. This practice has been continued in OASys, but it means that the assessment takes more time. Another aspect that gives ACE and OASys assessments more depth than LSI-R is that each section requires judgements on detailed aspects (e.g. whether the offender is in employment) as well as a judgement on whether the need area as a whole is linked to risk of further offending. This gives a more rounded picture requiring more professional judgement. Further depth is provided by the fact that OASys acts as a trigger for more detailed assessment of specific areas, such as risk of violence, if needed.

The value of these tools for needs assessment depends on the practical situations in which they are going to be used. There is a shorter version of OASys which can be used when there is not time to do a full assessment (e.g. Specific Sentence Reports) but even this is longer than LSI-R or ACE, and an even shorter assessment may be sufficient to decide on a suitable PSR proposal which matches service level to risk. For supervision planning a fuller assessment is desirable. But in both cases there seems to be a strong case for having a comprehensive assessment framework which encourages the practitioner to look beyond the immediate offence.

Value for assessment of risk of reconviction

Users also see risk assessment as a very important function of assessment tools (Aye Maung and Hammond 2000). In this section we consider the prediction of risk of reoffending rather than risk of serious harm. Risk/need tools have more often been validated in this way.

There has been a debate about whether third generation tools are better predictors of reconviction than second generation ones. Sutton and Davies (1997), for example, argued that, because they contain dynamic risk factors in addition to static ones, they are more effective in estimating risk of reconviction. In a study using PSR data collected via a variety of local probation monitoring systems, May (1999) found that dynamic variables such as drug use added only slightly to the predictive power of static factors alone. He noted that they were of more value for offenders with little criminal history (i.e. fewer static factors). It could be that the balance of static and dynamic factors may change over an offender's career, and that static factors are really dynamic ones which have worked their way through into a criminal record.

The study by Raynor et al. (2000) was the first to test LSI-R and ACE as reconviction predictors in the UK. The authors found that LSI-R was almost as predictive of reconviction over a 12-month period as the static predictor OGRS (65.4 per cent correct compared to 67.1 per cent). The same study found that ACE, although predicting at better than chance levels, did not perform as well as OGRS (61.5 per cent correct compared to 66.4 per cent). This may be due to the absence of a criminal history component in ACE. Validation work on OASys (Howard et al., in press) shows that it is about as predictive of reconviction over a 12-month period as OGRS using a different measure (ROC[1] area under curve is 0.74 compared to 0.77 for OGRS). It seems therefore that, as predictors of whether someone will be reconvicted over 12 months, risk/need tools are about as accurate as a good static predictor, but not better.

So far we have only considered the predictive power of total scores. But it is also important that criminogenic needs within risk/need tools are predictive of reconviction, since they are intended to pinpoint areas for intervention. Table 4.3 shows the extent to which component scores within LSI-R, ACE and OASys differ between those reconvicted and not reconvicted over a 12-month period. The number of asterisks indicates the degree of difference.

It is clear that there are similarities between the instruments. Almost all the need areas are indicative of reconviction regardless of instrument used. But OASys is the only tool showing a link between emotional well-being and reoffending. This suggests that the relationship is relatively weak or that it is difficult to establish using these kinds of general assessments. Within substance abuse it is drugs rather than alcohol which is the risk factor. The only other disagreement between the tools is that ACE seems unable to pinpoint criminogenic aspects of family and

Table 4.3 Difference in mean need scores between those reconvicted/not reconvicted (t-test significance level)

Need area (based on OASys)	LSI-R (N = 805)	ACE (N = 964)	OASys (N = 757)
Offence/offending history	***	n/a	Current offence ** Criminal history ***
Education/training/ employability	***	***	Education/training *** Employability ***
Financial management/income	***	***	***
Relationships	***		***
Accommodation	***	***	***
Lifestyle/associates	Companions *** Leisure ***	***	***
Drug and alcohol misuse	***	Alcohol Drugs ***	Alcohol Drugs ***
Emotional well-being		Emotional Physical	**
Attitudes	***	Attitudes *** Motivation ***	***
Thinking and behaviour	n/a	Personal skills ** Individual characteristics***	Thinking/behaviour*** Interpersonal problems**

Significance level: *** < 0.001   ** <0.01   * <0.05

personal relationships. The table shows that, to a large extent, the risk/ need dimensions of these tools have predictive validity.

To summarise, these tools give a valuable assessment of reconviction risk, but no more accurately than a static predictor. Where they gain is in being able to pinpoint the areas of criminogenic need that must be addressed to reduce that risk.

Value for assessing risk of serious harm

We noted already that risk of reconviction has played a more significant part in the development of risk/need tools than risk of harm. The management of risk of harm has become an important theme in probation work (see, for example, Kemshall 1996), but it has not been incorporated into risk/need assessment in the same way as risk of reconviction. One reason for this is that risk of serious harm is not a unified concept, but includes a variety of types of risk, e.g. to children, to staff, to self. Structured tools are used to assess specific risks, for example of sexual offending, but not as part of a general assessment. However, it is arguable that causing serious harm is just an extreme form of offending generally, and therefore risk/need tools should be able to predict serious offences such as violence in the same way as general offending.

LSI-R includes no risk of harm assessment. ACE has a short harm section, but this is not integrated into the rest of the assessment, and no separate score is produced. OASys has the most comprehensive treatment of harm. There are three aspects: firstly a judgement on risk of harm is required in relation to each of the 12 'need' areas, alongside the risk of general offending. Secondly a risk screening form is completed for every person. Thirdly, a full assessment of serious harm is required where appropriate. This process results in the offender being placed in one of four risk of harm categories, and a risk management plan being drawn up if necessary.

The reliability and validity of these harm assessments in ACE and OASys has not yet been investigated. However, some research has been done on whether the risk of reoffending scores in LSI-R and ACE are also predictive of serious reoffending (Raynor at al. 2000). Two measures of seriousness were used: whether the first reoffence was serious,[2] and whether it resulted in a custodial sentence. The results showed higher scores for those reoffending seriously, but the authors were only cautiously optimistic and warned against using scores as the only assessment of risk of serious harm. Mixed results were found with the juvenile assessment tool *Asset* (Baker et al. 2002).

Further research is needed on how far risk of harm assessments are reliable (replicable), and whether assessed risk levels do indeed pinpoint those who are likely to cause serious harm. The latter is difficult to test given the relative rarity of serious or violent reoffending. But the issue is important because of the risk either that serious cases will be missed, or, more likely, that cases will be placed unnecessarily in a high-risk category.

Matching service levels to risk

Combining assessments of risk of reconviction and risk of harm makes it possible to apply the 'risk principle' that allocation of resources should follow risk. A number of probation areas[3] have developed a targeting matrix based on the principles in Table 4.4 to ensure that use of resources such as programmes is focused appropriately.

Table 4.4 Simplified targeting grid

Risk of serious harm	Risk of reoffending	
	Low	*High*
Low	Low service level based on minimum national standards	Medium service level focused on need assessment
High	Medium service level focused on risk management plan	High service level focused on need assessment and risk management plan

At present these grids use OGRS to assess risk of reoffending. It would clearly be preferable in future to use OASys, which will identify not only the reoffending risk but also the criminogenic needs to be targeted. An important research question is whether the dosages indicated by this method are justified by improvement outcomes. There appears to be little evidence on this yet in the UK probation setting.

Value for supervision planning and targeting interventions

ACE and OASys include a supervision plan document. These have a family resemblance in that they start from the main areas of risk/need identified in the assessment and involve setting an objective for the reduction of the risk and specifying what action will be taken to achieve the objective. In addition, the OASys form asks questions about who will do the work, the timescale and how progress will be measured. OASys assists the targeting of accredited programmes where appropriate. LSI-R does not include a preferred supervision plan document.

Aye Maung and Hammond's survey showed that users greatly valued tools as aids to supervision planning. The main way in which ACE and LSI-R helped was in highlighting issues to be addressed, but ACE also helped to decide the type of intervention, and with writing the plan and specifying objectives. OASys user feedback has not yet been published on its value for supervision planning, but it will be important to do so. The OASys forms for supervision planning, and the arrangements for targeting programmes, are complicated and may need some simplification in order to be practical for users.

Little research has been published so far on the extent to which supervision plans reflect the assessment of needs. Merrington (2001) analysed ACE data from three probation services and found that objectives were more likely to be set where problems were rated as 'very offending-related' (Table 4.5). It is disappointing that the 52 per cent figure is not higher though.

Table 4.5 Relationship between problem severity and whether objectives were set (N = 535 cases)

Problem severity	% with objectives set
Not offending-related	6
Slightly offending-related	21
Fairly offending-related	34
Very offending-related	52

Additionally, problems in the 'Very offending-related' category were not equally likely to have objectives set. The most likely were alcohol (83 per cent), drugs (80 per cent), mental/emotional health (69 per cent), aggression (62 per cent) and accommodation (60 per cent). The least likely were lifestyle (14 per cent), attitudes (16 per cent) and impulsiveness (22 per cent). Since lifestyle, attitudes and impulsiveness are highly predictive of reoffending, while alcohol and emotional health are not, this gives some grounds for concern.

OASys research has not so far examined whether setting of objectives reflects the needs assessment. But OASys can be useful in estimating the proportions of offenders suitable for particular programmes. For example, roughly 15 per cent of offenders were found to fit the criteria for general offending programmes, and 39 per cent of the probation sample seemed to require a detailed violent offender assessment (Howard et al. in press). But it is too early to say whether OASys is actually assisting this process.

What this section shows is the potential value of risk/need tools in supervision planning and targeting interventions. Whether this will be achieved depends largely on how valuable practitioners find them in their day-to-day practice.

Value for improving offender engagement

There is more than one way in which these tools can encourage involvement of the offender in the process of assessment and supervision planning. In the process of gathering data, all tools provide an agenda for raising issues with the offender (Aye Maung and Hammond 2000). Indeed they can help practitioners raise difficult questions, though Gibbs (1999) noted that ACE could be difficult to complete with uncooperative offenders. At the review stage, the tools can be used to discuss progress with the offender.

ACE and OASys both include an offender self-assessment. The main advantage these give at the initial assessment stage is the opportunity for discussion and comparison with the practitioner's own assessment. This comparison is greatly assisted if both assessments have a similar structure, but this is not generally the case. For instance, the OASys self-assessment is a 27-item problem checklist of questions which are not in the same order as in the practitioner form.

Nor should one assume that offenders' assessments will agree with those of practitioners. ACE research by Haslewood-Pócsik (2001) concluded that there was little agreement, with offenders feeling they had less problems, and especially less offending-related ones. Figure 4.1 illustrates this in relation to reasoning and thinking skills. It suggests that there is a need for discussion between practitioner and offender before a useful intervention plan can be agreed.

Overall, the potential of risk/need tools for improving offender engagement is considerable, especially where there is a self-assessment form. It is important that self-assessment should be seen as assisting involvement in the assessment process rather than just 'letting offenders have their say'. Having a similar structure to both forms is useful, perhaps even a scoring system which allows the offender to discuss priorities in the same way that staff can.

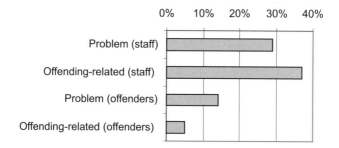

Figure 4.1 Percentage rating reasoning/thinking as a problem.

Value in measuring change

The ability to measure changes in risk and need levels over time is one of the major advantages of third-generation tools. It provides the practitioner with evidence of progress or the opposite, and should assist the review of supervision plans. Aye Maung and Hammond's survey showed that practitioners valued this aspect, but turning the potential into reality is more difficult. Research studies show staff reluctance to complete second assessments (Merrington 2001). Staff need to be persuaded of the value of using single-case designs to evaluate their work, and tools need to be short enough to be fitted into everyday practice.

Raynor et al. (2000) looked at the performance of LSI-R and ACE in measuring change. In the ACE sample 67 per cent of scores improved and only 29 per cent deteriorated. In the LSI-R sample 48 per cent improved while 36 per cent got worse. This shows the ability of both tools to measure change in both directions. They also looked at which areas of criminogenic need showed a change. The LSI-R sample was very small due to missing data (43), but the ACE sample (173) showed significant improvements in substance abuse, personal skills, individual characteristics, lifestyle and attitudes. There was also a slight deterioration in average motivation scores. They then compared the reconviction rates of offenders whose scores got worse with those who got better over a six-month period. Both instruments showed significantly higher rates of conviction for offenders whose scores deteriorated. For example, in an ACE sample, 69 per cent of those who deteriorated were reconvicted compared to 29 per cent of the improvers. Validation studies have not yet taken place to assess the ability of OASys to measure change, but this is expected during 2003. An important aspect of this is to assess whether changes are real or merely a 'disclosure effect' as described earlier. OASys has attempted to tackle this by allowing assessors to indicate whether a change in rating is due to a disclosure effect.

Perhaps the most important area for future research is to establish the relationship between interventions and the measurement of change. In a separate study of ACE, Merrington (2001) related the type of intervention method used to whether or not offending-related problems reduced or got worse. As Table 4.6 shows, nominal contact appeared the least effective, setting tasks or activities the most effective. Surprisingly, group work appears less effective, though it should be noted that the data were gathered in 1997–8, before the introduction of accredited programmes.

To summarise, risk/need tools such as LSI-R and ACE are capable of measuring change, and those changes can be related to probation inputs on the one hand and reconviction outcomes on the other. In future it is likely that OASys will become the major tool for measuring change over the period of a community rehabilitation order. While specific tools will continue to be used to evaluate the impact of accredited programmes, the best overall measure must surely be a risk/need tool such as OASys.

Table 4.6 Relationship between intervention method and problem reduction (N = 208 cases)

Intervention method	Frequency of use	% of cases where problem reduced
Nominal contact	15	20
Practical help	64	34
Talk/counselling (open ended)	279	42
Talk/counselling (about past)	93	43
Talk/counselling (present/future)	222	45
Activities (assessment/monitoring)	96	47
Activities (educational)	34	44
Activities (behavioural)	29	38
Activities (setting tasks)	32	53
Family work	23	39
Referrals (group work)	66	35
Referrals (in-house specialist)	77	44
Referrals (partnership)	66	41
Referrals (other external)	81	46
Other	21	43
All methods	*1,198*	*43*

Value to practitioners

So far we have considered rather 'technical' aspects of the value of risk/ need tools to practitioners: their value for needs assessment, assessing risk and so on. It is clear that staff appreciate the ability to work more consistently and defensibly. Indeed some research has shown improvements in the quality of practice, such as PSR writing and supervision planning, as a result (Roberts and Robinson 1998). But at the same time staff have expressed concerns that structured assessment tools will erode professional discretion, and deprofessionalise probation work (Robinson 2003). Robinson quotes staff fears that

> ... they're gonna replace our assessment skills with a tick-box system ... there was a big fear that it was going to de-professionalise us and that sooner or later our professional judgement's not going to be needed.

Robinson's research into LSI-R convinced her of the need to address the issue of professional ambivalence. Tools like OASys demand a lot of time and paperwork, and staff with large caseloads need to be convinced that their efforts are repaid. Tools need to be ways of structuring professional judgement and discretion rather than just ticking boxes. Issues of length and user-friendliness are critical. If staff see OASys as a way of removing discretion about supervision objectives and methods in order to achieve centrally set targets about programme numbers, then they are likely to become cynical and not take it seriously. If, on the other hand, they feel that OASys improves their own assessment practice, their supervision planning and the relevance of their interventions, and gives them feedback on effectiveness, then it is likely to be a success. This needs to be reflected in OASys training and backed up by user feedback surveys.

Value to managers

So far we have talked about the value of risk/need tools for the practitioner. Yet there is a strong feeling among some practitioners that their main purpose is to assist managers. We agree that they are of great potential value to managers, but this will only be realised if it takes second place to their value as practice tools.

There is little research evidence so far about their actual value to managers. Aye Maung and Hammond's survey included only a few managers. For them the most valuable aspects of ACE and LSI-R were in ensuring consistency of assessments and monitoring quality of assessments and supervision plans. These could be done through individual supervision and quality audits to improve practice.

But it is when the data can be aggregated and analysed to discern overall patterns that it becomes really useful to management. Need profiles can be used to plan specialist resources such as accredited programmes, partnerships or in-house specialisms such as accommodation or education, training and employment. Quality assurance can be used to ensure that case managers are making appropriate use of referrals. And as we have shown above, risk/need tools can be used to evaluate probation effectiveness. So far, however, managers can see the potential advantages, but few have experienced them in practice. Partly this is due to managers' lack of confidence with handling data, indicating an important role for local research staff. But a more substantial hurdle has been the development of IT systems capable of handling risk/need information and integrating it with other data on PSRs, plans, case records and programmes. LSI-R and ACE data were usually stored on separate research databases, if at all. Although the Probation Studies Unit at Oxford University and the Cognitive Centre each provided a valuable service, they could not give a quick turnaround of data at a local (team) level.

The computerisation of OASys was recognised as a priority early on. This was probably done to aid the individual practitioner rather than provide management data though, since OASys was considered too complicated to use as a manual tool. Computerisation has been a lengthy process and has delayed the roll-out of OASys. Also, eOASys, as it is called, does not yet integrate with case management data in the Case Recording and Management System (CRAMS) or programme attendance data. This stands in stark contrast to the situation in Youth Justice, where *Asset* assessments were built into the Youth Offending Teams' case management systems from the outset (see chapter by Baker, this volume).

It is too early to tell whether eOASys will realise the potential of risk/need tools for managers, but progress is being made.

Value for researchers

One benefit of risk/need tools which is not often discussed is their value for research. As researchers we have perhaps taken this for granted. LSI-R, ACE and OASys can be viewed as research questionnaires containing a large body of valuable quantitative and qualitative data. The databases they create allow a range of research issues to be explored, which range beyond the simple monitoring questions that managers might require on a daily basis. Some of these have been explored here, for instance whether probation interventions reduce the risk of reoffending. More theoretical investigations are possible: for instance the use of multi-variate analysis to explore the fundamental dimensions underlying criminogenic needs. A factor analysis of ACE data was done by Raynor et al. (2000) which showed that as many as eight factors were significant, suggesting that offending is genuinely multi-dimensional. Logistic regression was also used to explore the ability of need domains to predict reconviction. All this was done with data collected routinely by practitioners. One can contrast this approach with a conventional one-off research project, such as the Peterborough Youth Study, which used interviews with 1,957 school pupils to conduct a similar analysis of the relationship between risk factors and offending (Wikstrom 2002).

The advantage of using risk/need tools for research is that data are being collected in a standard way in large numbers across the whole country. Research can be conducted at a number of scales. It can be viewed on a continuum from simple investigations by a practitioner or local manager, though more ambitious projects by local research staff, to sophisticated national research projects. Also, analyses developed in one probation area can be replicated elsewhere.

Conclusions on the validity and value of assessment tools

This section has reviewed assessment tools from a number of different viewpoints: as need assessments, as risk predictors, as aids to super-vision planning, and so on. The shortest tool, LSI-R, is most valued by staff for risk assessment and it performs well as a dynamic predictor. ACE was more consciously developed as an aid to assessment, case planning and measurement of change, and it is valuable in these areas. Its offender self-assessment form is also appreciated as a way of engaging the offender. However, users are critical of the greater burden that ACE imposes as a result of its length. OASys, though similar in scope to ACE, adds further depth and coverage – for example in its risk of harm assessment. The complexity and time burden are also increased, but staff views on whether this is justified have not yet been gathered. OASys's technical performance has not been published yet, but some aspects – for example its ability to predict risk of reconviction – are understood to be good. Others, such as its ability to measure change, are not yet known. On the basis of its similarity to ACE, though, these could be expected to be good also.

The future for assessment tools in probation

Evidence-based practice means a focus on outcomes and greater effectiveness. What evidence is there so far that risk/need assessment tools will make probation more effective?

- There is evidence that they help to focus on and assess criminogenic needs.

- They are as effective at predicting reconviction as static predictors.

- Their ability to assess risk of serious harm reliably is not yet evident.

- They are starting to be used to match service levels to risk, but there is little UK evidence so far that these service levels are justified by improvement outcomes.

- They can assist with supervision planning and targeting interventions, but this process should not be manipulated to achieve national targets. Instead, they should be used to enhance professional decision-making and empower the case manager.

- They can also improve offender engagement with the assessment, planning and review process.

- They can be used to measure reduction of risk and needs across the order as a whole, and to assess the value of different probation inputs.

As OASys is the future assessment system for probation and prisons, it is important that the evidence of its 'technical' performance is made available to practitioners and managers alike. It is also important that gaps in our knowledge are plugged by future research, for example into its ability to measure change. But the technical potential will only be achieved if users' views are carefully sought and responded to, so that OASys is user-friendly for practitioners and seen to assist practice. A balance has to be struck between technical performance and fitness for purpose.

Notes

1 Receiver Operating Characteristic.
2 Defined as being in Home Office gravity category A–D.
3 For example, West Yorkshire and Merseyside.

References

Andrews, D.A. and Bonta, J.L. (1995) *LSI-R: The Level of Service Inventory – Revised*. Toronto: Multi-Health Systems.

Aye Maung, N. and Hammond, N. (2000) *Risk of Re-offending and Needs Assessments: The User's Perspective*, Home Office Research Study 216. London: Home Office.

Baker, K., Jones, S., Roberts, C. and Merrington, S. (2002) *Validity and Reliability of ASSET*. London: Youth Justice Board.

Bonta, J.L. (1996) 'Risk-needs assessment and treatment', in A.T. Harland (ed.), *Choosing Correctional Options that Work*. Thousand Oaks, CA: Sage.

Burnett, R. (1996) *Fitting Supervision to Offenders: Assessment and Allocation Decisions in the Probation Service*, Home Office Research Study 153. London: Home Office.

Gendreau, P., Little, T. and Goggin, C. (1995) *A Meta-analysis of the Predictors of Adult Offender Recidivism: Assessment Guidelines for Classification and Treatment*. New Brunswick, NJ: Department of Psychology, University of New Brunswick.

Gibbs, A. (1999) 'ACE: the assessment, case management and evaluation system', *Probation Journal*, 46 (3), 182–6.

Haslewood-Pócsik, I. (2001) *Practitioner ACE Assessments and Offender Self-Assessments: A Comparison*, ACE Practitioner Bulletin 5. Oxford: Probation Studies Unit.

Home Office (1999) *A Joint Risk/Needs Assessment System for the Prison and Probation Services*, Probation Circular 16/1999. London: Home Office Probation Unit.

Howard, P., Clark, D. and Garnham, N. (forthcoming) *An Evaluation and Validation of the Offender Assessment System (OASys)*. London: Home Office.

Kemshall, H. (1996) *Good Practice in Risk Assessment and Risk Management*. London: Jessica Kingsley.

MacDonald, G. (1993) 'Implementing the findings of effectiveness research in probation', in C. Roberts (ed.), *Improving Practice: Towards a Partnership between Information, Research and Practice*, Proceedings of the 9th Annual Research and Information Conference of the Probation Service. Warwick: University of Warwick.

McGuire, J. (ed.) (1995) *What Works: Reducing Reoffending: Guidelines from Research and Practice*. Chichester: Wiley.

May, C. (1999) *Explaining Reconviction following a Community Sentence: the Role of Social Factors*, Home Office Research Study 192. London: Home Office.

Merrington, S. (2001) *Objectives, Intervention and Reducing Risk*, ACE Practitioner Bulletin 3. Oxford: Probation Studies Unit.

Raynor, P., Kynch, J., Roberts, C. and Merrington, S. (2000) *Risk and Need Assessment in Probation Services: An Evaluation*, Home Office Research Study 211. London: Home Office.

Roberts, C. (1995) 'Effective practice and service delivery', in J. McGuire (ed.), *What Works: Reducing Reoffending: Guidelines from Research and Practice.* Chichester: Wiley.

Roberts, C. and Robinson, G. (1998) 'Improving practice through pilot studies: the case of pre-sentence reports', *Vista*, 3 (3), 186–95.

Roberts, C., Burnett, R., Kirby, A. and Hamill, H., (1996) *A System For Evaluating Probation Practice*, Probation Studies Unit Report 1. Oxford: Centre for Criminological Research.

Robinson, G. (2003) 'Implementing OASys: lessons from research into LSI-R and ACE', *Probation Journal*, 50 (1), 30–40.

Sutton, D. and Davies, P. (1997) *A Review of the Development of LSI-R in Britain.* Dinas Powys: Cognitive Centre Foundation.

Wikstrom, P.-O. (2002) *Adolescent Crime in Context.* Cambridge: University of Cambridge Institute of Criminology.

Chapter 5

Is *Asset* really an asset? Assessment of young offenders in practice

Kerry Baker

Introduction and context

Scope of the paper

Merrington (Chapter 4) has given an overview of the development and use of a number of different assessment tools and helpfully highlighted the range of functions that we could reasonably expect such tools to perform. In contrast, this chapter focuses on the development and use of one particular tool, namely *Asset*, the assessment tool introduced for use in the reformed youth justice system. More generally, a number of the issues discussed will be relevant to the broader debate about the role of risk assessment tools in the development of evidence-based practice.

What is Asset?

Design and development

Asset is the name given to the assessment profile currently used across England and Wales with young people who offend.[1] Before looking at the impact of *Asset* on practice in the youth justice system it is appropriate to give a brief outline of how and why it was introduced. One of the first initiatives of the newly formed YJB in 1998 was to commission the design of a risk/need assessment tool for use with young offenders aged 10–17. This had a clear symbolic value in two ways. Firstly, it was intended to provide a common framework for assessment practice within the new multi-disciplinary YOTs and, secondly, it was intended to be different from tools used with adults in order to reflect the particular risks and needs of young people who offend.

The design and development work was undertaken by the Probation Studies Unit of the University of Oxford and began in the spring of 1999. This was informed by the earlier work of Roberts and Burnett in developing ACE (Roberts et al. 1996; Merrington, this volume) and by subsequent initiatives to adapt ACE for use with younger offenders.[2] The design process involved a thorough review of the research literature relating to risk and protective factors for young people who offend and extensive consultation with practitioners, managers and specialists from a range of relevant services. The draft forms were piloted for a short period and subsequently revised before being issued to Youth Offending Teams (YOTs) with accompanying guidance. A national training programme was funded by the YJB although it was limited in scope and many practitioners did not receive any training in the use of *Asset* before its introduction into practice in April 2000.

Asset is now in use in all YOTs with young people at each of the different stages of the criminal justice system. An increasing number of youth justice teams in Scotland have also chosen to use *Asset*.

Components of Asset

Asset consists of a number of different elements which are briefly described below.

- *Core Asset profile*. This includes some static factors (e.g. criminal history) but focuses on dynamic factors. There are 12 main sections addressing key issues such as living arrangements, family and personal relationships, education, training and employment (ETE), neighbourhood, lifestyle, substance use, thinking and behaviour, and attitudes to offending. It also includes a section on positive factors and sections to screen for vulnerability and/or risk of serious harm to others.

- *Final Warning Asset*. This is a shorter version of the core profile which covers the same areas but in less detail.

- *'What do YOU think?'* This self-assessment form, to be completed by young people who offend, mirrors the sequence of the core profile and addresses similar issues so as to facilitate comparison between the views of young people and those of practitioners.

- *Risk of serious harm form*. This is only intended to be used with a minority of young offenders and provides a more in-depth assessment of whether a young person presents a real risk of serious harm to others.

- *Bail Asset*. This is similar in style to Final Warning *Asset* but with a focus on information that would be relevant to decisions about whether a young person is remanded to custody or receives bail.

- *Intervention plan*. This was introduced by the YJB as part of the relaunch of *Asset* in August 2003 (Wright 2003) and is intended to help practitioners make clearer links between the outcome of an assessment and the subsequent plan of work that is agreed with a young person.

The remainder of the chapter focuses on the core *Asset* profile and the 'What do YOU think?' form but it is important to bear in mind that *Asset* is a package of material for use in YOTs. Judgements about its value need to take this into account rather than focusing too narrowly on specific details of just one of the forms.

Opinions about Asset

When a tool such as *Asset* is introduced into practice at a national level it is inevitable that it will provoke a diverse range of responses. Views about *Asset* are likely to vary according to people's roles within the youth justice system such that we would expect to see different perspectives held by practitioners, managers, the YJB, courts, academics and staff from other agencies. Views from within role groups also vary, e.g. practitioners differ among themselves in their attitudes to *Asset* (Roberts et al. 2001).

The YJB clearly views *Asset* in a very positive way. For example, it was stated recently that 'More than any other aspect of the reformed system, this tool, properly used is capable of preventing further offending' (Youth Justice Board 2002a: 9). One reason for this is that *Asset* is seen as improving the quality of practice in assessment and planning. 'Prior to the introduction of *Asset* the process of assessing risks and planning interventions lacked rigour and was unable to quantify the issues or contribute effectively to the delivery of joined-up solutions' (Wright 2003: 5). *Asset* enables more effective targeting of resources through increasing diagnostic accuracy: 'Offenders who are most likely to continue to offend can be identified at the earliest stage and steps can be taken to prevent it with confidence' (Youth Justice Board 2002a: 9).

By contrast, others have been very critical of *Asset* and, in particular, of its use of numerical ratings. For example, in a recent account of developments in youth justice, Roger Smith refers to 'the spurious scientific accuracy offered by actuarial instruments such as the *ASSET* form' (2003: 211). A second strand of criticism has been that *Asset* concentrates too much on the negative aspects of a young person's life. 'Indeed, the preoccupation with risk is likely to generate a pre-disposition to "seeing the worst in people" and focusing unduly on the possibility of failure. Is it entirely a coincidence that its adoption as a key assessment tool has accompanied a surge in custodial sentencing?' (Smith 2003: 192).

These examples are intended to highlight the polarised range of views about *Asset*, although of course most people would be found somewhere along this spectrum of opinion rather than at the extreme ends. A user survey, for example, found that practitioners had a number of concerns about *Asset* such as its length, the potential intrusiveness of some of the questions, the time required to complete it well and uncertainty about using the ratings (Roberts et al. 2001). At the same time, however, practitioners were able to see the potential of *Asset* in areas such as promoting consistency, transparency and improved resource allocation. Burnett and Appleton (2004) also found mixed views about *Asset* in their case study of one particular YOT and this is similar to research findings regarding the use of tools with adult offenders (Aye Maung and Hammond 2000). The question we now need to consider is which of these views most closely reflects the emerging evidence about the use and value of *Asset*.

Investigating the use of *Asset*

Asset is a relatively new assessment profile and clearly there will be less evidence available than for longer established tools such as LSI-R. Increasing amounts of data are now available, however, and these come from a variety of sources. A two-year YJB-funded research project looking at the validity and reliability of *Asset* has provided a rich source of both quantitative and qualitative data (Baker et al. 2002[3]) and additional data are now emerging from other research studies, e.g. the evaluation of the Intensive Supervision and Surveillance Programme (Moore, this volume; Moore et al. 2004). Other sources of data include analysis of local *Asset* data by specific YOTs (for example, Jose 2001) and YOT quarterly returns to the YJB.

National Standards (Youth Justice Board 2000a) state that *Asset* (either the core profile or the final warning version as appropriate) should be completed at the beginning and end of an intervention.[4] It is difficult to obtain accurate figures on completion rates as it is likely that the data given by teams to the YJB include *Assets* completed retrospectively but evidence suggests noticeable variations between teams in this respect (Baker et al. 2002). This is supported by recent data which indicate completion rates for initial *Assets* varying from 30 per cent in some teams to nearer 100 per cent in others (PA Consulting 2003).

While this is a limited measure in that it gives no information about the quality of completed *Assets*, it is a useful starting point and gives one indicator of the impact of *Asset* on practice. The key finding here is that YOTs still vary considerably in their frequency of *Asset* completion.

Validity and reliability

This first section of evidence looks at those aspects of *Asset* use which are most amenable to measurement and quantification. These are frequently identified as among the key tasks for risk/need assessment tools (Merrington et al. 2003, Merrington, this volume).

Predictive accuracy

The core profile and final warning *Asset* both produce a numerical score and it is important to note that this is essentially derived from clinical judgement. In each of the 12 sections dealing with dynamic risk factors, practitioners are asked to rate (on a 0–4 scale) the extent to which they think the problems they have identified are associated with a risk of re-offending (Youth Justice Board 2000c). How accurate is this at predicting the occurrence, frequency and seriousness of reconviction?

The ability of *Asset* to predict the occurrence of reconviction within a 12-month period has been shown to be comparable to or slightly better than that of similar tools used with adult offenders in England and Wales (Baker et al. 2002). This finding was maintained for particular groups such as female, younger or ethnic minority offenders. Its predictive accuracy across the score range is illustrated in Figure 5.1.

Asset was shown to be able to distinguish between young people reconvicted more frequently within the 12-month period and those who were reconvicted less often. This was tested using both number of reconviction occasions and number of reconviction offences (Baker et al. 2002). Using risk/need assessment tools to predict the seriousness of reconviction is more difficult, however (Raynor et al. 2000). Using the original scoring system, *Asset* was not accurate at predicting the gravity of reconviction offences but was more accurate at distinguishing between young people receiving custodial sentences on reconviction and those receiving community penalties or fines.[5]

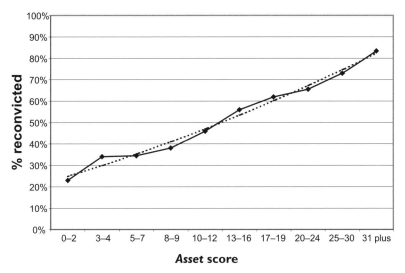

Figure 5.1 Current *Asset* score by percentage reconvicted.
The *Asset* scores of the sample were divided into ten equal sized groups for this analysis. The dotted line indicates the ideal fit between *Asset* score and reconviction whilst the continuous line shows the actual correlation obtained for this sample of young people.

Reliability

A common concern raised by YOT staff is that *Asset* is used inconsistently by different practitioners and teams (Roberts et al. 2001). This is understandable given the mutli-disciplinary nature of teams, the speed with which *Asset* was introduced and the lack of training. In this context, it would not perhaps be surprising to find evidence of significant variations in *Asset* use, particularly with regard to the ratings, but the initial evidence available suggests that this is less of a problem than might have been expected.

A fuller account of research in this area to date, including methodology,[6] is provided by Baker et al. (2002) but the key findings are as follows. Firstly, there were no significant variations in the ratings given by different professional groups once account was taken of case stage, e.g. police officers and social workers rated similarly at the final warning stage and probation officers/social workers rated similarly at pre-sentence report (PSR) and post sentence stages. There was some inconsistency between different YOTs (this was mainly at the PSR stage rather than for final warnings) but the level of consistency between the different teams within larger YOTs was good.

The initial results were therefore generally encouraging but it would be useful to have more evidence in this area, particularly if it could be based on a more recent data sample.

Measuring change over time

There is relatively little data currently available on this because it has been difficult to obtain sufficient numbers of end-of-intervention *Assets* to undertake meaningful analysis of patterns of change over time (Baker et al. 2002). Problems in this area were of two kinds: non-completion of forms and replication of earlier *Assets* without updating them or modifying the ratings. In some YOTs practitioners have either not found the time to complete end *Assets* or have not appreciated the importance of doing so in developing effective practice (Burnett and Appleton 2004).

The Youth Justice Board is funding ongoing research into this particular question and the project is due for completion in summer 2004. The results of this should provide clearer evidence about the ability of *Asset* to measure change over time.

Practice and culture

In addition to the issues discussed immediately above, Merrington identified a number of other, less quantifiable, functions that an assessment tool should perform. These can be difficult questions for which to obtain evidence but some initial indications of the impact of *Asset* in these areas is given below. This is drawn primarily from the study by Baker et al. (2002) which, in addition to the quantitative data used to test validity and reliability, also involved qualitative data, in particular semi-structured interviews with staff and analysis of completed *Asset* forms.

Explaining assessment conclusions

One of the key features of *Asset* is the emphasis on providing evidence to justify the assessments made. All through the core profile (and final warning version) there are evidence boxes which practitioners should use to explain the basis for their judgements. Similarly, the risk of serious harm form requires assessors to explain their conclusions. For example, if a practitioner states that a young person is likely to cause very serious harm to other people then one would expect that such a judgement could be backed up with clear and explicit reasoning.

The value of the evidence boxes is generally recognised by YOT staff. One worker, for example, said that 'we would be able to measure what we did as opposed to just relying on someone saying "did something serious" which I have seen.' Others valued the way in which the evidence boxes could be used to give a rounded picture of a young person. 'If somebody else wants to pick up and read what is there, a well thought out and filled in *Asset*, it's the actual evidence in it that brings everything together. It does give me a flavour of what young person I'm dealing with so I like to see a bit of evidence.'

Actual practice in this area appears to be variable, however, and examination of completed *Asset* forms provides examples of both good and poor practice. In the quote given below, for example, the assessor used the evidence box (in the 'family and personal relationships' section of the core profile) to record important details about a difficult situation in a young person's life but also to explain that this was not linked to the recent offending behaviour. 'Both grandparents have died recently within ten days of each other. No evidence to suggest this influenced the decision to commit the offence'.

In other cases, the use of evidence boxes was less constructive. In one case, for example, the initial *Asset* referred to 'bizarre behaviour at school' without explaining what this meant. The case had subsequently been transferred to another worker who did not know what this referred to or why it had been included in the original *Asset* form.

This is clearly an area in which many more examples could be given but the key finding here has been that practice is very variable and some practitioners are using the evidence boxes more extensively and effectively than others. An advantage of *Asset*, however, is that it at least makes assessments more explicit and can be used to promote greater transparency in decision-making.

Planning interventions

As yet there is little data available on the link between *Asset* and intervention planning comparable to the research findings available in relation to other tools such as ACE (Merrington 2001; Haslewood-Pócsik and Skinns 2000) although work in this area is underway as part of ongoing research.

Early findings suggested that *Asset* was often viewed by practitioners as an isolated piece of work and was not closely linked into other areas of practice such as pre-sentence report writing, reviewing the progress of an order or intervention planning (Roberts et al. 2001). To give one example in relation to planning programmes of work to be undertaken with young people, there was little evidence of practitioners incorporating positive factors identified in *Asset* into intervention plans. However, anecdotal evidence suggests that this situation is now changing. The YJB has recently issued an intervention plan to link in with *Asset* and we are also aware of a number of YOTs who have been doing their own work in this area to ensure that *Asset* becomes more integrated into practice.

Open and transparent practice

To what extent has the use of a common assessment framework promoted or facilitated the sharing of information both within teams and between YOTs and other agencies? One aspect of this is the opportunity that *Asset* presents for managers to oversee the quality of assessments being made within a team and to take action where appropriate (e.g. through supervision or provision of training) to improve practice. Again, practice was variable between teams with some managers regularly sampling the quality of completed *Assets* and others never doing so. Other problems included a lack of communication between managers and staff in some settings. For example, one practitioner stated that 'I know managers read them but I've never had any feedback on the *Assets* I've done so I don't know if I'm doing it well.'

A second issue concerns the transfer of information between agencies. There was some confusion about what happened when young people moved into the adult system as to whether *Asset* forms were always passed on to the Probation Service. The transfer of information to the secure estate has also been problematic in some cases. National Standards (Youth Justice Board 2000a) state that a completed *Asset* should always be sent to the secure estate when a young person receives a custodial sentence but practice was variable. Some YOT staff were concerned about how information might be used by other organisations and there may be issues to address concerning the provision of information or training for staff in relevant agencies about how to use and interpret the *Asset* forms that they receive.

Resource management

The scope for *Asset* to provide aggregate profile data of young people who offend has been demonstrated by Baker et al. (2002). This type of analysis can give both broad-brush descriptions of large samples of young people and more specific comparisons of the differences between particular groups, for example by gender or ethnicity. Evidence suggests that a small number of YOTs have begun to carry out similar analyses locally to assist in decisions regarding resource allocation but for the majority this is not yet something which they see as central to practice. This may increase with the forthcoming publication of a handbook for managers which will include some guidance on how to use *Asset* data as a basis for allocating resources within the YOT and as a tool for securing funding from other services.

Is it an asset?

Is it achieving what was required by the original specification?

A first step in assessing the value of *Asset* is to consider whether it has met the requirements set out by the YJB at the initial stage of design and development. It was intended that *Asset* should:

- cover those risk and protective factors most closely linked to offending by young people;

- produce a score for each young offender on the level of risk identified as an indicator of the service needs a YOT should put in place;

- measure changes in needs and risk over time both in the community and in custody;

- assist practitioners to plan a programme of interventions to reduce the risk factors and increase the protective factors associated with the young person;

- give an overall prediction of the likelihood of reconviction including its frequency and seriousness;

- contain triggers for further assessment in respect of more specific needs and risks.
  (Youth Justice Board 1998)

The evidence outlined above demonstrates that *Asset* is achieving some of these goals while in other areas further research is both required and ongoing (e.g. measuring patterns of change over time).

Fit for purpose

The list given by Merrington (this volume) of aspects of practice in which assessment tools need to demonstrate their value is broader than the specification set by the Youth Justice Board. Some of these issues – for example, the role of *Asset* in assessing young people who may present a risk of serious harm to other people – have not been discussed specifically in this chapter because of lack of space but it is anticipated that results of research in this area will be made available in the near future.[7] For the areas in which evidence is available it appears *Asset* is working well in terms of the 'technical' issues such as validity and predictive accuracy but that there is a lot of variation between YOTs in the extent to which it is impacting on wider practice, e.g. its use for allocating resources.

We might also want to add to Merrington's list some criteria which are more specific to assessment tools being used with young people, e.g. that a tool should take account of 'welfare' needs or should assist in identifying situations where statutory provision is not being given (such as a child not receiving any educational provision). *Asset* has the potential to contribute in this area as it incorporates questions about these broader issues (e.g. health needs[8]) but the evidence as to how YOTs are using this information is currently anecdotal rather than systematic.

What is the broader impact of Asset on practice and performance?

There are a number of practical issues that could be discussed here (e.g. the impact of *Asset* on the workload of youth justice staff) but I want to focus on three key themes that are central to practice.

Developing the knowledge base

Aggregate *Asset* data can help YOTs to be more informed about the profiles of the young people they are working with in any particular locality. Similarly, on a national scale *Asset* should be expected to provide useful data to help develop our knowledge about young people who offend. Clearly the use of data in this regard is dependent on the quality of *Assets* completed by practitioners but there are three main ways in which *Asset* can help to develop the knowledge base.

Firstly, it can support or reinforce existing research findings. For example, the links between educational difficulties and offending or the multiple problems faced by many 'looked after' young people (Youth Justice Board 2001a) were also found in the recent national *Asset* study (Baker et al. 2002). The second area is in providing data on groups who have sometimes been previously under-represented in research, e.g. female offenders and young people from ethnic minorities. As *Asset* is used with all young people from final warning stage onwards it has the potential to provide data on relatively large samples of particular groups. This can include, for example, highlighting differences between various ethnic groups, between male/female offenders and between those of different ages when providing an account of the assessed needs and risks of young people (Baker et al. 2002) which can help staff in choosing appropriate ways of working with particular young people.

Third, *Asset* data can highlight areas for further research. This could include, for example, work in relation to young people who commit particular types of offences. One example from recent research is that it appears that young people from a mixed ethnic or dual-heritage background were assessed by practitioners as having more risk factors and fewer protective factors than other groups of young people (Baker et al. 2002). The initial sample was relatively small and it would be necessary to investigate this further before reaching any conclusions but it illustrates how *Asset* can identify interesting issues for an ongoing research agenda to expand our knowledge base.

Routinisation and professional judgement

A criticism often made in relation to the use of assessment tools is that they deskill staff and lead to ways of working that involve repetitious completion of tasks within a rigid practice framework that restricts the use of professional judgement (Garrett 2002; Pitts 2003). A similar argument has been made against the use of *Asset*; for example, Smith refers to 'the conflicts inherent in a standardized instrument such as *Asset*, which confronts professional judgement with a routinised scoring system in such a way as to challenge many of the core beliefs of those who see a role for individual discretion and creative decision making in the youth justice system' (Smith 2003: 101).

However, this is to misunderstand both the purpose and the design of *Asset*. To use *Asset* well actually requires the use of considerable professional skill and expertise. Practitioners are asked to make decisions about a wide range of issues, from practical assessment of the suitability of a young person's accommodation arrangements to judgements about their self-perception, levels of victim awareness and motivation to change. Information to form the basis of these assessments needs to be gathered in a way that engages a young person and their parents/carers, thus challenging staff to work in a creative and dynamic way.

The ratings themselves are based on clinical judgement (such that it is not entirely accurate to refer to *Asset* simply as an actuarial tool). As practitioners are asked to rate the extent to which the issues identified in each section of *Asset* are associated with a risk of reoffending, it is quite possible for a worker to record details of problems in a young person's life but give a low rating because there is no evidence to suggest that these are the issues most closely associated with the offending behaviour (for example, the case involving bereavement cited on page 10 above). It is not an automatic system in which ratings are generated by the number of boxes ticked in any given area but rather it is a way of helping to structure and measure professional judgements.

The way in which the ratings are used in practice must also be considered. If they were to be used in a rigid way which prescribed exactly which services a young person received according to their total score then Smith's criticism would appear more reasonable. Alternatively, they can be used in a more flexible way to indicate the intensity of provision that might be appropriate or which of a range of programmes might be most suitable.

Risk and contextualisation

As a risk/need assessment tool, *Asset* obviously attaches a lot of weight to the assessment of risk – in particular risk of reconviction and risk of serious harm to others. This focus has been welcomed by some staff who feel that it has corrected a previous imbalance in practice. For example, one practitioner stated that:

> I don't think we actually looked at risk … I think we were aware that they might be at high risk of reoffending but the *Asset* brings out other issues. They might be at high risk because of an emotional or mental health problem that we perhaps didn't highlight before. You might be going in the house and doing an assessment and all of a sudden it comes out that when they were little they microwaved the dog. I think it's made us much more aware of risk but also what can be done with it to reduce it.

For other observers, however, this focus on risk and offending behaviour is viewed negatively. 'The preoccupation with the offender *as an offender* and nothing else, reflected by the use of instruments such as the *ASSET* form, creates an arbitrary and ultimately unsustainable separation between the young person concerned and his/her social characteristics and needs' (Smith 2003: 197).

I would argue that this represents a misunderstanding of *Asset* and that it is possible to use it in a way that combines an emphasis on risk with attention to other needs. There are three main reasons for this. Firstly, *Asset* includes questions about a range of areas, e.g. health, self-perception and positive factors, that can contribute to understanding the context in which offending behaviour occurs but also to identifying particular issues that may need to be addressed in addition to directly offending-related work. This can apply to the specific work carried out with individual young people and to the use of aggregate data. From the recent national sample, for example, it was found that lack of access to health care resources was regarded by practitioners as a problem for 9 per cent of the young people being assessed.

Secondly, if *Asset* is used appropriately it should enable practitioners to take account of the complexity of young people's lives and to look at the interconnections between different risk and protective factors. *Asset* was never intended to be used as an interview schedule (Youth Justice Board 2000b) or to prescribe a fixed range of questions that practitioners cannot deviate from. Instead it is intended to be used to structure the process of collecting, recording and analysing information, but it is clearly emphasised that this should be done in a way that engages young people (and their parents/carers) and encourages them to participate fully in the process of assessment and planning (Youth Justice Board 2002b).

Following on from this point, the third argument is that creative use of the 'What do YOU think?'(WDYT) self-assessment provides a clear opportunity for young people to express their own views about their circumstances, behaviour and the problems they may be facing. Once again, this has value both at the individual level and in terms of aggregate data. Analysis of a sample of these forms, for example, was able to show that a large proportion of those who completed the WDYT acknowledged that they found it hard to trust other people while a small but significant number recorded thoughts of deliberate self-harm or suicide (Baker et al. 2002). In addition, comparison of *Assets* completed by practitioners with responses given by young people on WDYT can highlight interesting differences of perspective. For example, of 265 cases in which young people said they were worried about something that might happen in the future, only 49 per cent of *Asset* forms contained an acknowledgement of this by practitioners.

Asset in the future

Progress so far

Asset has been developed and introduced into practice within a relatively short period of time and, as with the roll-out of any initiative on this scale, there have inevitably been some difficulties in implementation.[9] Nevertheless, it is now being used regularly across England and Wales and there is an increasing amount of evidence to suggest that it is a useful practice tool for the youth justice system. This chapter has highlighted the areas in which the evidence suggests that *Asset* is working well, the issues which are currently the subject of ongoing research and the areas in which more evidence would be desirable. Pursuing further research is clearly essential but it is also important to ensure that existing evidence is widely disseminated so that youth justice practitioners and managers can begin to engage with it and consider how it could inform the ways in which they work.

Making Asset more of an asset

Asset is clearly here to stay and, further, the Youth Justice Board has set a target for 100 per cent completion (Youth Justice Board 2001b). How therefore might we build on the progress made so far in order to make *Asset* an even stronger asset?

Changes to the tool itself

This could include changes in the style and presentation of *Asset* (both in paper and electronic formats) or more technical adjustments, for example removing some items found to have a weak association with recidivism. One important area for development will be to refine the rating system. For example, the addition of static factors and weightings has been shown to increase predictive accuracy (Baker et al. 2002). Over time, there may be sufficient evidence to justify the possibility of adding different weightings for ethnicity, gender or age. Bonta, for example, argues that 'risk/need scales may need to be differentially weighted according to race' (1989: 60). The advantage of such an approach is that it provides a closer reflection of young people's particular characteristics while retaining a common assessment framework.

Changes in systems

Practitioners might perceive *Asset* more positively if it was easier to use and easier to link to other areas of practice. Modifications to information technology systems could be important here, for example making it easier to update *Assets* during an order, allowing information recorded in *Asset* to be copied over to pre-sentence reports (PSRs) and enabling faster transfer of completed assessments between teams (or between YOTs and the secure estate). Another area for system change might be in relation to the nature and frequency of data transfers from YOTs to the YJB.

Changes of policy and culture

At a national level, this might include the Youth Justice Board placing greater emphasis on the use of *Asset* to inform planning and resource allocation so as to demonstrate its practical value. Within teams, managers may need to become more proactive at discussing *Asset*, providing feedback to staff or using *Asset* as part of the appraisal process. In some teams, or among some groups of practitioners, there is still a need for greater openness about assessment practice and a willingness to record the basis for professional judgements in a more coherent and systematic way.

Conclusion

It has rightly been argued that 'while standardised assessment tools have a real value in promoting consistency and in giving structure to practitioners' judgements, their uncritical application will be unfair and counter-productive' (Eadie and Canton 2002: 21). The key issue therefore is how to ensure that *Asset* is used appropriately and creatively within a practice framework that promotes high-quality assessment, values professional skills and engages young people and their carers.

On the basis of the evidence currently available, it is possible to conclude that *Asset* can be an asset in many ways. For practitioners, it gives comprehensive coverage of key risk and protective factors and provides an indicator of the likely risk of reconviction that can be used to inform subsequent service delivery. For young people, there are benefits to having higher quality assessments and intervention plans, particularly if practitioners make use of WDYT and incorporate young people's views into the planning process. For anyone working, or interested, in the field of youth justice *Asset* has the potential to be of significant interest because of its ability to help expand our knowledge about young people who offend. *Asset* has already had a significant impact on practice. This needs to be consolidated and further steps taken to ensure that it is used to the best possible effect.

Notes

1 *Asset* is not an acronym but for the first three years of its existence it was capitalised by the Youth Justice Board (YJB) and appeared in YJB documentation in capitals – perhaps to signify its central role within the new youth justice system.
2 For example, a version of ACE for young adult offenders was developed for the Probation Board for Northern Ireland.
3 Some additional qualitative material collected as part of this study and not reported by Baker et al. is cited in this chapter.
4 If a young person is sentenced to a Detention and Training Order (DTO), the core profile should also be completed at the point of release into the community.

5 Revised versions of the scoring system (i.e. including static factors and weightings) were more effective in predicting seriousness of reconviction offences (Baker et al. 2002).
6 Practical constraints meant that it was not possible to use the preferred method of comparing assessments of the same young person made by different practitioners at a similar point in time. As an alternative, comparisons were made using a score derived from static factors as a control.
7 In summary, practice is mixed. Some practitioners are using *Asset* to record thorough assessments of risks of serious harm to others but in some teams staff are much less clear about how to use this part of *Asset*. Its use is also influenced by whether or not teams have clear local policies on risk management.
8 Other improvements have been made in the revised version of *Asset* issued by the YJB in August 2003, e.g. the ETE (education, training and employment) section now includes specific questions about the amount of provision a young person receives.
9 Including issues around the development of electronic versions of *Asset*.

References

Aye Maung, N. and Hammond, N. (2000) *Risk of Re-offending and Needs Assessments: The User's Perspective*, Home Office Research Study 216. Home Office: London.

Baker, K., Jones, S., Roberts, C. and Merrington, S. (2002) *Validity and Reliability of ASSET: Findings From the First Two Years of Its Use*. London: Youth Justice Board.

Bonta, J. (1989) 'Native inmates: institutional response, risk and needs', *Canadian Journal of Criminology*, 31 (1), 49–61.

Burnett, R. and Appleton, C. (2004) *Joined-up Youth Justice: Tackling Youth Crime in Partnership*. Lyme Regis: Russell House.

Eadie, T. and Canton, R. (2002) 'Practising in a context of ambivalence: the challenge for youth justice workers', *Youth Justice*, 2 (1), 14–26.

Garrett, P. (2002) 'Yes Minister: reviewing the "Looking After Children" experience and identifying the messages for social work research', *British Journal of Social Work*, 32 (7), 831–46.

Haslewood-Pócsik, I. and Skinns, J. (2000) *Supervision Plans*, Probation Studies Unit ACE Practitioner Bulletin 2. Oxford: Probation Studies Unit.

Jose, S. (2001) 'Summary of the Results of a Study into the Reliability of *ASSET* Use in the Devon Youth Offending Service'. Exeter: Devon Youth Offending Service (unpublished).

Merrington, S., Baker, K. and Wilkinson, B. (2003) 'Using risk and need assessment tools in probation and youth justice', *Vista*, 8 (1), 31–8.

Merrington, S. (2001) *Objectives, Intervention and Reducing Risk*, Probation Studies Unit ACE Practitioner Bulletin 3. Oxford: Probation Studies Unit.

Moore, R., Gray, E., Roberts, C., Merrington, S., Waters, I., Fernandez, R., Hayward, G. and Rogers, R. (2004) *National Evaluation of the Intensive Supervision and Surveillance Programme: Final Report to the Youth Justice Board*. London: Youth Justice Board.

PA Consulting (2003) 'Delivery Plan for 100% Completion of *ASSET* in All Required Cases'. London (unpublished).

Pitts, J. (2003) *The New Politics of Youth Crime: Discipline or Solidarity?* Lyme Regis: Russell House.

Raynor, P., Kynch, J., Roberts, C., Merrington, S. (2000), *Risk and Need Assessment in Probation Services: An Evaluation*, Home Office Research Study 211. Home Office: London.

Roberts, C., Baker, K., Jones, S. and Merrington, S. (2001) *The Validity and Reliability of ASSET: Interim Report to the Youth Justice Board*. Oxford: Centre for Criminological Research.

Roberts, C., Burnett, R., Kirby, A. and Hamill, H. (1996) *A System for Evaluating Probation Practice*, Probation Studies Unit Report 1. Oxford: Centre for Criminological Research.

Smith, R. (2003) *Youth Justice: Ideas, Policy and Practice*. Cullompton: Willan.

Wright, C. (2003) '*ASSET*: success proves it essential', *Youth Justice Board News*, July, 5.

Youth Justice Board (1998) *Specification for the Design of a Risk Assessment Tool for Youth Offending Teams and Secure Establishments*. London: Youth Justice Board.

Youth Justice Board (2000a) *National Standards for Youth Justice*. London: Youth Justice Board.

Youth Justice Board (2000b) *ASSET: The Youth Justice Board's Assessment Profile. Guidance Note 1*. London: Youth Justice Board.

Youth Justice Board (2000c) *ASSET: Explanatory Notes Version 1*. London: Youth Justice Board.

Youth Justice Board (2001a) *Risk and Protective Factors Associated with Youth Crime and Effective Interventions to Prevent It*. London: Youth Justice Board.

Youth Justice Board (2001b) *Corporate Plan 2001–02 to 2003–04 and Business Plan 2001–02*. London: Youth Justice Board.

Youth Justice Board (2002a) *Building on Success: Youth Justice Board Review 2001/ 2002*. London: Youth Justice Board.

Youth Justice Board (2002b) *Assessment, Planning Interventions and Supervision: Key Elements of Effective Practice Source Document*. London: Youth Justice Board.

Chapter 6

Exploring effective educational interventions for young people who offend

Geoff Hayward, Martin Stephenson and Maggie Blyth

The interrelationship between education and youth crime has long been recognised. The question posed in *The Times* in 1867: 'Which is best, to pay for the policeman or the schoolmaster – the prison or the school?' (Furlong 1985) has never been satisfactorily answered. Public opinion and social policy has seesawed between these options ever since. Similarly the professional response has often been to adopt polarised positions whereby learning is the prerogative of teachers and the criminal justice remit is confined to offending behaviour. The Youth Justice Board is attempting to devise and implement a new synthesis whereby mainstream education recognises its duty to prevent offending and those working in youth justice understand that virtually all their interventions revolve around the promotion and support of learning. In order to achieve this it will be necessary to blend the evidence base across education and youth justice, modify the design and research methodologies and adopt new skills and knowledge across professional boundaries. This chapter addresses these issues in three sections. First, we examine the relationship between education and offending. Second, we describe the Youth Justice Board's new education and training strategy intended to deal with the issues raised in the first section of the chapter. Finally, we review our current understanding of what works in relation to the educational interventions which lie at the heart of the YJB strategy.

The link between education and offending

There are three main areas where there appears to be significant linkages between education and offending by young people:

1. Detachment from mainstream education.
2. The impact of custodial sentences.
3. Educational underachievement, particularly with respect to literacy and numeracy.

The research base in each of these areas is uneven and, in some instances, non-existent. It is likely, however, that these three aspects are related and that the barrier to learning represented by low levels of basic educational attainment is a significant factor in pushing young people out of formal learning and further towards the margins of society. What is known, as revealed by meta-analyses, is that school participation and delinquency are quite strongly and inversely related, and that the most effective intervention programmes for reducing offending are those which help young people who offend to enter and sustain themselves within the labour market (Lipsey 1995).

Detachment

The association between being out of school and offending has received considerable attention over the last few years – particularly in the context of the significant rise in permanent exclusions from school which occurred during the 1990s. The latest research is starting to indicate that exclusion in itself could have an independent impact on offending (Berridge et al. 2001). However, there have been no studies so far looking in detail for a given area at the relationship between the scale and nature of juvenile offending and the out-of-school population. In relation to those young people who have not attended school for a significant period of time but were not formally excluded, remarkably little is known about their numbers or experiences. For instance, there are no national statistics on how many young people have not attended school for, say, the last six months. There is not even an official definition of what constitutes long-term non-attendance. There are potentially large numbers of young people out of the school system for lengthy periods of time and therefore at risk of offending who are not being effectively monitored.

The interaction of systems can also put further barriers in the way of young people who are already excluded and make their return to mainstream education more difficult. For example, young people not attending school are more than three times as likely to offend than those attending school (although the causal relationship of these two facts is not clear) (Graham and Bowling 1995). Research has also shown that excluded young people who commit offences are much more likely to receive custodial sentences as those who are not excluded (Parker et al. 1989).

Even less is known about transmission mechanisms. In the case of permanent exclusion, for example, a strong link with offending behaviour has been shown (Home Office 1988; Audit Commission 1996) but is it because offenders are more likely to be excluded or does this exclusion have an independent effect on offending? If it does have an independent effect on offending, how does this occur? A variety of explanations, either singly or in concert, could be the case:

- increased opportunity for offending;
- greater association with delinquent peer groups;
- increased conflict within the family;
- greater surveillance by the police.

Although it is currently impossible to be precise about the numbers of young people outside of mainstream education, the scale of the problem can be illustrated through the following extract from an Audit Commission report on attendance and exclusion (Audit Commission 1999):

> On any one day, just under 400,000 (5 per cent) of the 8 million pupils who should be in school are not there. Absence un-authorised by the school (pupils truanting or parents keeping them off without permission) will account for just over 40,000 of these. In the whole school year, over 6 million of the 8 million pupils in England and Wales are likely to have at least one authorised absence; over 12,000 pupils will be permanently excluded from their schools and over 150,000 will be excluded for a fixed period.

Similarly, as the Audit Commission's 1996 report on young people and crime concluded:

> Reducing the number of pupils who are not at school for reasons of truancy or exclusion could significantly reduce the number of

young offenders in a local area. Half of truants offend, but only one quarter of non-truants do. If half of the truants returned to school, and the returned truants were as likely to offend as the non-truants, the percentage of offenders in the age group could be reduced from 35 to 30 per cent. Similarly, three-quarters of excluded pupils offend, but only one-third of those who are not excluded.

Similar conclusions were reached in a later study (Reid 1999):

> The consequences of truancy are enormous. Consider a few simple facts. Forty per cent of all street robberies in London, and a third of car thefts, 25 per cent of burglaries and 20 per cent of criminal damage were committed by 10 to 16 year-olds in 1997 and were blamed on truants. Truancy is the greatest single predictor of juvenile and adult crime. Two-thirds of young offenders begin their criminal activities while truanting.

The most recent study of this issue argued that it was the simple fact of absence from school that represented the real link with youth crime rather than being in a particular category such as permanent exclusion. It concluded that social policy needed to measure and then take steps to reduce the total out-of-school population in a given youth offending team area in order to prevent offending (Youth Justice Board 2001).

Custody

Ironically there are grounds for suspecting that the criminal justice system itself exacerbates its problems of detachment by lowering attainment and increasing risk factors for further offending. This is exemplified by the impact of custody. The criminal justice system in its interaction with the education system appears, partly as a punitive reaction to offending, to detach young people from mainstream schooling. Indeed, the legislation was recently amended to enable head teachers to remove a young person from the school roll when they receive a custodial sentence (Education Pupil Registration Amendment Regulations 1997). The very formation of youth offending teams may have acted to absolve schools of their duty to provide education for all young people, including those who have offended. There is a tendency for the focus of professional attention to be on behaviour rather than educational attainment.

Custody appears to have three intrinsic weaknesses. It curtails decision-making and planning skills in those who require them the most. Learning is provided in such an abnormal environment that the subsequent application of this learning in the community is extremely limited. By removing young people who have only a tenuous attachment to formal education (even if only to a pupil referral unit with part-time provision) further dislocation is caused for a young person, their parents/carers and the relevant professionals.

For the 3,000 children and young people in custody at any point in time, a review of the pre- and post-custodial education and training experiences of young people assessed the continuity and effectiveness of work begun in the first half of the Detention and Training Order through into the second half of the sentence (Youth Justice Board 2001). While for some young people there was an increase in the volume of education that they received in custody, and for many young people there was a positive shift in attitudes towards formal education, there were some extremely negative consequences. While between one-quarter and one-third had no education, training or employment provision arranged immediately prior to their entry into custody, this had risen to nearly 60 per cent by the time of their release into the community on average only three months later. There was a significant increase in part-time educational provision, and where young people did continue in education, there was a 70 per cent discontinuity in the courses and materials they followed compared to those undertaken in custody.

Reintegration into mainstream school, on either a full- or part-time basis, was uncommon with only 13 per cent of those released being offered places in mainstream schools and only half of these actually attending (7 per cent). An even smaller proportion had college placements arranged (10 per cent), although attendance was proportionately much higher. Not surprisingly perhaps, just over a quarter had offended in the first month following release.

Another study found that 'the most dominant theme in educational breakdown was primarily organisational or system failure rather than the fault of the young people concerned'. The stigma attached to these young people was so great, and negotiations between custodial institutions and the often distant local education authority (LEA) so difficult, that 'it was suggested that education authorities often initiated problems either through delays, or because of inadequate or inappropriate provision' (Hagell, Hazel and Shaw 2000).

Underachievement

Raising the educational attainment of young people who offend has been identified as one of the most effective means of reducing criminogenic risk factors. Studies have indicated that the route to rehabilitation for most young offenders is through the attainment of normal milestones often denied to them because of their marginalised status – learning to read and write, attending school, gaining qualifications, getting a job, entering further education and training, finding somewhere to live and maintaining stable family relationships. Historically, young people who have offended have not achieved these milestones because they have not had access to, or have had great difficulty in participating in, mainstream educational services, both pre- and post-16. For the Youth Justice Board's Basic Skills Initiative (2000), INCLUDE carried out a survey on the basic skills needs of young people with whom Youth Offending Teams (YOTs) are working. This survey revealed reading ages averaging six years behind chronological ages.

The levels of literacy and numeracy of many young people (aged 10 to 17 years) as measured on their reception into custody are very low. For those of compulsory school age (15- and 16-year-olds in this sample) about half had literacy and numeracy levels below that expected of an 11-year-old. Almost a third (31 per cent) had literacy levels at or below that expected of a seven-year-old and over 40 per cent had numeracy skills at or below the level expected of a seven-year-old (Youth Justice Board 2001). Low attainment also potentially weakens other interventions to prevent offending. It is not simply that the very low reading skills might compromise the learning in the programmes, but equally that limited oral skills could be a barrier for interventions such as programmes to overcome offending behaviour.

Examination of the influence of schools has concentrated on their effects on pupils' academic achievement and attendance rather than on their disruptive behaviour, exclusion or offending, and the consensus here is that schools do have a substantial effect on the academic progress of their pupils and on attendance (Rutter, Giller and Hagell 1998). The evidence that exists on the direct impact of schools on behaviour indicates that this operates through two mechanisms:

- the ethos of the school;
- the intake balance.

It is likely that schools have an important influence on the development of resilience. Several studies have found, for example, that schools helped young people to acquire, through positive experiences, a greater ability to plan their lives. Young people from high-risk backgrounds who were enabled to adopt this approach were less likely to join peer groups with anti-social behaviour and this had a beneficial impact on their life choices, for example regarding employment (Rutter, Giller and Hagell 1998).

It may well be that resilience is more likely to be developed in normal settings such as mainstream schools. While behaviour can be modified in a segregated setting, it is the transfer of learning to the everyday world that is the real challenge. A reintegration model that groups together young people on the basis of their anti-social behaviour – in an environment that is very different from mainstream school – would appear to have a limited chance of success in terms of equipping them for a return to mainstream school. Even positive behaviour, when it is learned in 'abnormal' environments, will not easily survive the challenge of transferring to a school, college or workplace.

The Youth Justice Board's learning and skills strategy

In recognition of the importance of learning and skills provision in assisting with the aim of preventing offending, a strategic approach towards the access, participation and progression of young people in education has been adopted (Youth Justice Board 2003a):

> Ensuring young people are in full-time education, training or employment is the single most important factor in reducing the risk of offending. The Youth Justice Board will, therefore, continue to prioritise the engagement of young people in education and training. We aim to improve access to education, training or employment in the community and for those young people making the transition from custody to the community on Detention and Training Orders.

In doing so the Youth Justice Board has attempted to apply the principles of effective practice in relation to preventing offending in an educational context with, for example, the principle of 'dosage' being reflected in requirements for the volume of learning for young people in the youth justice system and work being undertaken on 'responsivity', that is, matching interventions to learning styles. There is also recognition of the inherent difficulties of applying the same methodologies and hierarchy of validating evidence to educational issues.

Having first made significant contributions to the evidence base the Youth Justice Board has constructed its Learning and Skills Strategy around the three crucial areas identified above:

- detachment from education;
- the negative impact of custody;
- increasing the literacy and numeracy skills of young people who offend.

With a view to reducing the numbers of young people detached from mainstream education the Youth Justice Board has used its position as a non-departmental public body to lobby government departments, particularly the DfES, and established partnerships with bodies such as the Connexions Service National Unit, the Adult Basic Skills Strategy Unit, the Offenders Learning and Skills Unit and the Learning and Skills Council.

The YJB, in line with its policy of encouraging mainstream services, particularly schools and FE colleges, to provide for young people who offend, has required through its National Standards (Youth Justice Board 2004) that youth offending teams have effective protocols with LEAs and Local Learning and Skills Councils to ensure access to suitable education and training provision. Similarly the roll-out of the Intensive Supervision and Surveillance Programme contains a requirement for a full-time educational component within it. In order to strengthen the evidence base, a two-year research study has been commissioned to identify the scale and salient features of young people detached from education and the most effective means of reconnecting them.

To counter the negative impact of custody, the Youth Justice Board has adopted a twin-track approach of reducing the numbers in custody and attempting to introduce a comprehensive education reform programme to transform Young Offender Institutions into Secure Learning Centres. It has produced a detailed *National Specification for Learning and Skills for Young People on a Detention and Training Order* (Youth Justice Board 2002) supported by significant new resources and detailed monitoring systems, and targets to monitor the volume of learning received in custody, its impact in terms of learning gains and continuity subsequently in education and training in the community. In recognition of the crisis of attainment in relation to literacy and numeracy among young people who offend and its importance as a risk factor in their offending, the YJB has also devised and introduced the PLUS strategy as an integral part of the *Skills for Life* strategy in conjunction with the Adult Basic Skills Strategy Unit (DfES) and managed by the YJB, the Offenders Learning and Skills Unit (DfES) and the Arts Council England.

The YJB has set demanding targets relating to education and training in order to assure progress in this area. These targets are incorporated in its plans for both Youth Offending Teams and the Juvenile Secure Estate

(Youth Justice Board 2003a). The corporate and business plan has 11 overarching targets for its three-year period, with Target 7 being to: 'Ensure that at least 90 per cent of young offenders are in suitable, full-time education, training and employment during and at the end of sentence by March 2004'. In addition there are 13 specific targets set for youth offending teams, at least four of which are closely related to the effective delivery of education and training to young people on a Detention and Training Order.

In order to reach these and other crucial targets the Youth Justice Board has introduced an effective practice strategy (see also the chapter by Fullwood and Powell). This strategy is characterised by recognition of both the weaknesses of the evidence base and the need to secure local managerial and practitioner ownership. Consequently it is based not on accredited programmes but rather on key principles that have been derived from the existing evidence. Out of the 15 areas of effective practice identified, education has been set as a priority.

This effective practice strategy in turn is supported by the Youth Justice Board's Human Resources and Learning strategy which has as its centrepiece a new qualification: the Professional Certificate in Effective Practice (Youth Justice).

Implementing the vision

The remainder of this chapter examines how evidence can inform and enable the implementation of the YJB strategy, especially the educational interventions which lie at its heart.

Does participation in education reduce recidivism?

There have been a number of research studies that have tried to measure the effectiveness of educational intervention programmes with offenders, but these are bedevilled by poor research design. For example, Tolbert (2002: 19) identifies the following as being major limitations of studies investigating the relationship between educational intervention and recidivism:

- Most do not take into account other services and factors both inside and outside of prison that may affect recidivism rates, such as drug treatment programmes, post-release services and family support

- Most of the results are vulnerable to self-selection bias – the methodologies do not adequately account for participant characteristics.

- Most do not follow released inmates for a long enough period of time.

- Most vary in their definitions of recidivism; a nationally [US] recognised definition of recidivism does not exist.

- Most are unable to measure various levels of improvement in inmates' behaviours.

- Most are based on correctional educational records that are often poorly kept by institutions.

An exception is Porporino and Robinson's (1992) research on the effectiveness of a Canadian Adult Basic Education (ABE) programme. Using random and matched comparison group designs, Porporino and Robinson (1992) concluded that the recidivism rate of participants in the ABE programmes was significantly lower than that of the comparison group. In the US, Steurer, Smith and Tracy (2001), using a longitudinal design involving 3,400 inmates released from correctional institutions in Maryland, Minnesota and Ohio prior to 1999, found that participation in state correctional education programmes lowered the likelihood of reincarceration by 29 per cent. Saylor and Gaes's (1997) research on the Post-Release Employment Project (PREP) found that there was a 33 per cent drop in recidivism among 7,000 federal prisoners who participated in vocational and apprenticeship training between 1983 and 1987. Tolbert (2002: 1–2) concludes that:

> These programmes lead to lower recidivism rates, according to advocates, because they provide inmates with the knowledge, skills, attitudes, and values needed to succeed in society and to avoid future criminal activity.

Such evidence both substantiates the assumptions underpinning the YJB's strategy and identifies the need for a systematic basic skills intervention, such as the PLUS Strategy, for young offenders.

What are the features of successful programmes?

Meta-analytic studies provide the best evidence about the general features of successful programmes. These include maintaining programme integrity, providing appropriate assessment, provision of one-to-one support and providing a community base. Providing a vocational focus also seems to be important in some programmes. Vennard and Hedderman (1998), reproducing the principles drawn up by reviewers of the What Works literature, list the following as characteristics of effective intervention programmes with offenders:

- *Risk classification* – more intensive programmes should be targeted at higher-risk offenders while those of lower risk should receive lower or minimal intervention.

- *Targeting criminogenic needs* – that is, looking at factors which contribute directly to criminal behaviour, as outlined in research, such as anti-social attitudes, drug dependency, low levels of educational and vocational skills and poor cognitive skills.

- *Programme integrity* – programmes should be carried out by trained staff in accordance with aims and objectives that do not change and methods that are consistently applied.

- *Responsivity* – research shows that the best results are obtained if teaching styles match offenders' learning styles, with most offenders requiring active, participatory approaches rather than loose, unstructured and overly didactic methods.

- *Treatment modality* – most effective interventions are those which are skills-based, designed to improve problem-solving and social interaction and which also include a cognitive component to address attitudes, values and beliefs which support offending behaviour.

- *Community base* – programmes provide mechanisms for offender reintegration back into community-based education, training and employment programmes.

This list provides important clues for designing educational interventions for young offenders and the YJB strategy does place, for example, an appropriate emphasis on targeting those with low levels of educational attainment and poorly developed vocational skills. Furthermore, the YJB Human Resources strategy is intended to develop the capabilities in staff needed to ensure programme integrity. Tolbert (2002) identifies two additional features of effective correctional education programmes that are relevant here:

- the need to make the programmes participatory so that they address learners' needs outside prison or outside of an intervention such as the Intensive Supervision and Surveillance Programme;

- the need to link prison education programmes to post-release services.

The YJB's policy clearly acknowledges these needs. For example, the PLUS Strategy has been designed so that it is complementary to the Adult Literacy and Numeracy curriculum frameworks and also introduces learners to objectives-led approaches to teaching being advocated for adult basic skills instruction in the community. This provides the potential for learners to make a smoother transition from basic skills provision within the Youth Justice System to community-based provision.

Designing effective basic skills interventions

The meta-analytic studies suggest some broad principle for designing effective interventions. However, the details of such interventions, what Vennard and Hedderman (1998) refer to as 'treatment modality', still need to be worked out and the effectiveness of the different components of a programme's design in raising attainment in basic skills needs to be established. It is at this level of analysis that the evidence base becomes very weak and fragmentary. The problem is not a dearth of basic skills programmes for offenders, but a lack of studies that have employed the research designs needed to tease out the contributions being made by different parts of an instructional design – such as methods of assessment, materials being used, pedagogical strategies employed and the role of information technology – to gains in basic skills attainment.

Currently the best advice available about the detailed design of basic skills instruction takes the form of lists of rather general statements that can be construed as guidelines for 'good teaching'. The *Skills for Life* strategy, for example, contains recommendations for teaching using the Adult Literacy and Numeracy Curricula. This, combined with the training programme for basic skills tutors and learning support assistants, provides an important source of advice for designing instruction but the extent to which it is based upon causal evidence is open to question. This point is well made by Brooks et al. (2000: 138):

> One very significant finding needs to be stated immediately. If the question is put as 'What factors have been shown by research to be *causally* related to progress in adult basic skills?' the answer is *none*. For a factor thought to be causally related to progress to be proven so it is necessary to set up an intervention or training study. Matched experimental and control groups must, over a period of time, receive treatments that differ only in the factor being investigated (all other factors being controlled), and must be tested

both before and after treatment. Only if the experimental group makes statistically significantly more progress that the control group can it validly be inferred that the difference in treatment caused the difference in progress. It is clear from the analysis of impact studies … that *barely a single intervention or training study has been successfully carried out in the adult basic skills field. This is the most significant gap in the research literature identified in this review.* (Emphasis in the original)

Greenberg et al. (2002: 208) also point to the weak knowledge base:

There has been very little research on effective reading instruction for adults with limited reading skills. The situation today has not changed much from the late 1980s when Bowren (1987: 208) bemoaned the fact that research on reading instruction for adults 'has long floundered as an educational stepchild. While the research in reading instruction is voluminous, that in reading for the adult population is meagre'. Similarly Bristow and Leslie (1988: 214) stated that 'practitioners … currently have little research-based information regarding instructional techniques effective with … [the adult literacy] population.' More than ten years later, a literature review indicates that reading instruction for adults continues to lack a theoretical and developmental-based approach to reading acquisition.

This is clearly an area where the knowledge base underpinning effective instructional design requires rapid development.

Motivation and attitudes to learning

One area where more research evidence is available concerns how contextual factors can affect motivation and attitudes towards learning, and how these can be managed by taking account of the interaction of learner characteristics, the learning context and learning processes in producing desired learning outcomes. For example, Sutton (1982) argues that the coercive prison environment makes implementing educational programmes problematic. To meet this challenge, Kerka (1995) and Talbot (2002) suggest that educational programmes must be designed to be sensitive to 'prison culture'. Here, Kerka (1995) cites the Principles of Alphabet computer-assisted programme as one that works in prison because it aligns with prison culture but also offers offenders the opportunity to exert agency. Thus this programme:

- was advertised as a 'reading lab' rather than as a straightforward literacy class;
- involved pairing learners according to race ethnicity or the prison 'pecking order';
- relieved tedium through the use of computer-assisted instruction;
- taught skills that matched the short-term self-interest of the learners thereby aiding motivation and providing rapid positive feedback;
- involved using computer disks that allowed learners rare opportunities for privacy.

Recognising that the previous experiences and needs of learners is also crucial for effective instructional design. A danger here is stereotyping offenders in terms of their prior educational experiences and attainments. Nonetheless, Sutton (1992) argues that offenders do show some common characteristics across countries and regions which are closely interrelated with previous educational experiences and perceptions of current needs. Kerka (1995) identifies the following as learner characteristics which should be considered when designing educational interventions for offenders:

- the negative schooling experiences of many offenders;
- their lack of self-confidence in relation to learning and education;
- their likely poor attitudes towards education.

Kerka (1995) claims that such characteristics interact with prison routines – lock-downs, head counts, attending court, meeting with lawyers – and peer pressure to discourage attendance at, and reduce attainment in, educational programmes. Such findings are echoed by Brooks and colleagues:

> The major motive for entering basic skills provision appears to be a self-desire for self-development (including work-related motives) and a better self-image, and the major barrier appears to be sensitivity to the stigma attached to poor basic skills. (2000: 57)

> *Young adults in particular, are sensitive to the stigma attached to poor basic skills and this acts as a real deterrent.* (2000: 49, emphasis in the original)

Effective instructional designs will, therefore, need to provide very positive experiences if young offenders are to be motivated to participate in and learn though prison- and community-based basic skills instruction. However, the formation of such motivation cannot be left solely to those providing basic skills instruction, whether in the secure estate or in the community. A whole-institution approach is likely to prove more effective (see next section).

Fortunately, motivation is one of the better researched concepts in educational psychology and the principles developed by educational psychologists to inform the development of motivating learning environments (see Graham and Wiener 1996, and Stipek 1996) map closely to key features of effective prison education programmes identified by Sutton (1992), Kerka (1995) and Tolbert (2002). Thus, all of these authors recognise the need to provide a learner-centred learning experience that:

- involves the student;
- uses an individualised approach;
- involves the students in formative assessment;
- provides formal recognition for progress.

Once again these are rather general statements. They still need to be interpreted and operationalised in the form of an appropriate instructional design that takes account of the characteristics of both learners and the learning context. Two examples indicate how this might be achieved.

Offenders are too often constructed in policy discourse as being educationally deficient. However, all individuals bring some resources to a situation that can be built upon. Recognising and using such resources, in combination with the identification of individual learning needs, seems to be a hallmark of effective basic skills instruction. For example, Boudin (1993) used women prisoners' concerns about AIDS as an issue around which to organise instruction. The instructional form, writing and performing a play, drew upon a key resource of this group of learners: a well-developed oral tradition.

Family literacy programmes also develop the idea of needs and resources as a means of producing effective instructional designs, with the added advantage of enabling offenders to view themselves and to be seen by others in roles other than that of an offender. In addition, family literacy programmes have high retention rates, typically over 90 per cent and almost always over 80 per cent (Brooks et al. 2000: 52). The Arts Enrichment strand, for example, within the PLUS Strategy provides the opportunity to both embed basic skills learning in addition to mobilising the resources and interests of the learners. This should, if effective, lead to enhanced motivation, commitment and learning.

Infrastructure for effective delivery

The evaluation of Literacy and Numeracy Strategies (Earl et al. 2003) highlighted the need both to provide support for teachers and schools, and to apply pressure to achieve change. The PLUS Strategy provides support through a developing HR strategy, a network of advisers, and the provision of learning support assistants and instructional materials. The YJB targets provide the pressure for change. Thus some basic building blocks are in place. However, some major institutional issues are identified within the literature which must be addressed if programme implementation is going to be effective.

For example, Tolbert (2002) suggests that a decentralised criminal justice system can lead to duplication of effort and inconsistencies in the education offered to offenders. LoBuglio (2001: 117–18) describes these inconsistencies as follows:

> This fragmented system has a deleterious effect on correctional education programs as the correctional population moves among these institutions. An accused offender may begin his correctional experience in a local jail, wind up in a state prison after receiving a criminal conviction, and get parole for good behaviour at the same time that he serves a sentence of probation, which might require him to attend a day reporting center. As offenders move within and between these institutions, they rarely are provided a consistent and uniform level of educational programming.

The US evidence is that the 'correctional philosophy' within prisons is crucial to the success of education programmes. For example, for class attendance to be encouraged and strictly enforced by the prison staff, the education programmes need to have strong and constant support from the governors and prison officers. If this support does not exist then the programme will suffer, as described by LoBuglio (2001: 123):

> Correctional education programs depend on the cooperation of correctional officers who let inmates out of their living units and monitor classroom activities along with performing a host of other duties. Wardens and superintendents who value rehabilitative programs make sure that the incentives are properly structured

and that correctional staff willingly and consistently ensure the smooth operation of these programs. Institutions that have prison administrators who are indifferent to rehabilitation programs and are plagued by labour-management disputes often have poorly functioning programs that are cancelled for a variety of security reasons.

The US research reviewed by Tolbert (2002) also emphasises the crucial importance of governance structures on correctional education programmes. Contrasting state delivered correctional services with those that are contracted out, Tolbert (2002: 5) points out that:

> There are pros and cons to each type of governing structure, with each type having a notable effect on the correctional education program in areas such as funding, teacher certification requirements, whether instructors are viewed as correctional officers or simply as instructors, and the acceptance of education in the correctional institution.

These findings are reminiscent of those from both the ECOTEC Audit (YJB 2001) and the evaluation of the PLUS Programme. The movement of young people within the youth justice system, and inconsistent liaison between those providing educational services and those with custodial responsibilities within the secure estate both served to reduce the effectiveness and efficiency of programme delivery.

This problem is exacerbated by the short length of many Detention and Training Orders (DTOs) which limits the time available in the custodial part of the sentence to undertake meaningful educational work. Porporino and Robinson's (1992) research suggests that a minimum of three months of structured, ongoing educational input is needed to make quite modest gains in basic skills. The construction of 'stable learning platforms' is therefore a priority to ensure access on a regular basis to educational services during the custodial part of the DTO, and to maximise the benefit for those on short sentences. In addition, community follow-up is crucial if meaningful gains in basic skills are to be made. Developing the community side of the PLUS Strategy is a clear priority.

Institutional incentives to participate also need to be considered. For example, in the US, most states and the Federal Bureau of Prisons provide positive and/or negative incentives for inmates to enrol in education classes, such as earlier eligibility for parole, extending visitation privileges and reinstating days required to be served prior to being eligible for parole (Tolbert 2002). The US also has regulations that affect educational provision in state prisons. For example, the Federal Bureau of Prisons has a mandatory policy requiring inmates who do not have a high school diploma to participate in literacy programmes for a minimum of 240 hours or until they obtain their General Educational Development test (GED). Enrolment in education programmes is also required in many states if the inmate is under a certain age, as specified by that state's compulsory education law.

Conclusion

This limited review of the literature supports the importance placed by the YJB on education and training to reduce recidivism among young offenders. Meta-analytic studies also provide broad design principles for constructing educational interventions. The gap in the research evidence lies in making causal connections between features of programmes, such as assessment and different teaching strategies, and gains in basic skills attainment.

However, we cannot wait for evidence to be produced before starting to design and implement basic skills programmes for young offenders in the community and the secure estate. Rather we need to develop such knowledge while developing and implementing programmes. During this knowledge-building phase it will be sensible to use a wide conception of what is to count as evidence in order to collect as much intelligence as possible about what might work.

One possibly fruitful source of such intelligence is the voluminous literature on learning to read and write derived from research with young children. In addition, the growing literature about effective offender education programmes, which is largely a literature about prison education programmes, can also be drawn upon. Combining the two should allow the production of a tentative design matrix that indicates the desirable features that should be included within the instructional designs of educational interventions for young offenders.

New research also needs to be undertaken. Thus there is an urgent need in this knowledge-building phase to consider the types of research questions to be asked and the sorts of research designs appropriate for answering those questions. Such questions need to range from the technical design features of basic skills instruction to wider issues of culture and managing change within the Youth Justice System. Here, well conducted design experiments and practitioner research are likely to be more useful during this knowledge-building phase than randomised control trials (RCTs), not least because they can be undertaken more rapidly and at a fraction of the cost of an RCT. Once more intelligence on which to base programme design has been collected, and once those programmes have been given time to bed down, then research can move to a knowledge-evaluation phase using more experimental approaches. Such a process is analogous to the conduct of a drugs trial: the trial, properly using an RCT design, takes place at the end of a long process of research and development, not at the beginning of the process.

However, what will emerge from this process will be neither a prescriptive manual that teachers or other practitioners can un-thinkingly apply to solve problems nor 'teacher-proof' materials. Such 'command-and-control' approaches, based upon an engineering model of social science research, tend not to work because they can neither take account of the subtle and nuanced differences between contexts that practitioners find themselves in, nor the diverse needs of the learners. Rather, what is likely to emerge are principles and 'rules of thumb' that can be used to expand the rationality of practitioners, helping them to think through their practice and so develop the way they work with young people.

References

Agyris, C. and Schon, D.A. (1982) *Theory in Practice*. San Francisco, CA: Josey-Bass.

Audit Commission (1996) *Misspent Youth*. Audit Commission: London.

Audit Commission (1999) *Missing Out*. Audit Commission: London.

Berridge, D., Brodie, I., Pitts, J., Porteous, D. and Tarling, R. (2001) *The Independent Effects of Permanent Exclusion from School on the Offending Careers of Young People*, RDS Occasional Paper 71. London: Home Office.

Boudin, K. (1993) 'Participatory literacy education behind bars', *Harvard Educational Review*, 63, 207–32.

Bowren, F.F. (1987) 'Adult reading needs adult research models', *Journal of Reading*, 31, 208–12.

Bristow, P.S. and Leslie, L. (1988) 'Indications of reading difficulty: discrimination between instructional and frustration-range performance of functionally illiterate adults', *Reading Research Quarterly*, 23, 200–18.

Brooks, G., Giles, K., Harman, J., Kendall, S., Rees, F. and Whittaker, S. (2000) *Assembling the Fragments: A Review of Research on Basic Skills*. London: DfEE.

Earl, L., Watson, N., Levin, B., Leithwood, K., Fullan, M. and Nancy Torrance with Jantzi, D., Mascall, B. and Volante, L. (2003) *Watching & Learning 3*. Toronto: OISE.

Furlong, V.J. (1985) *The Deviant Pupil: Sociological Perspectives*. Milton Keynes: Open University Press.

Graham, J. (1988) *Schools, Disruptive Behaviour and Delinquency: A Review of the Research*, Home Office Research Study 96. London: HMSO.

Graham, J. and Bowling, B. (1995) *Young People and Crime*, Home Office Research Study 145. London: Home Office.

Graham, S. and Weiner, B. (1996) 'Theories and principles of motivation', in D.C. Berliner and R.C. Calfee (eds), *Handbook of Educational Psychology*. New York: Macmillan, pp. 63–84.

Greenberg, D., Fredrick, L.D., Hughes, T.A. and Bunting, C.J. (2002) 'Implementation issues in a reading program for low reading adults', *Journal of Adolescent and Adult Literacy*, 45 (7), 626–32.

Hagell, A., Hazel, N. and Shaw, C. (2000) *Evaluation of Medway Secure Training Centre*. London: Home Office.

Hiebert, E.H. and Raphael, T.E. (1996) 'Psychological perspectives on literacy and extensions to educational practice', in D. Berliner and R.C. Calfee (eds), *Handbook of Educational Psychology*. New York: Macmillan, pp. 550–602.

Kerka, S. (1995) *Prison Literacy Programs*, ERIC Digest No. 159. Columbus, OH: ERIC Clearinghouse on Adult Career and Vocational Education.

Lipsey, M. (1995) 'What do we learn from 400 research studies on the effectiveness of treatment with juvenile delinquents?' in J. McGuire (ed.), *What Works: Reducing Reoffending*. Chichester: Wiley.

LoBuglio, S. (2001) 'Time to reframe politics and practices in correctional education', in J. Comings, B. Garner and C. Smith (eds), *Annual Review of Adult Learning and Literacy*, Vol. 2. San Francisco: Jossey-Bass.

Malen, B., Croninger, C., Muncey, D. and Redmond-Jones, D. (2002) 'Reconstituting schools: testing the "theory of action"', *Educational Evaluation and Policy Analysis*, 24 (2), 113–32.

Parker, H., Sumner, M. and Jarvis, G. (1989) *Unmasking the Magistrates: The 'Custody or Not' Decision in Sentencing Young Offenders*. Milton Keynes: Open University Press.

Porporino, D. and Robinson, F. (1992) *Can Educating Adult Offenders Counteract Recidivism?* Report of the Research and Statistics Branch. Ottawa: Correctional Service of Canada.

Reid, K. (1999) *Truancy and School*. London: Routledge.

Rutter, M., Giller, H. and Hagell, A. (1998) *Antisocial Behavior by Young People*. Cambridge: Cambridge University Press

Saylor, W. and Gaes, G. (1997) 'Training inmates through industrial work participation and vocational and apprenticeship instruction', *Corrections Management Quarterly*, 1, 32–43.

Steurer, S., Smith, L. and Tracy, R. (2001) *Three States Recidivism Study*, prepared for the Office of Correctional Education, US Department of Education. Lanham, MD: Correctional Education Association. http://www.ceanational.org/documents/3statefinal.pdf/.

Stipek, D.J. (1996) 'Motivation and instruction', in D.C. Berliner and R.C. Calfee (eds), *Handbook of Educational Psychology*. New York: Macmillan, pp. 85–113.

Sutton, P. (1992) *Basic Education in Prisons: Interim Report*. Hamburg, Germany: Unesco Institute for Education.

Tolbert, M. (2002) *State Correctional Education Programs: State Policy Update*. Washington, DC: National Institute for Literacy.

Vennard, C. and Hedderman, J. (1998) 'Effective interventions with offenders', in P. Goldblatt and C. Lewis (eds), *Reducing Offending: An Assessment of Research Evidence on Ways of Dealing with Offending Behaviour*. London: Home Office.

Youth Justice Board (2001) *An Audit of Education and Training Provision within the Youth Justice System*. London: Youth Justice Board.

Youth Justice Board (2002) *National Specification for Learning and Skills for Young People on a Detention and Training Order*. London: Youth Justice Board.

Youth Justice Board (2003a) *Youth Justice Board for England and Wales Corporate Plan 2003–04 to 2005–06*. London: Youth Justice Board.

Youth Justice Board (2003b) *Education, Training, and Employment: Key Elements of Effective Practice*. London: Youth Justice Board.

Youth Justice Board (2004) *National Standards for Youth Justice*. London: Youth Justice Board.

Chapter 7

Probation interventions to address basic skills and employment needs

Ilona Haslewood-Pócsik and Gráinne McMahon

This chapter will examine two probation interventions to improve the basic skills and employment potential of adult offenders through two separate pathfinder projects – the Basic Skills Pathfinder and the Employment Pathfinder – launched by the former Home Office Probation Unit, now the National Probation Directorate, and funded as part of the Crime Reduction Programme. While the first author was an evaluator of the Employment Pathfinder and the second author was an evaluator of the Basic Skills Pathfinder, both projects are discussed in tandem within this chapter for the following reasons. First, the large sample of offenders from the evaluation of the Basic Skills Pathfinder provides an opportunity to examine: the basic skills and employment needs of offenders in a probation context; the extent of the overlap between the two needs; and the associations of these needs with other offender characteristics. Second, the different approaches adopted in the implementation of the two pathfinders will be compared and contrasted in order to draw out some of the reasons why they were implemented with limited success, which may also have some implications for the future. We hope that this juxtaposition of the findings from each project will help to inform the future development of such initiatives so that they are better tailored to the needs of offenders.

The Basic Skills Pathfinder was operational between 2000 and 2002, and the Employment Pathfinder between 2001 and 2003. The Research, Development and Statistics Directorate of the Home Office commissioned the evaluation of both pathfinders, and two separate teams within the Probation Studies Unit in the Centre for Criminological Research, University of Oxford, were contracted to carry out the work.

Both evaluations were carried out in collaboration with the Department of Educational Studies and the ESRC Research Centre on Skills, Knowledge and Organisational Performance (SKOPE) also at the University of Oxford and, in the case of the Employment Pathfinder, in partnership with London Probation Area.

The full report of the evaluation of the Basic Skills Pathfinder has been published on the Home Office website (McMahon et al. 2004). A report on Phase I and II of the Employment Pathfinder evaluation has also been published on the Home Office website (Haslewood-Pócsik et al. 2004). However, some of the points raised here will rely to a greater extent on the findings of the Basic Skills Pathfinder evaluation because it collected information on a much larger offender sample than the Employment Pathfinder. Nevertheless, the issues discussed should, we hope, make a useful contribution to the pursuit of evidence-based practice in the National Probation Service.

This chapter will take the following format: We will commence with a summary of what the two pathfinder programmes and their evaluations set out to achieve. An overview of previous research on the basic skills and employment needs of offenders will follow. The next section will explore the basic skills and employment needs of offenders, and the significant associations of basic skills needs and unemployment with other offender characteristics, based on data collected as part of the Basic Skills Pathfinder. Consideration will also be given to the extent of the overlap between the two needs in this section. Next, the selection criteria and take-up rate of the basic skills and employment interventions will be discussed, and a number of reasons will be suggested as to why the pathfinders experienced high attrition rates and the implications of this for the National Probation Service. In conclusion, we will offer a few useful points distilled from the pathfinder evaluations as well as raise a number of questions which may contribute to marking out the future direction of innovative work in this area.

The pathfinders and their evaluations

Both of these pathfinders were aimed at providing interventions designed in accordance with effective practice principles (Chapman and Hough 1998). The effective practice initiative in the Probation Service advocated not only the necessity of distinguishing between offenders' needs in general and their offending-related needs, but also of building on research evidence in establishing what interventions seemed effective, for whom and under what circumstances. The importance of consistent implementation, monitoring and evaluation of such interventions was also emphasised by the initiative.

The Basic Skills Pathfinder and its evaluation

In devising the Basic Skills Pathfinder, the Home Office was mindful of the scarcity of information on offenders' basic skills needs and their link with reoffending, and drew on the available research evidence of the time, mainly originating from North America, in particular the research carried out in Canada by Porporino and Robinson in 1992 (discussed below in more detail). The Basic Skills Pathfinder was carried out in seven probation areas (nine prior to amalgamation of some services in April 2001) throughout England.

The primary objective of the Basic Skills Pathfinder was to measure the effectiveness of improving offenders' literacy and numeracy skills and to examine how improvements related to reducing reoffending rates. Prior to the commencement of the evaluation of the Basic Skills Pathfinder, the seven selected probation areas had already implemented basic skills programmes which differed largely in assessment and content. In order to be able to collect consistent data, and to ensure that the eligibility for basic skills provision was the same in all seven areas, the evaluation team stipulated a number of changes to the seven programmes, mostly related to the assessment materials. In this respect, the evaluation formed the core of the Basic Skills Pathfinder and had the following aims:

- To provide a baseline estimate of the basic skills needs in the population of offenders on whom pre-sentence reports were prepared by the Probation Service over a period of one year.

- To investigate the relationships in the data collected on the sample in order to examine the potential precursors to having a basic skills need and/or being unemployed, for example problems with drug abuse.

- To measure the progress of offenders who accessed basic skills provision in terms of improvements to their basic skills, pursuit of further education or training and/or gaining and maintaining employment. The evaluation also sought to measure actual improvements in basic skills from level to level.[1]

- To examine the attrition rates from basic skills programmes and the reasons why attrition takes place with a view to informing implementation practice.

- To identify good practice in screening, assessment, monitoring, teaching and learning, and implementation.

A three-stage process was devised for selecting offenders for basic skills tuition and in order to collect data for the evaluation:

1. Screening for basic skills needs, which should have been carried out with all offenders at the pre-sentence report stage.

2. If the screening indicated a probable basic skills need and the offender received a Community Rehabilitation Order (CRO) or a Community Punishment and Rehabilitation Order (CPRO), then at the commencement of community supervision he or she should have been referred to the next stage of the process where an in-depth basic skills assessment was undertaken.

3. If the in-depth assessment found further evidence of a basic skills need, the appropriate offenders should have been referred to basic skills provision.

A fourth stage was also envisaged where outcomes from basic skills provision (improvements in basic skills and accessing further education or training and employment) would be examined but, as will be explained in the last section of the chapter, the high attrition from the Basic Skills Pathfinder evaluation process meant that the data were not available to carry out these analyses.

The Employment Pathfinder and its evaluation

Compared with basic skills-related services, more extensive employment and training-related services were already in place for offenders in the late 1990s in the Probation Service. Therefore, the first question to consider in planning the Employment Pathfinder was whether the already available employment provisions were effective in helping offenders gain and retain employment and in reducing reoffending. It was concluded that there was little evidence of the effectiveness of the existing interventions in reducing reoffending, mainly due to the lack of rigorously evaluated programmes. A new pathfinder intervention was therefore designed, which began with a review of the available research, mostly from other countries, on what seemed to be effective (Home Office Probation Unit 1999).

The primary aim of the Employment Pathfinder was defined by the designers as 'improving the effectiveness in getting offenders into jobs, as a means of reducing reoffending'. The target group was restricted to those who met the following criteria: long-term, hard-to-place offenders with a medium to medium-high risk of reoffending, who had previously completed a general cognitive offending behaviour programme. The Employment Pathfinder also sought to determine approaches which addressed the particular disadvantages faced by minority ethnic offenders in the labour market.

The Employment Pathfinder intervention was planned to incorporate a number of elements:

- a specific assessment of offenders' employment needs;

- an employment skills programme using a cognitive-behavioural approach to improve problem-solving and other employment-related 'soft-skills' (e.g. social skills);

- support in developing other employment-related skills (e.g. CV writing) and in handling disclosure issues;

- effective partnerships with the Employment Service and potential employers to assist offenders with finding and sustaining jobs;

- a case management system that motivated, reinforced and supported offenders' learning from the pathfinder interventions.

The evaluation plan included a process evaluation of the implementation, programme monitoring, an evaluation of the outcomes (including a two-year reconviction study) and a cost-benefit analysis. However, the evaluation process was not interlinked with the implementation of the pathfinder to the same degree as was the case with the Basic Skills Pathfinder.

Basic skills, employment and offending: findings from previous research

The basic skills, qualifications and employment of offenders and ex-offenders became the subject of growing government policy and research interest towards the end of the 1990s. As the author of a recent literature review of this topic noted, more is known about the needs of 'captive' offender groups – that is, those under the supervision of the Probation Service or in custody – than about any other offender or ex-offender groups (Rolfe 2001: 241). Even for these groups, however, data on offenders' basic skills levels, qualifications and employment status are not generally and systematically available in an aggregate format. It is anticipated, however, that the nationwide introduction and routine use of the OASys assessment system within the Probation and Prison Services will improve this situation. In the meantime, the Basic Skills Pathfinder evaluation has provided a baseline estimate of basic skills needs and qualifications among a large sample of offenders, and the connection of these and other factors, such as permanent exclusion from school, with employment status.

Basic skills needs and offenders

In examining some potential precursors to the onset of offending behaviour in schoolchildren, Graham and Bowling (1995) concluded in their research that the strongest correlates in young people were contact with delinquent peers, truancy and low parental supervision. Those who truanted from school and those who were excluded from school were more likely to begin to offend. This seems consistent with findings from other research. Berridge and his colleagues reported that 65 per cent of their sample of those excluded from school (n = 343) had been cautioned or convicted of a criminal offence some time in their lives, while 44 per cent of males and 17 per cent of females in the sample had committed three or more offences (Berridge et al. 2001). Current work with young offenders, as discussed by Hayward, Stephenson and Blyth in this volume, indicates that there are also significant links between detachment from mainstream education and educational under-achievement, particularly with regard to literacy and numeracy. It can be reasonably assumed that these educational difficulties continue and remain prevalent through adulthood in the offending population.

The Prison Service began to screen prisoners for basic skills needs on a large scale in 1999. It came as no surprise that the Prison Statistics for England and Wales for 2000 (Home Office 2001) showed higher basic skills needs among a large sample of inmates (at least 90,000) than the levels estimated in the general population (Department for Education and Employment (DfEE) 1999). Approximately one-third of inmates were below Level 1 in reading, one-half in writing and more than one-third in numeracy in all adult establishments. These proportions were 2 to 5 per cent larger in young offender institutions.

Mair and May (1997) reported that 42 per cent of their probation sample (n = 1,273) had left school before the age of 16 and that 49 per cent left at age 16. One-fifth of females and 13 per cent of males said that they had entered full-time further or higher education. Overall, 48 per cent of the males and 51 per cent of the females in the sample had no qualifications. Similarly, the evaluation of the probation employment, training and education (ETE) schemes, Asset in London and Springboard in Surrey[2] (Sarno et al. 2000) quoted proportions of between approximately one-third to just under one half of offenders who had no formal qualifications (although the actual percentages differed by project, and also by year in at least one of the projects).

With respect to the links between poor educational achievement and employability, Stewart and Stewart (1993) found that offenders tended to leave school before the compulsory age of 16 and attended school irregularly while they were enrolled and, as a result, had poorer basic skills and lower levels of qualifications, if any. The authors then concluded that most of their sample (n = 1,389) were not sufficiently prepared for any possible employment opportunities and, as such, their subsequent work experience was unskilled and erratic.

Employment and offenders

Some authors have suggested that, generally, crime levels have tended to be related to periods of high unemployment (e.g. Box 1987; Downes 1993), and that, after the 1970s, the crime–unemployment link became remarkably strong due to a change in the character of unemployment which became endemic, long-term and clustered around certain geographical areas (Chiricos 1987).

Various sources have quoted a consistently low rate of employment, compared with the general population, among offenders supervised by the Probation Service during the past decade or so (allowing for some local variations). Mair and May (1997) reported that only 21 per cent of their sample on probation orders and combination orders were employed in 1994, when their survey was completed. The corresponding figure reported by the Association of Chief Officers of Probation in 2000 was 26 per cent (based on pre-sentence report data) (ACOP 2000). The employment status of prisoners entering custody was marginally better on the whole: about one third of male prisoners and one-fifth of female prisoners were in employment at this point (Social Exclusion Unit 2002). However, none of this compared favourably with the over 60 per cent among the general working-age population who were reported to be in employment even during the economic downturn of the early 1990s (Mair and May 1997).

There is recent evidence to suggest that strong links exist between unemployment and reconviction. In the reconviction study carried out by May (1999) on a sample of over 7,000 offenders under probation supervision it was found that within two years of the commencement of a community sentence, offenders who were unemployed were significantly more likely to be reconvicted than those who were employed. Moreover, unemployment and drugs were consistently found among the various combinations of problems which were strongly associated with reconviction.

It is also suggested by a number of authors that the link between unemployment and reoffending is complex and may be indirect, and that it exists in interaction with a range of other social and demographic variables (e.g. Tarling 1982; Downes 1993; Rolfe 2001). Some evidence also suggests that literacy levels, gaining employment and level of earnings are related (Carey et al. 1997), and that those who improve their basic skills will raise their status on the occupational scale and, thus, also improve their chances of employment (Bynner et al. 2001). However, neither of these studies were specific to an offender or ex-offender population.

Interventions to improve basic skills and employment

Previous research has highlighted strong links between poor basic skills, unemployment and offending behaviour. It is important to note, however, that much of the research in this field has been judged to be methodologically flawed by critics because of low sample sizes and the use of disparate assessment instruments, and therefore should be treated with caution (see Porporino and Robinson 1992; Pearson and Lipton 1999).

Perhaps one of the most widely quoted pieces of relevant research was carried out by Porporino and Robinson (1992) on a sample of prisoners in Canada. The authors found that, with regard to recidivism, 30 per cent of the sample (n = 899) who had completed the Adult Basic Education course (equivalent to the high school diploma) were returned to prison, compared with 36 per cent of those who were released before completion (n = 462) and 42 per cent of those who withdrew from the course (n = 375). Interestingly, it was reported that 'higher' risk offenders benefited from the course more than 'lower' risk offenders. Overall, a 33 per cent reduction in offending behaviour was reported for offenders who had completed the education course. Carrying out research in England and Wales, Bridges (1998) found that twice as many unemployed offenders under probation supervision who received help with their employment found a job, as did those who did not receive help (n = 739). These findings indicate that interventions with offenders' unemployment can lead to significant gains.

Previous research also highlighted some findings on the actual take-up of opportunities to improve the literacy and employment situation of offenders, which may continue to ring true in the light of the findings presented in this paper. Mair and May's (1997) survey revealed that the proportion of offenders addressing their employment needs gradually decreased during the period of supervision. For example, while 42 per cent of the interviewed offenders recalled discussing employment problems at their last session with their supervising officer, just 22 per cent recalled actually attending an 'in-house' training and employment unit. Although for a sample in which only 21 per cent were employed, it would be reasonable to expect a considerable overlap between the offenders who undertook the two activities (discussing employment problems and attending a training/employment unit), the study did not specifically mention this.

Mair and May (1997) noted that only 3 per cent of offenders reported contacting an external agency for help with reading, writing and numbers at the encouragement of their supervising officer. A few years later, the evaluators of the Springboard probation ETE scheme in Surrey recorded that, in those cases where the reason for the referral to the project was known (approximately 1,200), the referring officer specified literacy needs in only 9 per cent of referrals (Sarno et al. 2000). The evaluators noted that this might to some extent reflect offenders' initial reluctance to reveal that they had literacy problems. Such reluctance to disclose basic skills needs, and lack of incentives to learn were also observed in the Social Exclusion Unit's investigation of provision for prisoners and ex-prisoners (Social Exclusion Unit 2002). The Social Exclusion Unit identified a need to persuade offenders of the merits and relevance of attendance at basic skills and education sessions, for example by linking basic skills levels with other available activities such as prison workshops. This did not often happen, however. The authors of the report also pointed out that individual problems tended to be addressed separately; consequently, those prisoners who had more than one problem, as was often the case, found it difficult to access the relevant provisions to address all of them.

The literature on basic skills and employment interventions, however, suggests that it was not only the lack of offenders' interest which determined whether they engaged with basic skills and employment schemes. Davis et al. (1997) noted that, in the general context of the low priority given to basic skills work in the Probation Service at the time, whether an offender received some basic skills service or not depended more on the interest and knowledge of the individual staff member who supervised the offender than on area-wide policies or systems.

Roberts et al. (1996), Bridges (1998) and Downes (1998) referred to the uneven referral practice of probation staff to various employment schemes and services, concluding that only a certain proportion of them tended to refer offenders to the schemes. One explanation for the lack of referrals was that those who did not refer seemed to doubt whether the schemes, which were often short term and/or low profile, were able to improve the employment prospects of offenders (Downes 1998).

Basic skills and employment: needs and associations

The findings in this section are based on the dataset collected as part of the Basic Skills Pathfinder evaluation, since screening data (conducted at the pre-sentence report stage) were collected on a large sample of offenders. The sub-sample of those who were sentenced to CRO or CPRO will also be used in this section. However, the sample to which a particular finding relates will be clearly identified throughout.

Basic skills and employment needs

Over 10,000 screenings were collected on offenders at the pre-sentence report stage. Of these, 32 per cent were found to have a *probable* basic skills need (i.e. below Level 1). This is higher than would be expected in the general population, but roughly comparable with the large sample of offenders assessed in prison (see DfEE 1999 and Home Office 2001 above). When broken down by sentence, those who were sub-sequently sentenced to a CRO or a CPRO showed the highest level of probable basic skills needs (39 per cent), higher than among those who were sentenced to custody (30 per cent), and much higher than among those who received a Community Punishment Order (CPO) (19 per cent).

Altogether, approximately 400 offenders had a more in-depth basic skills assessment at the next stage (initial assessment procedure for basic skills needs) which found that 64 per cent had literacy skills below Level 1 and 44 per cent had numeracy skills below Level 1. However, not all of these 400 offenders met the actual criteria of the Basic Skills Pathfinder evaluation (which was that they should have been screened at the pre-sentence report stage and found to have a probable basic skills need, and also that they should have been sentenced to either a CRO or a CPRO). Nonetheless, approximately half of them had been screened for basic skills needs at the pre-sentence report stage and, for these, highly significant relationships were found in this sample between having a probable basic skills need and scoring below Level 1 in in-depth assessment of their literacy and numeracy.

Among the total sample of over 10,000 offenders who were screened at the pre-sentence report stage, 38 per cent were employed, which was considerably higher than the ACOP figure of 26 per cent (ACOP 2000). In the sample who were later sentenced to a CRO or a CPRO, a somewhat lower proportion (32 per cent) were employed, but this was still much higher than the comparable sample in Mair and May's (1997) study which was just 21 per cent. The employment rates in the seven participating probation areas showed some variation, as follows: the percentage of offenders subject to a CRO or CPRO who were in employment ranged between 11 per cent and 39 per cent in the seven pathfinder areas, but six out of the seven areas had a considerably higher rate of employment than that reported in Mair and May's (1997) study, based on 1994 data. Although there is not enough evidence to draw a firm conclusion that the higher employment rate among supervised offenders was due to the more vigorous economic conditions during the data collection period, this may have made a positive contribution as a general background to the variations of the local market conditions in the pathfinder areas.

Among the *unemployed* offenders in the entire pre-sentence report sample, 38 per cent were found to have a probable basic skills need compared to 24 per cent of those who were employed. In the smaller CRO/CPRO sample, 40 per cent of those who were unemployed had probable basic skills needs, whereas the proportion was again lower (29 per cent) for those who were employed. Interviews with 215 unemployed West Yorkshire offenders on a CRO/CPRO or post-release licence conducted as part of the Employment Pathfinder evaluation also contained questions about basic skills. Only 40 interviewees among the total sample (19 per cent) said that they thought they had a problem with basic skills. This percentage did not seem higher than existing estimates concerning the general population, and seemed lower than the 40 per cent with probable basic skills needs in the unemployed sub-sample of the Basic Skills Pathfinder evaluation. However, it is quite possible that this percentage would have been higher if interviewees' basic skills had been tested.

The analysis therefore showed that the association between probable basic skills needs and unemployment was statistically significant in both the entire screening and specific CRO/CPRO samples of the Basic Skills Pathfinder evaluation. However, it is also worth bearing in mind that the relationship between unemployment and basic skills needs is not absolute, as a large proportion of offenders who had probable basic skills needs were employed and the majority of those who were unemployed did not have a probable basic skills need.

Offender characteristics associated with basic skills needs and unemployment

In addition to the basic skills screening data, detailed background information was also collected on the pre-sentence report sample as part of the Basic Skills Pathfinder evaluation. This comprised criminal history, drug misuse, school attendance, educational qualifications and employment history data. As would be expected, particularly within this population, there were strong statistical associations between a number of these characteristics. However, these associations cannot be taken to infer causal relationships.

Three major types of characteristics were associated with *both* offenders' probable basic skills needs and unemployment: age at data collection, history of school attendance and level of qualifications, and risk of reconviction status as measured by OGRS2 scores.[3] For this analysis OGRS2 scores were grouped into three levels of risk: 'low', 'medium' and 'high'. These three categories had significant associations with probable basic skills needs and unemployment even after controlling for the effects of other variables.

The effect of the *age* of offenders on basic skills needs was different from the effect of age on unemployment. While younger offenders (18 to 21 year olds) were more likely than older offenders to have probable basic skills needs, the probability of being unemployed was significantly lower for those aged 18 to 25 and 31 to 40 compared with offenders who were 51 and over. With respect to offenders aged 51 or over, however, there is a possibility that a higher proportion of them were out of work because of incapacity or illness.

The *history of school attendance and highest level of qualification achieved* had a similar effect on both probable basic skills needs and unemployment: offenders who were poor attendees at school and who finished school with poor qualifications were, unsurprisingly, more likely to have probable basic skills needs and be unemployed than those who attended regularly or left school with some qualifications. Offenders who had no qualifications were much more likely to be unemployed than those with Level 2 qualifications or above.

The *risk of reconviction status* of offenders was also inversely associated with both probable basic skills needs and the employment status of offenders: those who were assessed as having a 'medium' or 'high' risk of reconviction were more likely to have probable basic skills needs than offenders in a 'low' risk category. The probability of being unemployed was significantly higher for offenders categorised as at 'medium' risk of reconviction compared with those in a 'low' risk category and much higher for offenders in a 'high' risk category of reconviction.

The survey conducted among 215 unemployed West Yorkshire offenders as part of the Employment Pathfinder evaluation found that offenders' age at interview, level of qualifications, and offending history/risk of reconviction status were also associated with interviewees' *employment history*. Those with a more extensive work history (measured by the length of interviewees' longest employment, the duration of their most recent jobs and the number of their previous job types) tended to be older, had left full-time education later and had a higher level of qualifications. The duration of their most recent jobs, however, was not directly related to the time spent in education or level of qualifications.

In addition, data from the Basic Skills Pathfinder evaluation suggested that the probability of being *unemployed* was also associated with offenders' sex and with drug abuse. *Women* in the sample were much less likely to be in employment than men; however, it is possible that the women in the sample were not in work because they were full-time carers. Offenders who were judged to be *abusing drugs* (or both alcohol and drugs), were significantly more likely to be unemployed than offenders who were not. Offenders who were abusing alcohol only were no more likely to be unemployed than those who did not abuse alcohol.

The survey conducted as part of the Employment Pathfinder evaluation included following up 91 per cent of the total sample of 215 offenders approximately three months after the original interviews. Altogether, 26 per cent of the follow-up sample obtained a job during the follow-up period, and 18 per cent of them still had a job at the time of the follow-up interview. Despite the modest sample size and the limited scope and timescale of the follow-up work, evidence was found that employment history, offending history/risk of reconviction status and recent or current drug use were not only closely interrelated but appeared also to be the determinant factors in offenders' success in obtaining employment. A more extensive criminal history/higher risk of reconviction and the use of drugs (currently or within the past 12 months) seemed to work against obtaining a job. A longer period spent in continuous employment and having had a greater range of job types in the past, indicating a substantial work history, increased offenders' likelihood of obtaining a job within the follow-up period. In addition, current age, age at leaving full-time education and level of qualifications seemed indirectly related to obtaining a job, through other, directly related employment history factors such as the length of the longest job and the number of past job types.

Thus the Basic Skills Pathfinder evaluation and the Employment Pathfinder evaluation found evidence that offenders with a history of poor school attendance, and who had no (or only Level 1) qualifications, who were judged to be abusing drugs, who were at a 'medium' or 'high' risk of reconviction and who had poor basic skills were much more likely to be unemployed than other offenders and less likely to succeed in finding employment. These findings support and further develop May's earlier finding (May 1999) that both unemployment and drug abuse were significantly associated with reconviction.

Given the strong associations between basic skills needs, employment needs and other problems or characteristics above, it is not surprising that the National Probation Service faced difficulties in implementing basic skills and employment provision within a community supervision context. It is also possible to use the findings above to explain, in part, the high attrition rates from the pathfinder programmes. However, the relationship between the variables is complex and is worth exploring further in future research.

Participation in the pathfinders

The number of offenders who accessed the provisions of the Basic Skills Pathfinder evaluation and Employment Pathfinder was below expectations. The low numbers, in turn, limited the evaluation of the pathfinders' effectiveness. This section will look at the approaches taken by the two pathfinders to draw up the selection criteria for offenders, and at possible reasons for low participation.

Differing approaches to drawing up selection criteria

The two projects used very different selection criteria for determining who should have access to the services provided by the probation areas. The approach taken by the Basic Skills Pathfinder will be described as the 'catch-all' approach, and the Employment Pathfinder's approach as 'criteria-based'. Paradoxically, neither of them resulted in a sufficient number of participants. The 'catch-all' approach adopted in the implementation of the evaluation of the Basic Skills Pathfinder specified that *all* offenders should have been screened for basic skills needs when the pre-sentence report was prepared (the PSR stage), and that all those who were screened 'positively' and who were then sentenced to a CRO or a CPRO were eligible for the next stage of the process. This stage involved completing a more detailed basic skills assessment, which should have resulted in a referral to basic skills provision if further evidence of a basic skills need was found. This was expected irrespective of whether offenders might have any other needs. The Employment Pathfinder's approach, on the other hand, was seen as 'criteria-based' because the implementation plan specified that offenders should be referred to the Employment Pathfinder intervention only if they were long-term unemployed, if their offending was likely to be related to lack of employment, and if they had already successfully completed a cognitive-behavioural general offending behaviour programme during their community sentence or while in prison.

Although neither project provided a truly open access to every offender under probation supervision, the Basic Skills Pathfinder evaluation team advised probation areas that offenders who did not precisely meet the referral criteria (e.g. who were sentenced to a CPO rather than a CRO/CPRO) should not be automatically debarred from accessing basic skills provision if they or their supervising officer indicated that they could benefit from it. In contrast, the Employment Pathfinder was not opened up to all of those who wanted to access an employment programme, nor even to all those who were assessed as having an employment need. Offenders' employment needs had to be related to their offending, but more importantly, eligibility for the programme was tied to prior participation in a cognitive-behavioural offending behaviour programme. This, in effect, linked the success of the Employment Pathfinder to the success of the implementation of cognitive-behavioural general offending behaviour programmes in the pathfinder areas involved. As the cognitive-behavioural programmes in these areas began to suffer from high attrition rates, the pool of offenders who successfully completed or nearly completed them, as well as satisfying the other (employment-related) eligibility criteria, quickly evaporated, and thus referrals made to the Employment Pathfinder were low. The National Probation Directorate took steps to remedy the situation a few months before the end of the Employment Pathfinder's operational phase by opening the programme up for a larger number of offenders through relaxing the cognitive-behavioural programme criterion. However, this measure did not result in an immediate increase of referrals and the total number of participants in the employment skills programme remained low.

Ultimately, the outcomes for both projects were limited by high levels of attrition from the programmes. In the case of the Basic Skills Pathfinder evaluation, offenders 'dropped out' or were 'lost to' the process for reasons other than lack of eligibility or suitability. Attrition in the Employment Pathfinder was, at first, mainly caused by the pathfinder being reliant for its target population on other programmes which had themselves high attrition rates. However, after relaxing the dependence on these programmes for referrals, the remaining time proved too short for setting up a comprehensive referral system similar to that of the Basic Skills Pathfinder evaluation. The few referrals were therefore acquired in a haphazard way and were mainly used for test-running a core element of the pathfinder: the employment skills group-work programme.

The next subsection will examine in more detail the points at which attrition occurred and the reasons for this when the 'catch-all' approach was used in the Basic Skills Pathfinder evaluation. It is commonly known that many programmes within community supervision suffer from high attrition rates although the reasons for this may differ from programme to programme. This subject is currently given a high level of attention by the National Probation Directorate and hopefully the points below will contribute to the emerging body of knowledge.

Where and why did attrition happen in the 'catch-all' approach?

Two different sources of data were collected during the evaluation of the Basic Skills Pathfinder to calculate attrition rates: the number of screenings and in-depth assessments received, and the monitoring and evaluation data collected by the pathfinder projects. Although there were some discrepancies between the figures in these sets of data, it was still possible to examine how offenders 'dropped out' of basic skills programmes at various stages.

From the assessment instruments returned to the evaluation team from all the probation areas and concentrating solely on those offenders who met the evaluation criteria, it was found that:

- of the 12,422 court reports prepared during the evaluation period, 10,252 offenders were screened for basic skills needs;

- of these, 1,003 were found to have a probable basic skills need and were sentenced to a CRO or a CPRO;

- of these, 194 attended the initial assessment procedure for basic skills needs.

In total, 191 offenders commenced basic skills provision. However, it was not clear from the received data how many of the 194 offenders who underwent the in-depth assessment took up basic skills provision, or how many of the 191 who commenced basic skills tuition were in the group of 194 offenders who attended the initial assessment procedure for basic skills needs. The staff involved in the Basic Skills Pathfinder evaluation reported that not all offenders who accessed basic skills provision had a basic skills need or were on a CRO or a CPRO. It may be assumed, therefore, that the number of offenders who commenced basic skills provision as a result of the pathfinder selection process is even smaller than 191. Lastly, only 20 interviews were conducted with offenders who were nearing the end of their basic skills provision, which is indicative of even further attrition and, as only 13 post-intervention assessments were received, information on the progress of offenders was limited and could not be analysed statistically.

The reasons for attrition were examined primarily through case material, quantitative data and interviews conducted with the staff involved in the Basic Skills Pathfinder evaluation. Case material was collected on two groups of offenders: (1) the 'experimental' group, that is those who accessed basic skills provision, and (2) the 'comparison' group, that is a random sample of offenders who were found to have a probable basic skills need at the pre-sentence report stage and who were sentenced to a CRO or a CPRO, but who *did not* access basic skills provision. It was concluded that the potential explanations for the high attrition rates could be broken down into two main types: those which concerned the offender and his/her needs on community supervision, and those which concerned the implementation of programmes within probation culture. Both of these will be discussed below.

Offender focus: offenders' characteristics and motivation
One of the most striking findings from the Basic Skills Pathfinder evaluation was that offenders tended to experience other difficulties in addition to poor basic skills, such as accommodation problems, drug abuse and unemployment, which, it was found when case material was analysed, may have acted as potential barriers to offenders accessing basic skills provision. As will be discussed later, more immediate or more pressing issues tended to be given priority by the supervising probation staff over improving offenders' basic skills.

Offenders living in temporary or unstable accommodation were less likely to attend the initial assessment procedure for basic skills needs than those living in their own or semi-permanent (rented) accommodation. This might have been because their case manager was more concerned with addressing their accommodation situation and prioritised that instead of basic skills tuition. In addition, offenders who were not judged to be abusing drugs were more likely to attend the initial assessment procedure for basic skills needs, suggesting that treatment for substance abuse was perhaps given precedence over addressing basic skills needs. This did not apply to offenders believed to be abusing alcohol.

Offenders who were assessed as at a 'low' risk of reconviction were also more likely to be referred to the initial assessment procedure for basic skills needs, and then to basic skills provision, than 'higher' risk offenders. One possible explanation for this is that many offenders who were in a 'higher' risk category might have been referred to offending behaviour programmes at the beginning of their supervision instead of basic skills provision, as the level of risk of reconviction was an important referral criterion for the offending behaviour programmes.

In addition to all this, and not surprisingly, it was found that offenders' motivation was paramount to their success in accessing and remaining on basic skills provision. Offenders who were poor attendees at school were less likely to attend the initial assessment procedure for basic skills needs, implying a potential motivational issue. Also, reports from the basic skills tutors involved in the pathfinder evaluation and from the offenders who were interviewed highlighted that offenders in need of basic skills provision may not have been sufficiently motivated to take-up tuition. Some of the reasons stated by offenders for non-participation, classified by the evaluation team as motivational issues, were:

- work commitments that were believed to be more important than improving basic skills;

- other problems like drugs rehabilitation which were also believed to take precedence for offenders over improving basic skills;

- denial that a problem exists with basic skills;

- embarrassment that a problem exists;

- lack of interest in improving basic skills and not realising the potential benefits;

- believing that basic skills are not an actual or important problem in everyday life.

The Social Exclusion Unit (2002) found a similar reluctance among some prison inmates to take up basic skills tuition and concluded that offenders needed to be convinced by prison staff of the value of improving these skills. The Basic Skills Pathfinder evaluation also suggested that pre-sentence report writers had an important role in performing a similar task. At this early stage, it seemed possible to increase offenders' understanding of what is involved in improving basic skills and to highlight its potential benefits. At the commencement of community supervision and throughout the community sentence, the case manager's role was likewise pivotal in ensuring that basic skills provision was included in the supervision plan and that motivational strategies were employed to encourage the offender to take up and regularly attend basic skills provision.

Probation-related issues: case management practice and staff motivation
The analysis of the case material revealed that the inclusion of basic skills work and the importance placed upon it in the supervision plan affected whether or not an offender was likely to access basic skills provision. Basic skills needs were included in a similar number of pre-sentence reports in the comparison group as in the experimental group but in considerably fewer supervision plans. The reason for this seemed to be mainly the order of priorities drawn up in the supervision plan.

The evidence suggests that offenders in the comparison group were considered by probation staff to have a greater number of problems to be addressed by the Probation Service which took priority in their supervision plans. These included addressing alcohol and drug abuse, cognitive behavioural work, addressing health/depression/self-harm issues, payment of fines to the court or seeking accommodation and employment. This coincides with the findings outlined above on offenders' characteristics and motivation.

Those probation officers who expressed commitment to improving offenders' basic skills thought that such work could normally only take place once other needs had been addressed and other programmes had been completed. Unfortunately, a number of the offenders who could have accessed basic skills provision following other interventions had, by then, been breached for non-compliance or had reoffended and received custody or had had their community sentence revoked. Thus the opportunity was not often presented for referral to basic skills tuition at a later stage.

In addition, it was suggested by much of the evidence from the interviews conducted with staff involved in basic skills work in the seven probation areas that there may have been some motivational issues for probation staff with regard to addressing offenders' basic skills needs. This was closely connected with the nature of probation culture and traditional methods of working with offenders. Although many of the probation staff interviewed were aware of the high level of basic skills needs within the offending population and the potential links between poor basic skills and offending behaviour, most did not see addressing basic skills needs as integral to their work with offenders. This was for two main reasons. While many probation officers recognised that a systematic assessment process was important within probation for ascertaining offenders' needs, this was juxtaposed with the belief that having to complete numerous assessment materials, including those for basic skills, was 'deskilling' to their profession. Related to this was the perception that basic skills provision, as a service to offenders, was an aspect outside of core probation practice because offenders were, in the main, taught by personnel who were not 'traditionally' part of the Probation Service. In essence, it was reported at the time, that the concept of 'farming out' offenders for work to be carried out by others was often not considered conducive to successful intervention with offending behaviour and alien to probation practice.

The implications of attrition

Aside from some of the reported effects of the high attrition rates from the Basic Skills Pathfinder evaluation such as wasted resources, the fundamental implication is that the Probation Service faces an uphill struggle in improving offenders' basic skills. Overall, through further attrition during basic skills programmes, the average number of basic skills sessions attended by offenders was only six, while the most common number was two. It has been estimated by the Basic Skills Agency that it takes several hundred hours to improve an individual's basic skills from one level to the next, although the basis for this claim is unclear. This does, however, illustrate the difficulty faced by the National Probation Service in improving offenders' basic skills and provides further indication of where some of the focus of the National Probation Directorate should potentially lie.

Although great strides have been made to increase the priority given to basic skills work in the probation service in recent years, the evidence above suggests that much work is still to be done both on offenders' motivation and on changing probation culture. To this end, the evaluation found that it is important to increase staff awareness of the significance of basic skills work with offenders as much as possible. This may also require a gradual alteration of traditional perceptions of probation practice whereby probation staff feel more comfortable with the use of specialist outside agencies for basic skills work with offenders.

Next steps after the two pathfinders

Following the findings from the Basic Skills Pathfinder evaluation, the National Probation Service decided to implement a national basic skills strategy across all probation areas in England and Wales. To this end, service delivery targets have been put in place for probation areas. For 2002/03, the targets were 6,000 starts on basic skills programmes and 1,000 qualifications at any level. The targets are much higher for 2003/04: 12,000 qualifications, including 2,000 at Entry Level, 8,000 at Level 1 and 2,000 and Level 2. A 'start' implies offenders commencing to attend basic skills tuition (National Probation Directorate 2003).

The Employment Pathfinder will be followed by a freshly designed Phase II. The design process of Phase II will reconsider the potentially most effective forms of employment service provision, as well as build on the experience of the first pathfinder (now known as Phase I). The latter will include strengthening of the already existing partnerships with other agencies and further development, then application of the new employment skills groupwork programme. Lessons from Phase I, such as those relating to the selection criteria and the referral system, will also be useful in ensuring that the pathfinder maximises the number of participants it recruits and retains. Phase II was scheduled to commence early in 2004.

Conclusions

In summary, some of the findings presented above confirmed, but some also differed from, previous research findings. The present research confirmed that the level of basic skills needs was higher in the offender population than in the general population. The proportion of offenders with probable basic skills needs was a few percentage points higher in the CRO/CPRO population, and lower in the CPO population, than the known custody figures. The research also confirmed the existence of significant associations between basic skills needs, employment needs, drug use and risk of reconviction status, an association found by previous research with employment in focus. The value of basic skills screening and tuition in improving offenders' employment prospects was therefore further supported by the findings.

However, the need for skilled judgement in targeting offenders is evident if we consider that although a significant overlap exists between basic skills and employment needs, a large number of unemployed offenders on community supervision, according to preliminary screening, did not have a basic skills need. The findings presented in this chapter differed from previous research in that a higher proportion of offenders were employed both in the entire pre-sentence report sample and the community supervision sample. However, this figure may have been influenced by the choice of geographical areas participating in the Basic Skills Pathfinder evaluation as well as the more buoyant economic conditions at the time of the data collection. This further underlines the value of systematic, routine collection of aggregate data on the basic skills and employment profile of offenders, both at national and local levels.

It could be argued that the differing approaches taken by the two pathfinders to offender selection and participation led to a similar end. Whereas the Employment Pathfinder only managed to recruit a small number of offenders from the start, the Basic Skills Pathfinder evaluation experienced attrition at all stages of the process. The high attrition experienced by the latter may have important implications for the success of the basic skills provision currently implemented nationally in the National Probation Service, both in terms of feasibility and achieving set targets.

The design failure versus implementation failure dichotomy is also worth considering in the light of the low numbers yielded by the two different pathfinder projects. At first sight, it might be suggested that the Employment Pathfinder suffered from design failure (i.e. offenders' eligibility for the pathfinder was unduly restricted) and the Basic Skills Pathfinder evaluation from implementation failure (i.e. the design was not put into practice as intended). However, it is difficult to substantiate such a claim on the basis of studying the few cases available from the projects, since low numbers do not lend themselves easily to interpretation. The findings above, as well as the already discussed observations of the Social Exclusion Unit in respect of prisoners and ex-prisoners (Social Exclusion Unit 2002), suggest that other factors, such as offenders' motivation and present working practices within the Probation Service, may play just as important a part as the dichotomy above.

Beyond the immediate concern of implementing interventions and meeting targets, however, lay a more fundamental question which was raised both by some of the associations between offender characteristics and by the reasons why take-up remained below expectations. This is the question of determining the most effective strategies for responding to multiple problems presented by offenders. This incorporates a number of more specific questions. For example, which areas of concern should be focused on first in working with individual offenders, and how should interactions between the identified areas be taken into account? In what sequence should interventions take place, and on what timescale? These are all important issues which the Basic Skills and Employment Pathfinders as well as other pathfinders which concentrated on specific areas of probation work have highlighted, but to which they have not by themselves been able to provide definitive answers.

Notes

1 The basic skills levels can be categorised as follows: pre-Entry – below National Curriculum level 1; Entry level – National Curriculum level 1; Entry 2 – National Curriculum level 2 (the level of a competent seven-year-old); Entry 3 – National Curriculum level 3; Level 1 – National Curriculum levels 4 and 5 (the level of a competent 11-year-old); and Level 2 – GCSE A* to C.

2 The *Asset* and Springboard projects in Inner London (now part of London Probation Area) and Surrey Probation Services were probation schemes with the main aim of helping offenders serving probation sentences into work. They also assisted offenders already in employment to improve their work opportunities. Some of the features of these schemes were that offenders were offered counselling, training, work placements and mentoring, and were also provided with sheltered employment schemes.

3 OGRS2 is used in the Probation Service to predict the risk of reconviction of offenders within the next two years and chiefly consists of static criminal history components. For further details on OGRS scores, see Copas and Marshall (1998).

References

Association of Chief Officers of Probation (2000) *Offender Employment Statistics Summary*. London: ACOP.

Berridge, D., Brodie, I., Pitts, J., Porteous, D. and Tarling, R. (2001) *The Independent Effects of Permanent Exclusion from School on the Offending Careers of Young People*. London: Home Office.

Box, S. (1987) *Recession, Crime and Punishment*. London: Macmillan.

Bridges, A. (1998) *Increasing the Employability of Offenders: An Inquiry into Probation Service Effectiveness*, Probation Studies Unit Report 5. Oxford: Centre for Criminological Research.

Bynner, J., McIntosh, S., Vignoles, A., Dearden, L., Reed, H. and Van Reenan, J. (2001) *Improving Adult Basic Skills, Benefits to the Individual and to Society*. London: Department for Education and Employment.

Carey, S., Low, S. and Hansbro, J. (1997) *Adult Literacy in Britain*. London: HMSO.

Chapman, T. and Hough, M. (1998) *Evidence-Based Practice: A Guide to Effective Practice*. London: HMIP.

Chiricos, T. (1987) 'Rates of crime and unemployment: an analysis of aggregate research evidence', *Social Problems*, 34 (2), 187–212.

Copas, J. and Marshall, P. (1998) 'The offender group reconviction scale: a statistical reconviction score for use by probation officers', *Applied Statistics*, 47 (1), 159–71.

Davis, G., Caddick, B., Lyon, K., Doling, L., Hasler, J., Webster, A., Read, M. and Ford, K. (1997) *Addressing the Literacy Needs of Offenders under Probation Supervision*, Home Office Research Study 169. London: Home Office.

DfEE (1999) *Improving Literacy and Numeracy. A Fresh Start*, the report of the working group chaired by Sir Claus Moser. London: Sudbury.

Downes, D. (1993) *Employment Opportunities for Offenders*. London: Home Office.

Downes, D. (1998) 'The role of employment and training in reducing recidivism', *European Offender Employment Forum, Bulletin No. 6*.

Graham, J. and Bowling, B. (1995). *Young People and Crime*, Home Office Research Study 145. London: Home Office.

Haslewood-Pócsik, I., Merone, L. and Roberts, C. (2004) *The Evaluation of the Employment Pathfinder: Lessons from Phase I, and a Survey for Phase II*, Home Office Online Report 22/04. http://www.homeoffice.gov.uk/rds/pdfs04/rdsolr2004.pdf

Home Office (2001) *Prison Statistics: England and Wales 2000*. London: Home Office.

Home Office Probation Unit (1999) 'Employment and Reducing Re-offending: A Literature Review'. London: Home Office Probation Unit (unpublished).

McMahon, G., Hall, A., Hayward, G., Hudson, C., Roberts, C., Fernández, R. and Burnett, R. (2004) *Basic Skills Programmes in the Probation Service: Evaluation of the Basic Skills Pathfinder*. Home Office Online Report 14/04. http://www.homeoffice.gov.uk/rds/pdfs04/rdsolr1404.pdf

Mair, G. and May, C. (1997) *Offenders on Probation*, Home Office Research Study 167. London: Home Office.

May, C. (1999) *Explaining Reconviction Following a Community Sentence: the Role of Social Factors*, Home Office Research Study 192. London: Home Office.

National Probation Directorate (2003) *Audit of Probation Areas' Arrangements for Basic Skills, April 2002 – April 2003*. London: Home Office.

Pearson, D. and Lipton, F. (1999) *The Effectiveness of Educational and Vocational Programmes: CDATE Meta-Analyses*. Toronto: Annual Meeting of the American Society of Criminology.

Porporino, F. and Robinson, D. (1992) *Can Educating Adult Offenders Counteract Recidivism?* Ottawa: Report of the Research and Statistics Branch of the Correctional Service of Canada.

Roberts, K., Barton, A., Buchanan, J. and Goldson, B. (1996) *Evaluation of a Home Office Initiative to Help Offenders into Employment*. London: Home Office.

Rolfe, H. (2001) *Barriers to Employment for Offenders and Ex-offenders, Part Two: A Review of the Literature*. London: Department for Work and Pensions.

Sarno, C., Hearnden, I., Hedderman, C., Hough, M., Nee, C. and Herrington, V. (2000) *Working Their Way Out of Offending: An Evaluation of Two Probation Employment Schemes*, Home Office Research Study 218. London: Home Office.

Social Exclusion Unit (2002) *Reducing Re-offending by Ex-Prisoners*. London: Social Exclusion Unit.

Stewart, G. and Stewart, J. (1993) *Social Circumstances of Younger Offenders Under Supervision*. London: Association of Chief Officers of Probation.

Tarling, R. (1982) *Unemployment and Crime*. London: Home Office.

Chapter 8

Offending behaviour programmes: emerging evidence and implications for practice

Colin Roberts

In the past five years in England and Wales, we have seen an unprecedented drive by the Prison Service, and now the National Probation Directorate – supported by the Correctional Services Accreditation Panel[1] – to achieve reductions in reconvictions, with the use of cognitive-behavioural programmes at the spearhead of a What Works policy agenda. The major emphasis in this agenda is the use of research and ongoing evidence-based practice to determine the type of programmes and interventions which should be prescribed and developed, the types of offenders who would be most suitable for different types of programme, and a vigorous adherence to delivery standards and high-quality delivery of these programmes and forms of intervention (Vennard et al. 1997; Underdown 1998).

The vast majority of the research evidence that has been used has come from meta-analyses and other studies undertaken in Canada (Andrews et al. 1990; Robinson 1995) and the USA (Sherman et al. 1997). These have explained that approaches using learning theory and cognitive psychology – which focus on faulty thinking and reasoning, which teach problem-solving skills, which improve problem identification and searching for alternative solutions – have been the most consistent in producing positive effects on reoffending, whether applied to offenders when in prison or when in the community. A limited number of studies of the effectiveness of these types of programmes has been done in Germany (Lösel 1995) and recently in Sweden (Berman 2002).

Until recently, the only major UK study of the effectiveness of such programmes was one carried out, over five years ago, by Raynor and Vanstone (1997) that utilised the Canadian Reasoning and Rehabilitation

Programme (Ross et al. 1986) and was called Straight Thinking on Probation (STOP), in the mid-Glamorgan Probation Service. This study showed that actual and predicted reconviction rates (44 per cent) were the same for offenders who undertook it (including completers and non-completers) and offenders who did not, after 12 months follow-up. Of the 107 offenders who were required to attend as a condition of their Probation Orders, 59 completed the programme successfully. These completers achieved lower than predicted reconviction rates after 12 months and were substantially less likely to receive custodial sentences upon reconviction. Yet this apparently favourable outcome was not maintained when the follow-up continued for 24 months.

We are now beginning to see a new series of research studies on the more recent use of cognitive programmes in prisons and by probation areas (Hollin et al. 2002) in England and Wales. Some critics of the recent extreme deployment and delivery of these types of programmes have highlighted the lack of strong research evidence in this country as well as various potential pitfalls to their likelihood of delivering positive outcomes (Mair 2004; Kendall; 2004; Merrington and Stanley 2000). Others, including some of the most eminent supporters and designers of these types of programmes, have pointed out that while they believe the principles on which they have been designed and used do have strong empirical research backing, it does not automatically follow that they will therefore produce widespread and significantly successful outcomes from their widespread use at present. Most of us would agree that we are in fact at the earliest stages of the What Works agenda and that we are making our first tentative steps in producing evidence of the effects of these types of programmes, and in identifying the wide range of factors that can affect outcomes.

Prison-based cognitive behavioural programmes

The Prison Service was the first to begin the process of assessing programmes for accreditation, and while the use of programmes in prisons has been gradual and carefully monitored, they are now widely available and the number of prisoners attending them has broadly reached the targets set. Three studies of the effectiveness of prison-based offending behaviour programmes have been undertaken by a team of prison psychologists in the Offending Behaviour Programme Unit of the Prison Service led by Caroline Friendship. All of these studies have used retrospective quasi-experimental designs with matched comparison samples of prisoners.

The first evaluation of prison programmes (Friendship et al. 2002)

The first study, published in 2002, was of 670 adult male prisoners serving sentences of two years or more who had voluntarily participated (pre-accreditation) in one of two cognitive skills group programmes run in prisons between 1992 and 1996. Their reconviction rates after two years of release from custody were compared with a comparison sample of 1,801 adult male prisoners who had also served two years or more but who had not participated in any cognitive programme.

The cognitive programmes that the 'treatment' sample participated in were Reasoning and Rehabilitation (R&R) consisting of 36 sessions totalling 72 hours, and Enhanced Thinking Skills (ETS) consisting of 20 sessions totalling 40 hours. Sixty-six (10 per cent) prisoners did not complete their programmes for a variety of reasons: prisoner chose to leave; prison transfers; early releases; illness or injuries; and prisoners who were asked to leave groups by staff.

The predictability of reconviction rates (called 'expected rates') were calculated by use of the Offender Group Reconviction Scale (OGRS), which uses static demographic and criminal history factors to predict the probability of reconviction in two years from release from custody. Firstly, a profile of the 'treatment' group was produced and, using this, a comparison sample was randomly selected, matching prisoners in similar age bands (five bands) and risk of reconviction bands. The actual reconviction rates were obtained from the Offender Index (OI) rather than from the Police National Computer (PNC).

The actual reconviction rates in Figure 8.1 are derived from the published findings (Friendship et al. 2002). A statistically significant difference was found for prisoners of medium–low risk of reconviction (with a 21 percentage points reduction for the 'treatment' group compared with a five percentage points reduction for the comparison group) and for prisoners of medium–high risk of reconviction (where a 21 percentage points reduction for the 'treatment' sample compared with a 10 percentage points reduction for the comparison group – a difference of 11 per cent). The 'low' and 'high' risk groups also showed a trend in the direction of greater reductions in reconviction rates for the 'treatment' sample, but the differences were not statistically significant. Logistic regression was used to assess the respective influence of 'treatment' and offender variables that could have influenced reconviction rates. This confirmed that both forms of cognitive skills programmes had produced a robust reduction in reconvictions compared with the reconviction rate for the comparison sample. It was concluded that the early evaluation results were encouraging indications of the

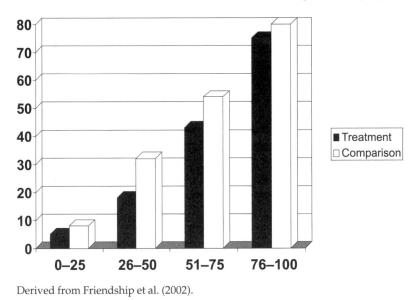

Derived from Friendship et al. (2002).

Figure 8.1 Two-year reconviction rates (prison groups) by levels of risk.

potential value of cognitive skills programmes, even though the programmes had not at that stage been 'accredited', nor had the delivery of the programmes in prisons been subject to rigorous site and delivery monitoring. It was hoped, therefore, that the results from post-accredited programmes and delivery monitoring might be even better than the positive results obtained in this first evaluation of the use of these types of programmes in prisons.

The second evaluation of prison programmes (Falshaw et al. 2003)

However, in the second evaluation of the use of cognitive skills programmes no significant differences were observed between prisoners who had voluntarily participated in the programmes compared with a large matched sample of prisoners who had not participated in them. In this second evaluation, 649 adult male prisoners who had voluntarily participated in one of two accredited prison-based programmes (either R&R or ETS) between 1996 and 1998 were compared with a random matched sample of 1,947 adult males prisoners who had not participated in programmes during their custodial sentences. In both samples the prisoners had been serving sentences of six months or more, and the actual reconviction rates were calculated for two years after their date of release from custody.

Again the OGRS calculations were used to estimate their probabilities of reconviction and each sample was subdivided into 'low', 'medium–low', 'medium–high' and 'high' risk of reconviction groups. Actual reconviction rates were obtained for both samples from the Offender Index (see Figure 8.2). As in the first evaluation, 10 per cent of the 'treatment' sample failed to complete their programmes for a similar variety of reasons.

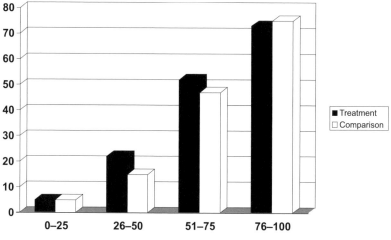

Derived from Falshaw et al. (2003).

Figure 8.2 Two-year 1996–98 reconviction rates (prison groups) by levels of risk.

The 'expected' reconviction rates were similar for both the 'treatment' and comparison samples; to that extent, the samples were well matched. This second evaluation also showed that the two-year 'actual' reconviction rates for both samples were virtually the same overall, being 40 per cent for the 'treatment' sample and 39 per cent for the comparison sample. There were no statistically significant differences in any of the four risk bands. There was a slightly lower reoffending rate for the 'treatment' sample in the 'medium–low' risk band (three percentage points reduction against the expected reconviction rate for the 'treatment' sample), but in the 'medium–high' risk band the reduction was the reverse and in favour of the comparison group (five percentage points reduction for the comparison group against the expected reconviction rate). In the 'low' and 'high' risk bands there were very slight differences of two percentage points and less.

Further analysis was undertaken to ascertain whether any particular factors had contributed to this result being different from the result of the first prison evaluation. This analysis involved: excluding non-completers from the 'treatment' sample; determining whether the length of time from programme completion to release date influenced programme impact on prisoners; excluding programme participants from prisons where there had been poorer quality delivery of programmes; examining differences between the results for the two separate programmes (R&R and ETS); and comparing the outcomes for prisoners who had participated in programmes early in the accreditation process and for those participating later in the process. None of these factors could adequately explain the result of the second evaluation. The researchers also considered whether the frequency of reconvictions and the differences in time to first reconvictions provided a different view of reconviction rates, but again this did not account for the similarity in reconviction rates of the 'treatment' and comparison samples.

The third evaluation of prison programmes (Cann et al. 2003)

A third evaluation of the prison-based cognitive skills programmes has recently been published. Both ETS and R&R programmes were assessed for two separate samples: adult men and young adult male offenders. One- and two-year reconviction rates for the programme participants were compared to retrospectively matched groups of adult and young adult offenders who had not participated in the programmes. In this study, the sample sizes were much larger than in the previous studies.

As in the previous studies, two-year expected reconviction rates were generated for the samples using the average OGRS score for offenders in each of the risk groups, demonstrating a reasonably accurate matching of programme attenders and the comparison groups in terms of static risk of reconviction factors.

When all programme starters were compared with the comparison groups in both samples, there were no statistically significant differences in reconviction rates at one and two years after release from custody. However, when programme drop-outs were excluded leaving only programme completers, there was a small but statistically significant difference in one-year reconviction rates between completers and the comparison groups. In the adults (Figure 8.3), the rates were 2.5 per cent lower than the comparison group, and in the young adults (Figure 8.4) it was 4.1 per cent lower. The greatest differences for programme completers occurred in the high-risk groups, achieving a 6.9 per cent lower reconviction rate in the adults and a 4.8 per cent lower reconviction rate in the young adults, compared with comparison groups. However, the lower rates of reconviction for programme completers at one year was not maintained after two years.

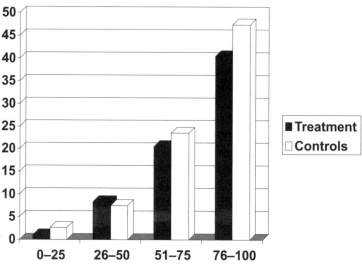

Derived from Cann et al. (2003).

Figure 8.3 Actual 12-month rates of reconviction for prison treatment and comparison groups by levels of risk (adult males).

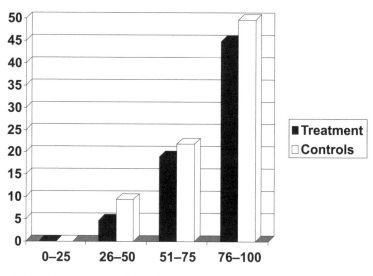

Derived from Cann et al. (2003).

Figure 8.4 Actual 12-month rates of reconviction for prison treatment and comparison groups by levels of risk (young adult males).

In the adults, 202 did not complete the programme (9 per cent) and in young adults, 220 of them did not complete the programme (14.9 per cent). There were considerable differences between the 'drop-out' rates for ETS, which is a shorter programme (22 two-hour sessions rather than 38 in R&R) and for R&R. The 'drop out' rates for ETS were 8.8 per cent for adults and 10.9 per cent for young adults, compared with 11.8 per cent for adults and 25.2 per cent for young adults attending R&R. The study reports that 'a substantial proportion of these offenders dropped out through their own choice'. The rate of reconviction for programme drop-outs was higher than the rate for the matched comparison groups for both samples. In the case of adults, 28.7 per cent of the programme drop-outs had been reconvicted in one year, compared with 17.0 per cent of the completers and 23.8 per cent of the comparison group. In the case of the young adults programme, 47.3 per cent of the drop-outs were reconvicted in one year, compared with 31.4 per cent of completers and 35.9 per cent of the comparison group. For the young adult offenders, this difference was statistically significant.

When you examine the three studies (Friendship et al. 2002, Falshaw et al. 2003 and Cann et al. 2003) you observe how the levels of risk of reconviction among participants (that is, OGRS risk groups) have changed over the eight years of the use of these programmes in prisons. Among adult males the proportion of high-risk offenders has decreased gradually from 38 per cent to 22 per cent, whereas the proportions in the two medium groups have gradually increased, such that in the 1998–2000 period 58 per cent of programme participants were in the two medium groups. The low group has shown some increases from 15 per cent to 23 per cent in 1996–98 but a drop to 20 per cent in 1998–2000 (Figure 8.5). Overall it appears that a higher proportion of the prisoners volunteering to participate in these programmes were in the lower and medium risk bands as the programmes spread to more prison establishments and became more commonly available.

Variations over time in the reconviction rates of prisoners who have participated in such programmes have been observed internationally and the results have generated three different types of explanation (Bonta 2002):

1. *Staff commitment and motivation.* That programme staff in the earlier, pre-accredited programmes who had volunteered to deliver them were more motivated and committed and therefore had had a greater impact as tutors than later post-accreditation staff.

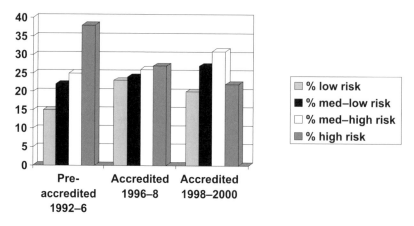

Figure 8.5 Proportionate risk levels from studies of adult male participants in prison programmes.

2. *Offender motivation and 'volunteering'.* Prisoners who had volunteered to attend the earlier pre-accredited programmes had higher levels of motivation to change and desist from future offending, compared with the post-accreditation volunteer prisoners whose participation was part of sentence planning arrangements and at a time when more prisoners could see short-term benefits from 'volunteering' to attend cognitive skills programmes (such as early release on Home Detention Curfew (HDC) or parole).

3. *Expansion and scale of programme delivery.* There had been rapid expansion in the number of prisons delivering programmes and in some prisons they were newly introduced, which may have affected the quality of learning experiences for prisoners in programmes at this stage so that expansion and delivery on a large scale had 'compromised' the quality of programme delivery (Gendreau et al. 1999).

Perhaps at this stage of our knowledge and understanding of the best use of cognitive skills programmes, the main conclusion to be drawn from the later prison evaluations is that we need to know a lot more about what works with whom. The researchers made the important observation that we should not assume that all offenders who participated in the programme, even though all did so voluntarily, will respond equally or uniformly to the programme. We need to identify which offenders have benefited from programmes and why they have done so, and also why some offenders who may appear at similar risk of reconviction do not benefit from such programmes.

Probation-based cognitive behavioural programmes

Researchers at the Probation Studies Unit[2] have been working for nearly four years on the study and evaluation of one of the cognitive programmes, developed by Professor James McGuire and in its accredited form now called 'Think First'. We produced two earlier reports on its development and use in three probation areas: Greater Manchester, Devon & Cornwall and Teeside. In the past two years we have undertaken a retrospective study, and recently completed a prospective study of it in its fully accredited form.

The prospective evaluation of 'Think First'

The prospective study was carried out on offenders required to attend Think First as part of a community sentence (CRO or CPRO) between September 2000 and March 2002, while offenders on licences were excluded. The accredited version has 22 sessions and includes provision for pre and post group sessions and careful monitoring of delivery including the use of videoing of programme tutors.

In this study a wide range of data was collected in each area, with the aid of local research staff. This included pre-programme information on offenders required to attend (criminal history data, demographic data, assessment data, a series of questionnaires for offenders, programme tutors and case managers and access to psychometric tests data); data obtained during the running of the programme (offender diaries, tutor questionnaires and case manager reports); and post-programme data (offender questionnaires, tutor and case manager questionnaires, postgroup psychometric, local and national reconviction data).

Unfortunately it was not feasible to match cases in the programme group and meaningful other comparison cases: selecting appropriate contemporary comparison cases proved impossible while ongoing data was also being selected. It is intended to construct a retrospective comparison group.

The main objectives of the prospective evaluation were to:

1. Identify factors associated with the completion of Think First.

2. Examine the effect of completion on treatment effect.

3. Investigate which variables appear to affect the programme's success.

4. Identify external factors that significantly influence the outcome of the programme.

5. Examine the effect of completion on reconviction.

Three sub-samples were identified:

1. *Non-starters*: did not attend any of the 22 sessions which were legally required (though may have received sessions before the 22 compulsory sessions).

2. *Non-completers:* attended one or more group-work sessions but did not complete Think First.

3. *Completers:* attended sufficient group work sessions to complete Think First.

In the retrospective evaluation it had been very difficult to distinguish non-starters from non-completers because records of non-attendance were poor. We therefore considered it important in the prospective study to differentiate between these two groups, and to examine the possible factors which might help to explain any differences in the outcomes for each category.

Although we were collecting data from offenders in the post-accredited version of Think First, in fact the three probation areas were still in the process of developing the formal pre and post group sessions in accordance with the management manual. We therefore were in a quasi-experiment situation where not all the offenders were expected to attend all pre or post group sessions, and on a limited basis we were able to compare offenders who had more or less experience of pre and post group sessions with the overall sample. However, in some cases the numbers for comparison were low and therefore results from small groups of offenders have to be treated with caution.

Attrition and programme attendance
We found three major effects of poor overall attendance rates for the programme:

1. Low completion rates: 42 per cent non-starters, 29 per cent non-completers, 29 per cent completers.

2. Early attrition: 50 per cent of non-completers lost by session four.

3. One in five programmes discontinued.

It was possible from the wide range of different type of data to identify some characteristics of the three groups of offenders (see Table 8.1).

Table 8.1   Characteristics of offenders

	Mean age	Mean OGRS	Total
Completers	29.1	58.7	141
Non-completers	25.8	68.5	141
Non-starters	27.0	71.8	208
Total sample	27.3	67.0	490

We were also able to identify other factors which were predictive of completion. Completers, compared with non-completers, were more likely to have the following traits. They were more likely to:

- be older (three years on average);
- be able to cope in groups;
- have better communication skills;
- have better problem-solving skills;
- have fewer practical obstacles;
- have more supportive influences;
- be in employment;
- be motivated to address problems.

There were differences between the criminal careers of completers and non-completers. The completers:

- had less entrenched criminal lifestyles;
- had fewer criminal associates;
- were less likely to have served custody in the previous two years;
- were less likely to have been breached;
- were more willing to consider desistance.

Reconviction rates
The prospective samples were submitted to the Home Office Research, Development and Statistics Directorate (RDSD) for PNC data analysis. Because the PNC stores actual offence dates, it was possible to remove pseudo-reconvictions (about 15 per cent of cases have pseudo-reconvictions) and measure time from previous sentence to date of first onset offences, not only subsequent sentence dates for reconviction. The probation areas had managed to obtain PNC identity numbers on 90 per cent of the cases. We were also able to verify data in Devon and

Greater Manchester via local police IT systems, accessed by our local researchers.

Reconviction rates for 6, 9 and 12 months were broken down by completers, non-completers and non-starters, and then analysed by: proportion reconvicted; proportion in which offences were more serious than previous ones; and proportion of reconvictions leading to custodial sentences. The differences on all three measures were significantly in favour of the programme completers – particularly at the 9- and 12-month stages, but also statistically at the six-month stage. Interestingly, non-starters were slightly less likely to be reconvicted than non-completers, but were much more likely to get subsequent custodial sentences (see Table 8.2).

Table 8.2 Attendance at Think First and reconviction

	Completer n = 116	Non-completer n = 115	Non-starter n = 174
Reconviction at 6 months			
% reconvicted	27	45 *	40 *
% with more serious primary offence (A up to F)	12	17 **	17 *
% receiving custody	1	5 *	16 ***
Reconviction at 9 months			
% reconvicted	36	64 ***	57 ***
% with more serious primary offence (A up to F)	15	26 ***	25 **
% receiving custody	1	14 ***	22 ***
Reconviction at 12 months			
% reconvicted	44	77 ***	74 ***
% with more serious primary offence (A up to F)	18	32 ***	29 ***
% receiving custody	3	16 ***	24 ***

The number of stars (*) indicate significance (two-tailed) departures from the reference category. * = $P < 0.05$; ** = $P < 0.005$; *** = $P < 0.0005$; chi square was used.

When first onset of reoffending was used as the measure of reconviction (i.e. date of first offence rather than date of court conviction and sentence) – providing an earlier indication of continued offending behaviour (a tougher test) – again the results were significantly lower rates for completers over non-completers and non-starters. This was the case using all three types of measures: proportion reconvicted; proportion committing more serious offences; and proportion receiving subsequent custodial sentences (see Table 8.3).

When the possible effects of different predicted probabilities of reconviction were taken account of by means of a logistic regression there were significant differences for offenders who completed who were from medium- and high-risk bands, but not those on the lower-risk band.

Table 8.3 Attendance at Think First and onset of first reconviction

	Completer n = 116	Non-completer n = 115	Non-starter n = 174
Onset of reconviction offence at 6 months			
% onset offence reconvicted	34	65 ***	59 ***
% with more serious primary offence (A up to F)	13	23 ***	28 ***
% receiving custody	2	16 ***	21 ***
Onset of reconviction offence at 9 months			
% onset offence reconvicted	41	69 ***	68 ***
% with more serious primary offence (A up to F)	15	24 ***	29 ***
% receiving custody	2	18 ***	24 ***

The number of stars (*) indicate significant (two-tailed) departures from the reference category. * = P < 0.05; ** = P < 0.005; *** = P < 0.0005; chi square was used.

The effect of completion on reconviction in different risk categories
Logistic regression was applied to the samples, taking OGRS2 risk differences into account within each risk band. Briefly, the key findings of this analysis were:

- *low risk* – no significant differences in reconviction rates between completers, non-completers and non-starters;

- *medium risk* – significant differences in reconviction rates: lower for completers than for non-completers and non-starters;

- *high risk* – significant differences in reconviction rates: lower for completers than for non-completers and non-starters and lower for non-starters than non-completers.

When offenders targeted for the programme were in the OGRS medium-risk banding (a score of 41 per cent to 74 per cent probability of reconviction in two years), as was originally recommended for accredited programmes, it was possible to demonstrate that Think First had a slight but not significant impact on lower-risk offenders on community sentences. However, when the medium-risk band was subsequently widened to include some lower-risk cases (31 per cent to 74 per cent probability of reconviction) no significant programme effect was found.

Overall, these results would appear to show encouraging findings with the possible positive effect of completing Think First on subsequent short-term offending, reconvictions and subsequent custodial sentences. However, because we had not been able to use random allocation methods or have a suitably matched comparison group of offenders who were not required to do Think First, we recognise that any claims for effectiveness cannot be safely made. We need still more rigorous and methodologically sound data about such programmes in the future.

At present, we can provide five possible interpretations of the results of the prospective evaluation. We can hypothesise that the outcomes are due to one or more of the following:

1. programme effect;
2. differences between offenders (measured and not measured);
3. interaction between programme effect and offender differences;
4. influence of other changes (e.g. employment);
5. interaction between all these factors.

While we may not be able to say with total confidence that Think First is having a significant effect on reoffending and reconviction, this prospective study is able to indicate more tentatively which factors correlate with positive outcomes and the potential benefits of such programmes.

By far the greatest and most important factor is attrition – that is, offenders not attending programmes or not completing programmes. Kemshall et al. (2002) distinguishes several factors – offender factors, programme factors, service delivery and organisational factors – and argues that attrition is located in interactions between them.

Offender factors

As already indicated in the characteristics of offenders who are likely to 'complete' – there are important offender factors potentially influencing attrition and likelihood of completion (see Figure 8.6).

Much attention is now being given to the motivation of offenders (Miller and Rollnick 2002). In the prospective study motivation was assessed in different ways (by offenders, tutors and case managers) at different times – before programmes, at the start of programmes, during them and after programme completion. We were not in a position to observe indicators of motivation at the pre-programme stage. However, it was possible to observe a lack of motivation just before or at the start of programmes and early in the course, and the best indicators were 'behavioural'. Motivation post-programme was observable by behaviour and verbal statements and attitudinal comments by offenders. As with most other studies, we found that motivation is multi-faceted

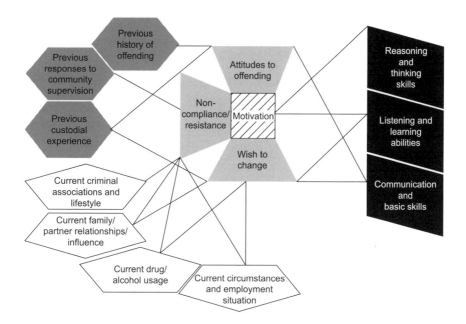

Figure 8.6 Offender factors.

and can be changeable over short time periods, and this is why there are no simple or precise measures of motivation.

We could, however, distinguish three distinctive aspects of 'motivation':

1. attitudes to offending
2. non-compliance
3. wish to change.

These were all being influenced by prior criminal history, current circumstances and relationships, and by a number of factors related to skills, such as reasoning, learning, communication and basic skills.

Again, previous criminal career factors were demonstrably important. We identified that the most motivated were those:

1. with less entrenched criminal careers;
2. with less strong criminal associations;
3. who had reached a point in their lives when they are willing to consider desistance (mean age of 30).

These factors link with a combination of current circumstances, including associations, relationships, employment, drug or alcohol usage and accommodation, to increase desire to change and provide more positive incentives (often called protective factors) to become law-abiding. Alongside these factors, we observed that skills and abilities (reasoning and thinking skills, learning ability, and communication and basic skills) also seem to enable some offenders more than others to benefit from community supervision and the content of programmes like Think First.

When one examines the evidence in the prospective study, issues of compliance were clearly of great importance. Bottoms (2001) has identified four primary sources of compliance: instrumental, normative, constraint-based and habitual. Our results suggest that offenders complied with Think First due to all four factors coming into operation. For example, completers were less likely to assess crime as worthwhile: perhaps because they had decided that the benefits outweigh the costs (a case of instrumental compliance) or perhaps because they had reached a point where they regarded offending as socially unacceptable (a case of normative compliance).

Core group work programme – content and experience
The major source of evidence on the core 22 sessions of Think First came

from the offenders who attended the programme – that is, mostly from completers although non-completers also provided ratings of early sessions. They were asked via questionnaires and a diary to rate the content and experiences they had of each session in Think First. A range of different types of data produced fairly consistent findings – irrespective of which service or groups. The session-by-session diary ratings by offenders are produced in a bar chart in Figure 8.7.

Ratings by non-completers were typically less favourable than those of completers but were consistent with completers' relative views of early sessions. They indicate that the first four sessions were rated significantly lower but that, over time, satisfaction with content and service rose steadily overall. Our finding that the content of the first four sessions were perceived as dull, unclear and boring by many offenders may go some way towards explaining the high drop-out rate in Think First by the fourth session. It is therefore worth examining the offenders' feedback on these sessions in more detail.

The most frequent offender criticisms were that it was boring and not helpful with current problems. The most frequently suggested improvements were that it should be: more challenging; more practical; more relevant to their own problems; more supportive in dealing with their problems. Other issues which were raised about the content of the core programme concerned basic skills levels of offenders (raised by tutors and case managers) and evidence of the effect of group dynamics

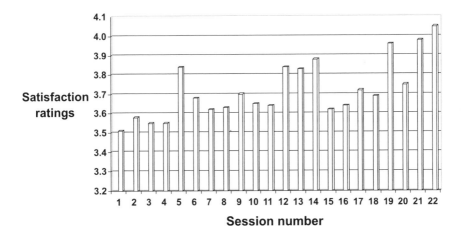

Figure 8.7 Offender satisfaction.

(largely negative – reported on both by offenders completing the programme and many course tutors).

Pre-group sessions and early identification

Pre-group sessions were introduced as part of the accreditation version of Think First. They only began to run the pre-group sessions during the sampling period from 2001, and therefore, by chance, we were able to collect data about whether offenders had been provided with and had attended some or most of these sessions. Although the numbers were relatively small and 'selection' effects were undoubtedly at work, the data collected does indicate that the provision of more sessions *before* the main group programme commenced was associated with improved completion of Think First and also, interestingly, with decreased onset reconviction rates (see Table 8.4).

Table 8.4 Pre-group sessions: completers and non-completers

Pre-group sessions	n	Completers (%)	Reconviction at 9 months (%)
Provided	136	35	47
Not provided	93	15	69
Attended	108	38	40
Not attended	28	14	76
Attended 2+	84	36	47
Attended 1/none	23	4	80

It was also possible to observe in data, collected by tutors in session 2 of the core programme, strong indicators in some offenders of the probability of non-completion, which supported the evidence of offender characteristics reported earlier.

Post-group sessions

Post-group sessions after offenders had completed the 22 main core group sessions were provided for 81 per cent of completers. Again, the numbers are small but the analysis indicates that providing and attending post-group sessions was associated with decreased reconviction rates as measured by onset of reconviction at nine months (see Table 8.5). These sessions typically involved offenders, tutors and case managers, and included booster sessions on problem-solving and on the application of Think First learning to real-life situations. While it is difficult to be certain that the content of post-group sessions across and within probation areas was consistent, analysis of this limited dataset shows a positive correlation between programme completion and attendance at post-group sessions. Programme completion was also associated with rehearsal of programme content in later one-to-one sessions with offenders.

Table 8.5 Post-group sessions and outcomes: completers only

Post-group sessions	n	Onset reconviction at 9 months
Provided	119	35
Not provided	28	63
Attended	84	32
Not attended	28	75
Attended 2+	76	28
Attended 1/none	23	67

Role of case managers and work undertaken with Think First offenders
The number of contacts offenders had with case managers before, during and after Think First was strongly associated with:

1. *attendance* – completers had significantly more contact with case managers during similar time periods;

2. *reconviction* – offenders not reconvicted had significantly more contact with case managers.

The key question was whether this was a cause or an effect of completion, and whether those offenders were more likely anyway to make and keep contact with case managers, irrespective of Think First attendance and the skills and abilities of case managers. This is clearly a complex and multi-faceted issue. We attempted to uncover the range of topics which were covered by case managers with offenders. Offenders who completed were more likely to cover *more* topics than non-completers and non-starters. The subjects that occurred most frequently with completers were employment, family issues, living arrangements and substance use (see Table 8.6).

Table 8.6 Offenders' attendance and issues discussed with case managers

	Completers n = 92 (%)	Non-completers n =117 (%)	Non-starters n = 173 (%)
Living arrangements	33	25	24
Employment/education	44	27	19
Lifestyle and associates	20	10	12
Family/personal	35	23	21
Substance use	23	12	16
Attitudes to offending	17	6	9
Motivation to desist	16	9	5

Possibly we have here some limited evidence of the complementary nature of case management supervision and Think First learning: it could be that offenders who are more likely to complete Think First are also more likely to discuss problems with their case managers, or there may be a two-way interaction between both elements. In interviews done with a small sample of offenders (n = 38) some months after they had completed Think First, we heard references to the beneficial effects of supervision being greater after Think First. A high proportion of these offenders had not been reconvicted by 12 months or had not had an onset reconviction at nine months.

Probation factors

If we combine these views of offender supervision we begin to see a model in which programme content and delivery are directly linked with an offender by case management work with offenders, as depicted in Figure 8.8.

In the Annual Report by HM Inspectorate of Probation (2003) there is a very interesting chapter on the Auditing of Accreditation Programmes. It reports on the audits of 35 Probation Areas and follow-up assessment of nine areas. Areas are rated on four criteria:

1. Committed leadership
2. Programme management
3. Quality of programme delivery
4. Case management.

The highest scores are for committed leadership (66 per cent); secondly, for programme management (63 per cent); thirdly, quality of pro-

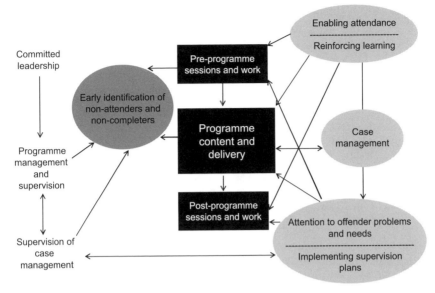

Figure 8.8 Probation factors.

grammes (60 per cent); and fourthly, case management (43 per cent). More analysis of their data indicates interesting relationships between the four criteria. There is a consistent positive relationship between committed leadership and programme management, but the quality of programme delivery and case management are both weak. The Inspectorate (HMIP 2003) did not find a consistent relationship between programme leadership and the quality of programme delivery:

> We have explored this issue further by analysing the scores *between* the four aspects of performance. Whereas *committed leadership* is, not surprisingly, fairly positively associated with *programme management* (a correlation of 0.50) both are weakly associated with effective *programme delivery* and *case management* (0.1 and 0.25 and 0.214 and 0.189 respectively). Furthermore, there is no relationship between the quality of *programme delivery* and *case management* (0.03).

Conclusion

Both the prison research studies on use of cognitive programmes in prison establishments and the Probation Studies Unit research on the

Think First cognitive programme in three probation areas demonstrate the difficulties of achieving high standard evaluation research results. Both also show complex, and on occasions apparently contradictory, findings about the relative value and effectiveness of this type of focused and structured offending behaviour work.

All the studies indicate the need for well-designed and rigorously executed evaluation studies. They all highlight issues about appropriate comparison groups, possible future use of random allocation methods in some studies, sizes of sample sub-groups and accurate and valid measures of reoffending and reconviction. It is also evident that evaluations should examine not only *input data* (for example, offender characteristics and previous criminal careers) and *short- and longer-term outcome data* (such as evidence that problem-solving skills have been acquired) but also *implementation process data*, including:

- selection and self-selection effects;
- attendance and compliance factors;
- completion;
- the quality and integrity of programme delivery;
- differences between groups (offender and tutor factors);
- quality and consistency of case management;
- the availability and quality of community support;
- assistance with resettlement (e.g. accommodation schemes, drug treatment).

These studies also demonstrate the importance of improving knowledge about the types of offenders who are most likely to benefit from programmes and the point in their criminal careers when they might benefit most in terms of desistance. Existing research about offender typologies and criminal careers could contribute to valid and rigorous analysis of key offender characteristics.

While the studies indicate that programmes of this kind have an influence on some offenders, for the majority the programmes *by themselves* are unlikely to deliver the outcomes in reducing offending that have been expected of them. Other significant offender factors play a part: their motivation to change, their attitudes to compliance and court orders, their basic and communication skills, their dependency on drugs and alcohol, and their neuro-psychological functioning are also important, alongside their cognitive abilities and problem-solving skills. Also, environmental and social factors contribute to reducing anti-social behaviour such as: access to employment, training and education, secure and appropriate accommodation, positive and strong family and partner support, reduced levels of anti-social associations, and the local neighbourhood and criminal opportunities. Therefore a range of factors will play a part in desistance from criminal behaviour. Nevertheless, the studies briefly described in this chapter do represent the start of a journey towards developing a better understanding and improving the delivery of What Works in the successful rehabilitation and resettlement of offenders.

Notes

1 Previously known as the Joint Prison/Probation Service Accreditation Panel.
2 Giok Stewart-Ong, Louise Harsent, Zainab Al-Attar and Colin Roberts.

References

Andrews, D.A., Zinger, I., Hoge, R.D., Bonta, J., Gendreau, P. and Cullen, F.T. (1990) 'Does correctional treatment work? A clinically relevant and psychologically informed meta-analysis', *Criminology*, 28, 369–404.

Berman, A.H. (2002) *Teaching a New Way of Thinking: An Evaluation of the Cognitive Skills Programme in the Prison and Probation Service, 1995–2000*. Stockholm: National Council for Crime Prevention, Stockholm, Sweden.

Bonta, J. (2002) *An Overview of What Works and Its Relevance to England and Wales*, Home Office and National Probation Service presentation at the Home Office, 12 March.

Bottoms, A. (2001) 'Compliance and community penalties', in A. Bottoms, L. Gelsthorpe and S. Rex (eds), *Community Penalties: Change and Challenge*. Cullompton: Willan.

Cann, J., Falshaw, L., Nugent, F. and Friendship, C. (2003) *Understanding What Works: Accredited Cognitive Skills Programmes for Adult Men and Young Offenders*, Home Office Research Finding 226. London: Home Office

Falshaw, L., Friendship, C., Travers, R. and Nugent, F. (2003) *Searching for What Works: An Evaluation of Cognitive Skills Programmes*, Home Office Research Finding 206. London: Home Office.

Friendship, C., Blud, L., Erickson, M. and Travers, R. (2002) *An Evaluation of Cognitive Behavioural Treatment for Prisoners*, Home Office Findings 161. London: Home Office.

Gendreau, P., Goggin, C. and Smith, P. (1999) 'The forgotten issue in effective correctional treatment: programme implementation', *International Journal of Offender Therapy and Comparative Criminology*, 43, 180–7.

Hollin, C., McGuire, J., Palmer, E., Bilby, C., Hatcher, R. and Holmes, A. (2002) *Introducing Pathfinder Programmes into the Probation Service: An Interim Report*, Home Office Research Study 247. London: Home Office.

HM Inspector of Probation (2003) *Annual Report for 2002–3 of Her Majesty's Inspectorate of Probation*. London: Home Office.

Kemshall, H. and Canton, R. with Bailey, R., Dominey, J., Simpson, B. and Yates, S. (2002) *The Effective Management of Programme Attrition: A Report from the National Probation Service (Welsh Region)*. Leicester: Community and Criminal Justice Unit, De Montfort University.

Kendall, K. (2004) 'Dangerous thinking: a critical history of correctional cognitive behaviouralism', in G. Mair (ed.), *What Matters in Probation*. Cullompton: Willan.

Lösel, F (1995) 'Evaluating psychosocial interventions and other penal contexts', in *Psychosocial Interventions in the Criminal Justice System, Proceedings of the 20th Criminological Research Conference 1993. Council of Europe Committee on Crime Problems, Criminological Research*, 32, 79–114.

Mair, G. (2004) 'The origins of What Works in England and Wales: a house built on sand?' in G. Mair (ed.), *What Matters in Probation*, Cullompton: Willan.

Merrington, S. and Stanley, S. (2000) 'Doubts about the What Works Initiative', *Probation Journal*, 47 (4), 272–5.

Miller, W. and Rollnick, S. (2002) *Motivational Interviewing: Preparing People for Change*, 2nd edn. London: Guildford Press.

Raynor, P. and Vanstone, M. (1997) *Straight Thinking on Probation (STOP): The Mid Glamorgan Experiment*, Probation Studies Unit Report 4. Oxford: University of Oxford Centre for Criminological Research.

Robinson, D. (1995) *The Impact of Cognitive Skills Training on Post-Release Recidivism among Canadian Federal Offenders*. Ottawa: Correctional Services of Canada.

Ross, R.R., Fabiano, E.A. and Ross, R.D. (1986) *Reasoning and Rehabilitation: A Handbook for Teaching Cognitive Skills*. Ottawa: University of Ottawa.

Sherman, L., Gottfredson, D., Mackenzie, D.L., Eck, J., Reuter, P. and Bushway, S. (1997) *Preventing Crime: What Works, What Doesn't, What's Promising*. Washington, DC: Office of Justice Programs.

Underdown, A. (1998) *Strategies for Effective Offender Supervision*. London: Home Office.

Vennard, J., Sugg, D. and Hedderman, C. (1997) *Changing Offenders' Attitudes and Behaviour: What Works?*, Home Office Research, Development and Statistics Directorate Research Study 171. London: Home Office.

Chapter 9

Intensive supervision and surveillance programmes for young offenders: the evidence base so far

Robin Moore[1]

The Youth Justice Board (YJB) has invested heavily in the Intensive Supervision and Surveillance Programme (ISSP) for dealing with persistent and serious young offenders. The programme is the most rigorous, non-custodial intervention available for young offenders and, in accordance with their promotion of an evidence-based approach, the YJB has proclaimed that it is founded on the 'best evidence as to what will reduce the frequency and seriousness of offending' (Youth Justice Board 2002b: 5).

This chapter looks at the historical context of ISSP, outlining the introduction of earlier intensive community programmes. The aims and objectives of ISSP, its targeting and its programme content are all considered in the light of findings from earlier evaluations and from a national evaluation of the first 41 ISSP schemes by the Probation Studies Unit.[2] The difficulty of measuring outcomes is recognised, and some of the emerging lessons considered. While the full outcomes of the ISSP evaluation will not be known until spring 2005,[3] the evidence base for intensive community programmes is clearly developing and various issues of importance have already materialised (Probation Studies Unit 2003). Particularly prominent questions are whether the aims and objectives for ISSP are compatible and whether reductions in re-offending rates and/or custody rates are achievable.

A brief history of intensive programmes

The YJB has claimed that ISSP is 'unique in both the amount and intensity of supervision and surveillance that is provided' (Youth Justice Board 2000b). While this is certainly true of the current youth justice system in England and Wales, ISSP is by no means the first intensive community programme. In the US, such programmes are well-established. As Tonry (1998: 691) stated, 'although ad hoc intensive supervision in individual cases presumably occurs in every probation system, no other country has adopted widespread programs of intensive probation'. The US Intensive Supervision Programme (ISP) for adult offenders dates back to the 1960s, and by 1990 an ISP had been initiated in every US state. By 1994 it was estimated that over 120,000 offenders were the subject of such a programme (Altschuler 1998; Petersilia and Turner 1992; Corbett and Petersillia 1994).

Intensive community programmes are less well-established in England and Wales, but there has been a general strengthening of community sentences. Notably, the Criminal Justice Act 1982 enabled courts to add further requirements to Supervision Orders in appropriate cases,[4] whilst the 1991 Act introduced the Combination Order, combining Probation and Community Service in a single sentence. As Cavadino and Dignan (2002: 145) noted, the latter was intended to be a 'particularly demanding non-custodial measure for some of the petty persistent property offenders'.

Alongside this strengthening of community sentences, there have been numerous attempts at developing intensive community programmes, although these have tended to be short-lived. One such attempt was the probation experiment known as IMPACT (Intensive Matched Probation and After-Care Treatment), which was initiated in the early part of the 1970s. Under this experiment, a more extensive use of resources was employed and the caseloads of the individual officers reduced, enabling them to spend greater time on individual cases (Folkard et al. 1974).

In the 1980s, the DHSS funded a wide range of Intermediate Treatment (IT) projects. Unlike the IT initiatives in the earlier decade which were provided for relatively minor offenders,[5] these new projects tended to be intensive in nature, targeting those 'high tariff' young offenders deemed to be at risk of custody (Bottoms 1995: v). In regard to these latter initiatives, Allen reported that '110 projects offering 3,389 places were set up by voluntary bodies in 62 local authority areas between 1983 and 1987' (Allen 1991: 48).

Further experiments in intensive probation were conducted in several probation areas in the early 1990s. These programmes, which targeted young adult offenders, marked a shift in approach. As Mair et al. (1994: 3) stated: 'In the past intensive meant more social work, more counselling, more guidance; while today, intensive tends to mean a more rigorous and demanding approach to working with offenders'. Later in the decade, Prolific Offender Projects were introduced. These combined intensive attention from both the police and probation services in an attempt to reduce property crime, particularly theft and burglary (Worrall and Walton 2000: 35).

ISSP can thus be seen as the latest in a long line of intensive community programmes. There were variant forerunners of ISSP in both Kent (Little et al. 2004) and Rotherham, but the first fully-fledged schemes were introduced from July 2001. By February 2002, the first 41 ISSP schemes were operational. Comprehensive coverage of the ten priority 'street crime areas' followed in September 2002 and nationwide roll-out began in October 2003. A further eleven schemes, operating under the title of the Intensive Control and Change Programme (ICCP), are now being piloted by the National Probation Service for young adult offenders (Home Office 2003).

The aims and objectives of ISSP and their compatibility

When ISSP was first established, the YJB set three key objectives as follows:

- to reduce the rate of reoffending in the target group of offenders by 5 per cent and reduce the seriousness of any reoffending;

- to tackle underlying problems of the young people concerned in an effective manner and with a particular emphasis on educational needs;

- to demonstrate that supervision and surveillance is being undertaken consistently and rigorously, and in ways which will reassure the community and sentencers of their credibility and likely success (Youth Justice Board 2000b).

A further implicit objective of ISSP was to reduce the number of custodial sentences made against young offenders. This was clearly demonstrated by the introduction of eligibility short-cuts to counter any increase in the use of custody resulting from other policy initiatives (see 'targeting' section below). It was further illustrated by the YJB's stated preference for ISSP over short Detention and Training Orders (DTOs). Notably, in their annual report for 2001/02, the YJB advocated an Intensive Supervision and Surveillance Order (ISSO) of at least 12 months, stating that 'ISSOs will be more cost-effective than short custodial regimes' (Youth Justice Board 2002a: 19).

Limiting the use of custody has been a much more explicit objective in the US,[6] where prison overcrowding has long been a particularly serious problem. Similarly, England and Wales has overcrowded prisons and the young offender custodial population expanded after the introduction of the DTO. In this respect, the political attractiveness of intensive programmes cannot be doubted. They provide a means for reducing the use of imprisonment and its associated costs without appearing soft on crime (Corbett and Petersilia 1994: 73).

The hopes for intensive programmes are thus wide ranging, but one needs to consider their compatibility. Commentators in England and Wales have in fact recognised that it may be difficult for all objectives to be met: 'IP (Intensive Probation) may not be able to satisfy equally well all of the demands which may be made of it. Will it be able to reduce offending, reduce the prison population, provide effective punishment, keep sentencers satisfied, and reduce costs all at the same time?' (Mair et al. 1994: 5).

Recent research findings, particularly in the US, fail to allay such doubts. High levels of breach have been common (Hill 1992; Giblin 2002), leading Petersilia and Turner (1992: 650) to conclude that: 'As higher risk offenders are placed in such programs, higher violation rates must be expected especially if the programs vigorously enforce their technical conditions.' Bearing in mind that a potential consequence of breach is imprisonment, there is a clear tension here between reducing the use of custody and providing tough community penalties which are rigorously enforced (Tonry 1998: 683).

Notably, the YJB has emphasised that strict enforcement is crucial to the success of ISSP and in providing reassurance to the community (Youth Justice Board 2002b). ISSP teams are required to deal with non-compliances according to National Standards (Youth Justice Board 2000c), but the YJB has stated that the additional resources available for ISSP provides the teams with the opportunity to set even higher standards. Thus consideration can be given to accelerating the decision to initiate breach proceedings following the wilful missing of an appointment instead of waiting for two formal warnings. The clear danger is that such a policy could seriously impinge upon any reduction in the use of custody. Muncie (1997: 138), in his critique of decarceration in the 1960s, referred to this risk as 'jeopardy': 'the risk of accelerating routes into custody through breaches of the conditions of community sentences'.

It is perhaps not surprising, bearing in mind this tension, that previous research found evidence of officers both differentiating between breaches and/or ignoring them and, in contrast, pursuing a policy of breaching as early as possible (Goodstein and Sontheimer 1997; Hill 1992; Latessa and Vitto 1988). Similarly, comments from the ISSP workers, during evaluation of the first 41 ISSP schemes, indicated that maintaining a balance between the desire for rigorous enforcement and the desire to keep the young person on the programme was far from straightforward:

> *ISSP Worker*: If I breached them for missing a first appointment then I'd be breaching them all. We all know that it's a court order that they're on, but if they don't show up we find out why. If there's no reasonable explanation and they're taking the mickey then we give them a warning. Next time it might be a formal warning. I think we're dealing with things properly. I tell the young persons that it's the last thing that I want to do but if they're not complying I will do it.

> *ISSP Worker*: Most of us see it as a last resort. We don't want to breach these young people unless we absolutely have to. Nevertheless we have to conform and make them conform.

Targeting and the impact upon custody rates

Analysis of the evidence base for intensive programmes generally, and ISSP in particular, is complicated by the fact that the programmes have varied greatly in the populations which they have targeted. In the US, this variability has had three dimensions:

1. *Age* – some of the programmes target adult offenders while others target young offenders.

2. *Stage in process* – some of the programmes are targeted at offenders pre-custody whilse others are post-custody.

3. *Risk* – some target low- to moderate-risk offenders, while others target high-risk offenders.

Taking these dimensions in turn, ISSP targets young offenders aged 10–17 years. Unlike many previous intensive programmes, it targets these offenders both pre- and post-custody. More precisely, the three routes onto the programme are:

1. as a condition of bail supervision and support;

2. as part of a community penalty, either a Supervision Order or a Community Rehabilitation Order;

3. as a condition of community supervision in the second half of a DTO.

ISSP is thus not an order in its own right and there were no new legislative powers relating specifically to the programme. For those serving a community sentence the programme lasts for six or four months, depending upon whether the order is part of a Supervision or Community Rehabilitation Order respectively. For those bailed or in the second half of a DTO the period of time is determined by the length of bail or the DTO. But the intention of the YJB, in adherence to their desire for ISSP to reduce the number of DTOs, is for the majority of young people to spend six months on the programme as part of a Supervision Order.

As for the level of risk posed by the offenders, ISSP targets the 'top end' of the offending spectrum; more specifically, it was aimed at 'the small group of prolific young offenders (aged 10 to 17) whom Home Office research suggests commit approximately a quarter of all offences committed by young people' (Youth Justice Board 2002b: 5). Eligibility criteria were developed to target this group, restricting the availability of ISSP to those young persons 'charged or warned for an imprisonable offence on four or more separate occasions within the last 12 months, and who had previously received at least one community or custodial penalty' (Youth Justice Board 2000b).[7] In addition, ISSP teams were given the flexibility to adopt further suitability criteria, encompassing factors such as the seriousness of offending, the need to target crimes that link to local crime reduction priorities, the motivation of the individual under consideration and, in DTO cases, the risk of reoffending on return to the community.

In April 2002 the YJB altered the eligibility criteria. This followed concerns that government initiatives on street crime, and robbery in particular, could lead to an increase in the use of custody for first-time serious offenders, while the implementation of section 30 of the Criminal Justice and Police Act of 2001 could lead to secure or custodial remands for young offenders with a history of offending while on bail. In addition, the term 'charging occasions' was creating difficulties for ISSP teams, some of whom were having difficulty achieving their numerical targets for ISSP referrals (Youth Justice Board 2002c).

As a result, the Board widened and refined the eligibility criteria to include offenders who:

- had been charged, warned or convicted of offences committed on four or more separate dates within the last 12 months and had received at least one community or custodial disposal; or

- were at risk of custody because the current charge or sentence related to an offence serious enough that an adult could receive a custodial sentence of 14 years or more (the 'serious crime' short-cut); or

- were at risk of custody because they had a history of repeat offending on bail and were at risk of a secure remand (the 'repeat offending on bail' shortcut) (Youth Justice Board 2002b: 5).

Thus ISSP began targeting 'serious' as well as 'persistent' offenders. The question raised, however, bearing in mind the implicit objective for ISSP to reduce the number of custodial sentences, is whether the schemes are successfully targeting those who are at genuine risk of custody. Unfortunately, there are numerous instances of diversionary programmes failing to target such offenders but targeting instead others who might have been dealt with more leniently (Bottoms 1995: 10), a failure sometimes referred to as the 'net-widening effect', a phrase coined by Cohen (1985: 44). When considering the introduction of ISSP, Cavadino and Dignan (2002: 304) were keen to highlight this danger:

[T]hese intensive and demanding (and easy to breach) schemes could be imposed on young people who would otherwise have received less intense, less stigmatizing treatment. This might actually have been more effective (or less damaging), and might have created less risk of catapulting the offender into custody when the enormous demands of the programme prove too much for a messed-up young person to comply with.

More positively, the high-tariff IT projects in England and Wales have been viewed as the 'most important factor' in reducing custody rates for young people in the 1980s (Pitts 2002: 418). Yet, in stark contrast, so-called 'net-widening' has accompanied the introduction of intensive programmes in the US, leading Tonry (1998: 683) to comment that 'the availability of new sanctions presents almost irresistible temptations to judges and corrections officials to use them for offenders other than those for whom the program was created'. But he further noted that those programmes particularly at danger of 'net-widening' are those in which the judges control the referrals. The danger of net-widening accompanying ISSP may thus be diminished by the ISSP teams themselves assessing both eligibility and suitability prior to making recommendations to the court.

Furthermore, there were some early indicators from the ISSP evaluation that extensive net-widening was being avoided. Early analysis of those young persons coming onto ISSP demonstrated that they were towards the 'top end' of the offending spectrum. They tended to have extensive criminal histories, with a mean number of ten recorded offences in the 12 months prior to their order (Probation Studies Unit 2003). Data were also extracted from the *Asset* assessments made at the beginning of the young persons' programmes (see Roberts et al. 2001 and the chapter by Baker in this volume). The mean *Asset* score, for an early sample, was 24.8 which is at the upper end of the medium–high score band, indicating a risk of reconviction within 12 months of 70 per cent. The corresponding mean score for a national *Asset* sample (Baker et al. 2002) was noticeably lower at 14.4, which indicates a risk of reconviction within 12 months of 49 per cent.

Programme content

The intensive programmes in the US vary greatly, not only in their targeting, but also their programme content, further complicating consideration of the evidence base for ISSP. As Petersilia and Turner (1992: 611) have stated, 'there is no generic ISP program. So many programs call themselves ISP that the acronym alone reveals little about any program's particular character. The only common characteristic of ISP programs is that they involve more supervision than routine probation programs.' But, notably, there is no standard as to how much more supervision is required before a programme is deemed intensive: 'In some jurisdictions, an increase from one to two contacts per month constitutes intensive probation, whereas requirements for others are several visits per day' (Goodstein and Sontheimer 1997: 335).

When ISSP was introduced, the YJB set out standards for both the supervision and surveillance components of the programme, to which the ISSP schemes are expected to adhere. In terms of intensity, the YJB has specified that, for those on six-month programmes, the first three months should entail a structured supervision programme of at least five hours a day during the weekday and access to support during the evenings and weekends. After three months there must be provision for day-to-day contact with the young person for at least one hour each weekday with access to support during the evenings and weekends. ISSP is thus much more demanding than many of its US counterparts, with attention having been paid to the What Works principle of 'dosage' which provides that 'programmes must be of sufficient intensity and duration to achieve their aims, especially with those who are chronic or serious offenders' (Utting and Vennard 2000: 22).

The content of the USA programmes varies in other ways. Potential programme components, as identified by Gendreau et al. (2000:197), are as follows:

1. greatly increasing contact between supervisors and offenders;
2. confining offenders to their homes;
3. enforcing curfews;
4. submitting offenders to random drug testing;
5. requiring offenders to pay restitution to victims;
6. electronically monitoring offenders;
7. requiring offenders to pay for the privilege of being supervised.

The content of ISSP, to a large extent, has been prescribed by the YJB. It has been specified that all programmes should contain the following five core supervision modules:

1. education and training;
2. restorative justice;
3. changing offending behaviour;
4. interpersonal skills; and
5. family support.

Other modules should be provided according to the needs of the individual, encompassing work to address risk factors such as mental health, drug or alcohol misuse, accommodation problems, as well as provision for counselling or mentoring, and engagement in some form of constructive recreation.[8] The availability of such a wide range of modules clearly adheres to the What Works principle of 'intervention modality', which identifies multi-modal programmes as the most consistently effective, in turn recognising that offenders have a variety of problems (Utting and Vennard 2000).[9]

Early analysis from the national evaluation of ISSP found that in many cases full programmes of supervision had been provided, although the breadth of service provision was variable (Probation Studies Unit 2003). As can be seen in Table 9.1, nearly all the young people were engaged in some form of education/training and some form of offending behaviour training.

Table 9.1 Engagement in supervision elements

Supervision element	Percentage engaged
Education/training	96%
Restorative justice	73%
Offending behaviour training	94%
Interpersonal skills training	85%
Family support work	79%

The YJB views community surveillance as a vitally important component of ISSP (Youth Justice Board 2002b). The objective is to ensure that the young people themselves are aware that their behaviour is being monitored and to provide reassurance to the community that their whereabouts are being checked. The ISSP teams are required to carry out checks at least twice daily, and they must have the facility for around-the-clock surveillance for those cases in which it is deemed necessary. At least one of the following four forms of surveillance has to be provided:

- electronic tagging;
- voice verification;
- tracking by staff; or
- intelligence-led policing.

In their evaluation of an intensive treatment programme, Bonta et al. (1999) found that the use of electronic monitoring encouraged compliance with the programme, and the tag has now become the most commonly utilised form of surveillance for young people on ISSP. Early analysis indicated that a young person had been fitted with a tag in 61 per cent of all ISSP cases (Probation Studies Unit 2003) and the percentage has since risen. In certain areas of the country, there were some initial ethical and moral concerns regarding the tagging of young people, but these concerns appear to have dissipated over time, with the value of the tag in providing structure and discipline and reducing peer pressure becoming widely accepted.

ISSP Manager: The tagging gives them some structure. Very few violate the tag, and quite a few say that they welcome it, having to be in at a certain time. There's no doubt that attending here, having their welfare needs met, is far less an infringement of their liberty as being locked up in a YOI (Young Offender Institution)... We've had one young person who wasn't tagged. He was a heavy drug user and we decided to track him, but in retrospect I wouldn't offer ISSP for him again without him being tagged.

ISSP Worker: The main thing is that it's [the tag] imposing some kind of order as they're expected to stay in their own homes. You might say that the tag is inappropriate if all the offences have been committed during the daytime, but it's still instilling some sort of order. It's a punishment as well, and I'm sure society likes the message it gives them.

Measuring outcomes

Having considered its targeting and programme content, one can now consider the likelihood of ISSP achieving its first key objective and reducing the rate of reoffending by at least 5 per cent, as well as reducing the seriousness of any reoffending. Previous evaluations of intensive programmes and their impact upon reoffending indicate that some caution is required. Reviewing the recent research in the USA, Gendreau et al. (2000: 198) concluded that 'when it comes to the matter of reducing offender recidivism, the conclusion is inescapable, ISPs have had little effect on offenders' future criminal activity'. Similar results were found in relation to the IMPACT experiment and the 'high-tariff' IT projects in England and Wales (Folkard et al. 1976; Bottoms 1995). Whether one should be surprised by this lack of impact is questionable. The evaluators of one of the forerunners to ISSP concluded as follows:

> Most innovative programmes in youth justice are handicapped by unrealistic expectations about what can be achieved. Almost by definition, persistent offending behaviour is extremely resistant to change ... it was unrealistic to expect that young people convicted several times prior to beginning ISSP would never be convicted during involvement with the programme and in the 24 months that followed. (Little et al. 2004: 228–9)

However, there have been some more positive results, and it is here that the variability in targeting criteria and programme content are of particular significance. Gendreau et al. (2000: 199–200) have drawn a distinction between those programmes with a treatment component

169

(e.g. counselling, supervised activities) and those with no treatment component. Reviewing the literature in more detail, they reported that 'the results were remarkably consistent. Under the "no treatment" condition ISPs produced a 7% increase in recidivism... ISPs that appeared to have had some treatment component tended to produce a slight decline in recidivism of 3%. ISPs that employed more treatment reported a 10% decrease in recidivism.' Such a distinction was earlier suggested by Corbett and Petersilia (1994: 77): 'The empirical evidence regarding ISPs is decisive: without a rehabilitation component, reductions in recidivism are as elusive as a desert mirage.' They thus concluded (1994: 74) that 'A persuasive case can be made for abandoning intensive supervision programs that seek only to control and punish offenders in favor of programs that give equal primacy to changing offenders.'

Bonta and colleagues also stressed the importance of distinguishing between high-risk and low-risk offenders. In their evaluation of an intensive rehabilitation supervision programme, they found a reduction in recidivism for the higher risk offenders only, leading them to conclude that 'the importance of matching treatment intensity to offender risk level and ensuring that there is a treatment component in intensive supervision programs is reaffirmed' (Bonta et al. 2000: 312). This clearly supports the What Works principle of 'risk classification', which stipulates that the level and intensity of the intervention should be matched to the seriousness of the offending and the risk of reoffending (McGuire and Priestley 1995).

These findings augur well for ISSP: the schemes target high-risk offenders and there is an emphasis upon 'treatment', with the second key objective being to tackle the underlying problems of the young people. It remains debatable, however, whether reconviction should be used as the paramount measure of effectiveness. Not only is a degree of recidivism inevitable when dealing with the most persistent offenders (Brownlee 1995) but the reconviction rates for young people on ISSP may be raised by the improved levels of surveillance. Such improvements in the level and speed of detection can be viewed positively: 'As programs move away from rehabilitation and toward surveillance and control, some might argue that higher arrest rates should be seen as an indication of program success, not failure, especially when dealing with high-risk probationers' (Petersilia and Turner 1992: 656). As pointed out by Worrall and Walton (2000: 36) in their evaluation of a Prolific Offender Project, this results in 'a "win/win" situation, which complicates evaluation and may raise questions about definitions of "success"'.

Whatever emphasis is placed upon reconviction, further outcome measures are needed for a more in-depth analysis of effectiveness.

Previous evaluations indicate that caseworkers themselves employ wider definitions of 'success'. In their evaluation of intensive probation for young adult offenders, Brownlee and Joanes (1993: 228) noted that 'it should be remembered that the philosophy and working practices of the project aim to address many aspects of an offender's life circumstances, not merely his or her offending behaviour'.[10] In the IMPACT probation experiment, the officers highlighted a wide range of outcome criteria. These included not only reconviction, but personality changes in the offenders, acceptance of new approaches by the probation service and increases in their own casework skills (Folkard et al. 1974).

Similarly, a number of the ISSP schemes were found to employ wide definitions of 'success'. In some of the 'more difficult' cases, any form of engagement with the young person was judged a success, along with any resulting changes in attitude or behaviour, criminal or otherwise.

> *ISSP Worker*: It depends how you measure success. To me, the kid I was talking about before, I would classify him as a success, being on the programme for two months. He's still with us, he's on a work programme, and attending his appointments. Some of them are going out and committing offences, but you have to measure what they'd done before. My own personal view is that the scheme is needed. We give them opportunities to go back to school or training. And the fact that we're addressing all the different needs, it can only be beneficial.

> *ISSP Manager*: Success comes in many forms, it depends how you define it really. It's about support and awareness and being functional for some young people, it's about giving them a direction ... having one to one and building professional relationships with their workers and seriously attempting to change their behaviour. Success is sometimes the completion element. Success is seeing them turn around and changing from an obnoxious young person to enjoying doing sport, or music or whatever they're into ... Success is knowing they they're not in court every week for petty silly things ... Success is when parents say thank you, and even write to say thank you. When a police officer sees a young person changing and so they become more proactive and supportive, when they go round to see if they're alright and to chat to a young person rather than arrest them and when they believe a young person who says they didn't commit a crime. When the housing department starts helping and a possible ASBO disappears. These are all elements of success.

An argument can thus be made that a limited impact upon reconviction should not be indicative of failure, provided progress is made in other ways, such as improvements in the young persons' attitudes or skills. Further weight can be added to this contention by recognising that the alternative of custody is much more costly, and potentially damaging in other ways. As the Children's Society (1989) has stated, 'penal custody leads to broken links with family, friends, education, work and leisure and causes stigmatization and labeling. Rather than reintegrating young people into the communities where they must learn to live, custody results in increased alienation and greater risk of further offending' (see also Potter 1998: 9).

The emerging lessons

The research evidence regarding the effectiveness of intensive programmes is clearly mixed, which is perhaps not surprising bearing in mind the differing forms of targeting and programme content. The best conclusion that can be drawn is that intensive programmes have 'worked well in some manifestations and not so well in others' (Mair et al. 1994: 124).

But what further lessons can be drawn from the evidence-base as to which programmes are likely to work well? The need for intensive programmes to provide quality contact, rather than simply more contact, has been highlighted, as has the associated need for a well-trained, supported and cohesive staff team (Goodstein and Sontheimer 1997; Lobley et al. 2001; Key 2001). Bearing in mind the 'multi-modal' nature of ISSP, establishing close liaisons with a range of departments and organisations appears critical, which, in turn, requires strong leadership (Altschuler 1998). It has been further suggested that there is a need for a degree of 'openness, creativity and flexibility' (Altschuler 1998: 383).

Further findings can be more accurately described as providing evidence of 'who works' rather than 'what works'.[11] Notably, the motivation of the offender and his/her willingness to change have been identified as crucial factors towards successful engagement (Folkard et al. 1974; Lobley et al. 2001). ISSP workers made comments to this effect.

ISSP Education Officer: They themselves have to have the maturity and the ability to see that they have a problem, they have to want to address it and they have to want us to help them. They will still blip, but they then come back to the general upward trend of wanting to do something about it.

ISSP Manager: There has to be some initial motivation there and a willingness to respond. What we've seen as essential are some stable foundations to build upon. Family support has been crucial. Where there is some ambivalence, a lack of motivation, no stable accommodation or where parents have not been supportive, we've found it difficult to move forward.

Similarly, in Chapter 7 of this volume, Haslewood-Pócsik and McMahon identify a lack of motivation as a reason for attrition on a basic skills pathfinder. The motivation of the young person can be considered when assessing suitability for ISSP, but deeming a person to be unsuitable on the basis of a lack of motivation is clearly controversial. After all, motivation can be seen as both 'modifiable' and an 'interpersonal phenomenon' (López-Viets et al. 2002:17; for further discussion, see Burnett in this volume).

Early findings from the ISSP evaluation indicated that a number of other personal factors influenced successful completion of the programme.[12] For instance, there were a number of significant associations between successful completion and individual items in *Asset*. It was very clear from these results that attitudes to offending and other people were inextricably linked to the progress of young people on ISSP. There were lower rates of completion where young people:

- displayed a lack of remorse;
- lacked understanding of the effect of his/her behaviour on victims;
- denied the seriousness of his/her behaviour, and believed that certain types of offence were acceptable and that certain people/groups were acceptable 'targets';
- had witnessed violence in a family context;
- had inadequate legitimate personal income;
- believed that further offending was inevitable.

There were further statistically significant associations between successful completion and scaled scores from Crime-Pics II, a criminal attitudes instrument administered to the young persons at the beginning of their programmes. The analysis indicated lower rates of completion where young people:

- thought that offending was an acceptable way of life;
- had less resolve to not reoffend;
- had less acceptance that offending had adverse effects on victims.

Finally, previous research has suggested that attention needs to be paid to preventing the offender from disengaging completely at the end of his/her planned programme (Mair et al. 1994: 119; Fraser 2003). Similar concerns were raised by a number of ISSP staff, indicating that there was some uncertainty as to whether ISSP would have a long-term impact upon the behaviour and attitudes of the young persons.

> *ISSP Manager*: What worries me is that the ISSPs last for six months and then they go back to whatever level of supervision, depending on the order, and the support's not there anymore. Some still contact us and some have gone onto Splash.[13] Basically, they still need more supervision. I've already seen it where the young person has finished their ISSP and once the supervision has reduced, the simple task of organising a taxi to get to school seems like too much hard work. So they don't go to school anymore … There should be an outreach service which they could use if they needed it, but you would need to maintain the same workers.

> *ISSP Manager*: There is a problem in that they have the 25 hours per week and then suddenly the carpet's been pulled from under them. I wouldn't like to predict what happens in the less intensive period. We need to think a lot more about what we do in this period … You can only hope that the work done in the intensive period has a lasting effect.

Conclusion

The evidence base for intensive community programmes is growing, but there is an obvious need for further research (McGuire 2002b). The reconviction rates for offenders subject to such programmes have been variable, but the research findings indicate that ISSP holds promise due to its targeting of high-risk offenders and its emphasis upon tackling the underlying problems of this target group. Whether ISSP will have a sustained impact upon custody rates remains unclear. 'Net-widening' has been a feature of the US programmes, but the danger of such an effect accompanying ISSP may be diminished by the ISSP teams assessing both eligibility and suitability prior to making recommendations to the court. A tension remains, however, between the objective of reducing the number of custodial sentences and the desire for strict enforcement so as to provide reassurance to the community. The greater the emphasis that is placed upon the latter, the greater the inroads that will be made into any potential fall in the use of custodial sentencing.

Notes

1 The author is the lead researcher on the national evaluation of the Intensive Supervision and Surveillance Programme. While the views expressed in this chapter are the author's own, he wishes to thank all members of the research team for their contributions to the evaluation project. Further thanks are due to Emily Gray for her comments on an earlier draft.

2 The evaluation is being conducted for the YJB by the Probation Studies Unit in the Centre for Criminological Research, University of Oxford, under the direction of Colin Roberts (see Probation Studies Unit 2002).

3 A 24-month reconviction study will be completed by this time, comparing offending rates in the 24 months pre- and post-intervention for both ISSP and comparison groups. The main evaluation report was submitted to the YJB in Spring 2004 (Moore et al., forthcoming).

4 Allen noted that 'these were designed to bolster the credibility of supervision orders and arrest the decline in their use by magistrates; in the words of the White Paper *Young Offenders* (Home Office 1980) "it was hard to resist the inference that in many cases courts do not have sufficient confidence in some of the existing non custodial disposals to make use of them instead of custodial sentences"' (Allen 1991: 45).

5 The term IT, which originally appeared in a 1968 White Paper, was given the following wide definition by the DHSS: 'The term should be taken to mean any intervention, through community-based programmes of supervised activities, guidance and counselling, planned to meet the identified needs of the following children and young people: (a) those who have offended; (b) those thought to be at risk of offending' (Bottoms et al. 1990: 137).

6 Petersilia and Turner (1992: 652) concluded that the US programmes were designed to serve 'three primary goals: (1) to conserve scarce prison space and money that would otherwise be spent on incarceration; (2) to keep offenders from committing crimes in the community while they are on probation; and (3) to impose a punishment less severe than prison, but more severe than routine probation'.

7 Persistency is thus defined by the eligibility criteria. There is in fact no commonly-accepted definition of 'persistence' and differing demarcations have been employed. For instance, the government has defined a persistent young offender (PYO) as 'a young person aged 10–17 years who has been

sentenced by any criminal court in the UK on three or more occasions for one or more recordable offences and within three years of the last sentencing occasion is subsequently arrested or has an information laid against him for a further recordable offence' (Home Office 1997), while the Youth Lifestyles Survey 1998/99 defined a PYO as 'someone who, in the last year, had committed three or more offences' (Home Office 2000).

8   For those on bail the programmes should be broadly similar, but the offending behaviour programmes and the restorative element are not suitable for those pleading not guilty.

9   Also known as the 'breadth principle' (Palmer 1992).

10 Furthermore, many of these 'life circumstances' can be predictive of reoffending (see the chapter by Merrington in this volume).

11 As McGuire (2002a: 3) has stated, 'both research and practice in this field have moved beyond the basic question of "what works" and the influences that may contribute to that. The focus is now upon more complex questions of what works, where, and with whom.'

12 Only those cases in which the young person was still attending at the end of the planned programme (or the point of sentence or subsequent ineligibility if a bail ISSP) were recorded as successful completions.

13 Splash programmes, funded by the YJB, offer recreational activities during the school holidays.

References

Allen, R. (1991) 'Out of jail: the reduction in the use of penal custody for male juveniles 1981–88, *The Howard Journal*, 30, 30–52.

Altschuler, D.M. (1998) 'Intermediate sanctions and community treatment for serious and violent juvenile offenders', in R. Loeber and D.P. Farrington (eds), *Serious and Violent Juvenile Offenders: Risk Factors and Successful Interventions.* Thousand Oaks, CA: Sage.

Audit Commission (1996) *Misspent Youth: Young People and Crime.* London: Audit Commission.

Baker, K., Jones, S., Roberts, C. and Merrington, S. (2002) *Validity and Reliability of ASSET Findings from the first two years of the use of ASSET.* Oxford: Probation Studies Unit.

Barton, W.H. and Butts, J.A. (1990) 'Viable options: intensive supervision programs for juvenile delinquents', *Crime and Delinquency*, 36, 238–56.

Bonta, J., Rooney, J. and Wallace-Capretta, S. (1999) *Electronic Monitoring in Canada.* Canada: Public Works and Government Services.

Bonta, J., Wallace-Capretta, S. and Rooney, J. (2000) 'A quasi-experimental evaluation of an intensive rehabilitation supervision program', *Criminal Justice and Behavior*, 27, 312–29.

Bottoms, A.E. (1995) *Intensive Community Supervision for Young Offenders: Outcomes, Process and Cost.* Cambridge: Institute of Criminology.

Bottoms, A., Brown, P., McWilliams, B., McWilliams, W. and Nellis, M. (1990) *Intermediate Treatment and Juvenile Justice.* London: HMSO.

Brownlee, I.D. (1995) 'Intensive probation with young adult offenders: a short reconviction study', *British Journal of Criminology*, 35, 599–612.

Brownlee, I.D. and Joanes, D. (1993) 'Intensive probation for young adult offenders: evaluating the impact of a non-custodial sentence', *British Journal of Criminology*, 33, 216–30.

Cavadino, M. and Dignan, J. (2002) *The Penal System: An Introduction.* London: Sage.

Children's Society (1989) *Penal Custody for Juveniles – the Line of Least Resistance.* London: Children's Society.

Cohen, S. (1985) *Visions of Social Control.* Cambridge: Polity Press.

Corbett, R.P. and Petersillia, J. (1994) 'Intensive rehabilitation supervision: the next generation in community corrections?', *Federal Probation*, 58, 72–8.

Flood-Page, C., Campbell, S., Harrington, V. and Miller, J. (2000) *Youth Crime: Findings from the 1998/99 Youth Lifestyles Survey*, Home Office Research Study 209. London: Stationery Office.

Folkard, M.S., Smith, D.E. and Smith, D.D. (1976) *IMPACT Intensive Matched Probation and After-Care Treatment: Volume II. The Results of the Experiment*, Home Office Research Study 36. London: HMSO.

Folkard, M.S., Fowles, A.J., McWilliams, B.C., McWilliams, W., Smith, D.D., Smith, D.E. and Walmsley, G.R. (1974) *IMPACT Intensive Matched Probation and After-Care Treatment: Volume I. The Design of the Probation Experiment and an Interim Evaluation*, Home Office Research Study 24. London: HMSO.

Fraser, P. (2003) *Sheffield Prolific Offender Project: First Evaluation Report.* London: NACRO.

Gendreau, P., Goggin, C. and Fulton, B. (2000) 'Intensive supervision in probation and parole settings', in C.R. Hollin (ed.), *Handbook of Offender Assessment and Treatment.* Chichester: Wiley.

Giblin, M.J. (2002) 'Using police officers to enhance the supervision of juvenile probationers: an evaluation of the anchorage CAN program', *Crime and Delinquency*, 48, 116–37.

Goodstein, L. and Sontheimer, H. (1997) 'The implementation of an intensive aftercare program for serious juvenile offenders', *Criminal Justice and Behavior*, 24, 352–9.

Graham, J. and Bowling, B. (1995) *Young People and Crime*, Home Office Research Study 145. London: HMSO.

Hagell, A. and Newburn, T. (1994) 'Persistent young offenders and persistent old myths', *Policy Studies*, 15, 51–9.

Hill, D. (1992) *Intensive Probation Practice: An Option for the 1990s.* Norwich: Social Work Monographs.

Home Office (1997) *Tackling Delays in the Youth Justice System: A Consultation Paper.* London: Stationery Office.

Home Office (2003) *Making the Right Choice: Helping Offenders Quit Crime – the Story So Far.* London: Stationery Office.

Key, J. (2001) 'The Rotherham experience of intensive supervision: a message from a seasoned practitioner', *Youth Justice Matters*, 10–12.

Latessa, E.J. and Vitto, G.F. (1988) 'The effects of intensive supervision on shock probationers', *Journal of Criminal Justice*, 16, 319–30.

Lipsey, M.W. and Wilson, D.B. (1998) 'Effective intervention for serious juvenile offenders: a synthesis of research', in R. Loeber and D.P. Farrington (eds), *Serious and Violent Juvenile Offenders: Risk Factors and Successful Interventions*. Thousand Oaks, CA: Sage.

Little, M., Kogan, J., Bullock, R. and Van der Lann, P. (2004) 'ISSP: an experiment in multi-systemic responses to persistent young offenders known to children's services', *British Journal of Criminology*, 44, 225–40.

Lobley, D., Smith, D. and Stern, C. (2001) *Freagarrach: An Evaluation of a Project for Persistent Juvenile Offenders*. Edinburgh: Stationery Office.

López-Viets, V., Walker, D.D. and Miller, W.R. (2002) 'What is motivation to change? a scientific analysis', in M. McMurran (ed.), *Motivating Offenders to Change: A Guide to Enhancing Engagement in Therapy*. Chichester: Wiley.

McGuire, J. (2002a) 'Integrating findings from research reviews', in J. McGuire (ed.), *Offender Rehabilitation and Treatment: Effective Programmes and Policies to Reduce Reoffending*. Chichester: Wiley.

McGuire, J. (2002b) 'Motivation for what? Effective programmes for motivated offenders', in M. McMurran (ed.), *Motivating Offenders to Change: A Guide to Enhancing Engagement in Therapy*. Chichester: Wiley.

McGuire, J. and Priestley, P. (1995) 'Reviewing "what works": past, present and future', in J. McGuire (ed.), *What Works: Reducing Reoffending: Guidelines from Research and Practice*. Chichester: Wiley.

Mair, G., Lloyd, C., Nee, C. and Sibbit, R. (1994) *Intensive Probation in England and Wales: An Evaluation*, Home Office Research Study 133. London: HMSO.

Meisel, J.S. (2001) 'Relationships and juvenile offenders: the effects of intensive aftercare supervision', *Prison Journal*, 81, 206–45.

Moore, R., Gray, E., Roberts, C., Merrington, S., Waters, I., Fernandez, R., Hayward, G. and Rogers, R.D. (forthcoming) *National Evaluation of the Intensive Supervision and Surveillance Programme: Final Evaluation Report to the Youth Justice Board*. London: YJB.

Muncie, J. (1997) 'Shifting sands: care, community and custody in youth justice discourse', in J. Roche and S. Turner (eds), *Youth in Society*. London: Sage/Open University.

Muncie, J. (1999) *Youth and Crime: A Critical Introduction*. London: Sage.

Palmer, T. (1992) *The Re-emergence of Correctional Intervention*. Newbury Park, CA: Sage.

Petersilia, J. and Turner, S. (1992) 'An evaluation of intensive probation in California', *Journal of Criminal Law and Criminology*, 83, 610-58.

Pitts, J. (2001) 'Korrectional karaoke: New Labour and the zombification of youth justice', *Youth Justice*, 1 (2), 3–16.

Pitts, J. (2002) 'The end of an era', in J. Muncie, G. Hughes and E. McLaughlin (eds), *Youth Justice: Critical Readings*. London: Sage, pp. 413-24.

Potter, M. (1998) 'Serious persistent young offenders', *Prison Service Journal*, 116, 9–10.

Probation Studies Unit (2002) *Intensive Supervision and Surveillance Programmes for Persistent Young Offenders in England and Wales. Evaluation Overview.* Oxford: Probation Studies Unit.

Probation Studies Unit (2003) *Intensive Supervision and Surveillance Programmes for Persistent Young Offenders in England and Wales. Practitioner Bulletin No. 2: Interim National Findings.* Oxford: Probation Studies Unit.

Roberts, C., Baker, K., Merrington, S. and Jones, S. (2001) *The Validity and Reliability of ASSET: Interim Report to the Youth Justice Board.* Oxford: Probation Studies Unit.

Smith, R. (2003) *Youth Justice: Ideas, Policy, Practice.* Cullompton: Willan.

Tonry, M. (1998) 'Intermediate sanctions', in M. Tonry (ed.), *The Handbook of Crime and Punishment.* Oxford: Oxford University Press.

Turner, S. and Petersilia, J. (1992) 'Focusing on high-risk parolees: an experiment to reduce commitments to the Texas Department of Corrections', *Journal of Research in Crime and Delinquency*, 29, 34–61.

Utting, D. and Vennard, J. (2000) *What Works with Young Offenders in the Community.* Ilford: Barnardos.

Worrall, A. and Walton, D. (2000) 'Prolific offender projects, and the reduction of volume property crime: targeted policing and case management', *Vista*, 7, 34-7.

Youth Justice Board (2000a) *ASSET: Explanatory Notes.* London: YJB.

Youth Justice Board (2000b) 'Intensive Supervision and Surveillance Programmes', unpublished YJB document.

Youth Justice Board (2000c) *National Standards for Youth Justice.* London: YJB.

Youth Justice Board (2002a) *Building on Success: Youth Justice Board Review 2001/2002.* London: YJB.

Youth Justice Board (2002b) *Intensive Supervision and Surveillance Programme (ISSP): A new option for dealing with prolific and serious young offenders.* YJB leaflet (updated June 2002)

Youth Justice Board (2002c) *ISSP Eligibility Criteria.* YJB letter to ISSP Managers, 22 April 2002.

Chapter 10

One-to-one ways of promoting desistance: in search of an evidence base

Ros Burnett

At first sight the subject of this chapter, depending on how it is labelled, might be perceived as either passé or as highly salient to present practice. If the chosen title had referred to 'counselling' or 'casework' of offenders or had alluded to the slogan 'advise, assist and befriend', each of which are fair descriptions of issues in the following discussion, then there was a danger of immediately losing the interest of many readers. Such labels were commonly used in the past to describe probation work and therefore might reasonably be construed as referring to methods that have been consigned to history. If instead the rubric selected for the chapter heading had included either of two current buzzwords, 'motivational interviewing' or 'pro-social modelling' – and each of these would also accurately label some of the chapter's content – then it likely would have raised expectations of a discussion that is forward-looking and relevant. Let me hasten to emphasise therefore that what follows is orientated to contemporary issues in offender management services. Yet, in the manner of the French proverb *Il faut reculer pour mieux sauter*, sometimes it is valuable to step back in order to leap forward and, in this spirit, the chapter will reconsider one-to-one practice in the past with a view to present and future advances. I will be referring primarily to probation practice, but the issues are equally relevant to youth justice work and, more broadly, to the newly named National Offender Management Services (NOMS).

An underlying common mechanism

Working with and talking to offenders on a one-to-one basis was, essentially, what the probation service set out to do when it was founded at the beginning of the twentieth century. Though the emphasis and theory base has varied, one-to-one interactions were the *modus operandi* of the service until relatively recently. Likewise, in youth justice work, practitioners had a caseload and worked with each young person on an *individual* basis. Front-line staff provided a mixture of counselling, brokering, practical help and family work, but the essence of their role was to provide a supportive relationship, based on the assumption that this relationship would be influential and would facilitate change (Monger 1964; Rayner 1985; Williams 1995).

'Individual work' may be preferred as a generic term in preference to the cosy-sounding label of 'one-to-one', perhaps too redolent of cosy conversations or mobile phone companies, but the latter at least has the merit of being in current use within the title of an accredited intervention: the *Priestley One-to-One Programme*. For present purposes, it serves as a convenient umbrella term under which to bring together a number of approaches and methods which have been applied under different labels but which seem to have some commonality. For example:

- volunteer befriending
- mentoring
- advise, assist and befriend
- casework
- task-centred casework
- probation
- supervision
- intensive supervision
- counselling
- psychoanalysis
- psychotherapy
- motivational interviewing.

This is not a comprehensive list and basic labels and concepts such as 'talking' and 'helping' as well as professional concepts such as 'the therapeutic alliance' and 'client engagement' could also be included. It is intriguing to ponder the elements that unite and divide each of these. Clearly there are important differences between some of them. For example, they might be distinguished according to the degree of training and expertise required. Other points of difference relate to aims, theory base and the balance of time spent on talking and other activities. Yet, more important than their differences, I would suggest, is their commonality in applying interpersonal processes to assist change.

Whether consciously or instinctively, the practitioner (or volunteer) utilises interpersonal processes to reshape or modify what the recipient thinks, feels and does (e.g. showing an interest, reflective listening, interpreting and summarising, modelling, and encouraging). Research is needed to identify more precisely how these processes come into play in motivational interviewing and in desistance counselling. Crucially, in my view, these factors work by influencing heart and mind and thereby have a greater potential to result in deep-seated behaviour change than is likely to follow from instrumental behaviour change during a period of supervision. In other words, such processes can serve to mobilise or bolster the offender's self-efficacy and intrinsic motivation to desist from further crime.

To help in explicating how these interpersonal processes might bring about such change I shall draw on the approach of William Miller, the leading proponent of motivational interviewing (Miller and Rollnick 1995) – and also the work of Felix Biestek (1961), the 'old master' of casework in probation. Though these two approaches may seem 'strange bed-fellows', there are remarkable similarities between the principles and techniques laid down by each of them. Miller and colleagues (López-Viets et al. 2002: 17) describe the processes underlying 'motivational interviewing' as follows. They explain that:

Motivation
- is *modifiable*
- is an *interpersonal* phenomenon, something that occurs and changes within the context of human relationship
- is often quite *specific*
- is *intrinsic* as well as extrinsic

Intrinsic motivation for change is engaged by eliciting it from, rather than installing it in, the person.

This analysis of motivation can also be applied to, for example, 'hope', 'self-efficacy', 'perceptions', 'attitudes'. All such within-person variables that influence behaviour are dynamic and liable to change in the course of interpersonal transactions. This argument is congruent with the underlying assumption of symbolic interactionism (Mead 1934) and social cognitive theory (Bandura 2001) that subjective meaning is moulded within human relationships.

Most desistance researchers would contest such a strong focus on psychological processes and within-the-person variables. For example, Farrall (2002) has pointed out that work with offenders should be at least as much about addressing environmental causes of crime. To use the sociological jargon, work with offenders should be concerned with 'social capital' at least as much as 'human capital'. It hardly needs to be said that if people are homeless and hungry or 'out of their mind' because of drug abuse, those are the priorities. When basic needs are being met, however, there is scope for important work with offenders that addresses both subjective and objective factors influencing offenders. Social casework was generally concerned with both, as Biestek's (1961: 3) explanation makes clear. He wrote that 'The purpose of casework ... is to help the client make a better adjustment ... The means to this purpose are the mobilization of dormant capacities in the individual, or the mobilization of appropriate community resources, or both, depending upon the needs of each client'.

This model was called the 'casework relationship' and the relationship between the practitioner and the client was described as the 'medium' or the 'channel' for this mobilisation of capacities and resources (1961: 7). It is perhaps worth pondering whether there has to be a *relationship* as such. Such interpersonal processes can apply within one-off meetings (strangers on a train) or in groups, or indirectly via the influence of famous role models. Nevertheless, these interpersonal processes are clearly more likely to take effect if trust and familiarity are developed, for which several meetings would normally be a pre-requisite. Conversely, a single meeting, with no prospect of further contact, would be a poor basis for a 'working alliance' to be established. Studies examining experiences of casework and probation (Brown 1998; Rex 1999) or counselling (Kelly 1997) indicate the significance that clients (or offenders) can attach to their relationships with practitioners and the impact of this on their self-perceptions and life choices. For individuals who do not have close or trusting relationships in their personal life, it is quite possible for the practitioner to become a 'significant other', albeit in an obviously circumscribed way.

The interpersonal skills of the practitioners are crucial here. They include the social and interpersonal skills that most people acquire in the normal process of becoming functioning human beings who care about and depend on others. They also include skills and techniques that can be taught and practised for a purpose: to influence, help or change others. It is unclear which of these are the most powerful. McGuire (2002b) has pointed out that interpersonal skills and the ability to develop relationships with others have 'rarely [been] addressed in direct fashion in outcome research in the offender field. Evidence from adjoining fields [though] such as mental health indicates that [they are] pivotal' (2002b: 28). For example, Rollnick and Miller found that a confrontational, challenging style was unsuccessful when attempting to motivate and engage clients, whereas a supportive and empathic style was effective. Miller and Rollnick (1995) emphasise that the 'spirit' of the working relationship is crucial to outcome.

Although these rather elusive matters of style and personal qualities have rarely been investigated by researchers in the offender field, they are certainly mentioned by *practitioners* in the offender field (Leibrich 1991; Burnett 1996; Brown 1998). In a study of changes in youth justice, Burnett and Appleton (2004) found that practitioners generally welcomed the new emphasis on evidence-based practice and case-management approaches, but they continued to regard practitioners' working relationships with young people as crucial to bringing about change.

The evidence against traditional one-to-one practice

Yet according to meta-analytical reviews of 'what works', casework (or counselling) was categorised among methods that were ineffective. The importance once attached to relational aspects of work with offenders was also adversely affected by shifts in sentencing policy and political thinking about crime (Rex 2002) but individual casework was shown in a particularly bad light in highly influential Home Office literature about effective practice in reducing offending, that distilled the 'what works' findings:

> Programmes which draw on cognitive skills and cognitive methods are reported as achieving higher levels of effectiveness than those which employ group or individual counselling and favour traditional non-directive therapy. (Vennard, Sugg and Hedderman 1997)

> The learning styles of most offenders require active, participatory approaches rather than traditional client-centred counselling. (Home Office 1999)

> [T]raditionally probation work has involved individual counselling but research shows that the best results are obtained if teaching styles match offenders' learning styles – and most offenders require active, participatory approaches (e.g. role play)

rather than loose, unstructured or overly didactic methods. (Vennard and Hedderman, 1998: 104)

Such conclusions seem to be based on overgeneralised descriptions of traditional practice. In the first quotation above, cognitive-behavioural methods are contrasted against individual counselling and traditional therapy as if they are mutually exclusive, whereas one-to-one counselling can of course be cognitive-behavioural in approach. Priestley, for example, uses the term 'cognitive counselling' (Priestley 2003). Guidelines on meeting the principle of 'responsivity' often specify that group work is more suited to offenders' learning styles and imply that the role of the offender in one-to-one sessions is passive and non-participatory. Yet some qualitative studies of standard relationship-based work suggest precisely the opposite.

The principles of effective practice have usefully been promulgated but they are not set in stone. Leading researchers investigating the effectiveness of interventions, including McGuire and Lösel, have pointed out that meta-analytical reviews of research to determine effective practice in reducing crime do not yet provide all the answers or clarification required:

There has been a perception that, in summarising the findings of [meta-analytical] reviews ... this somehow amounts to a claim that everything is now known that needs to be known about how to implement effective crime prevention with persistent offenders. This is hardly the position. The ... findings represent only the clearest or more consistent trends emerging from the meta-analytical reviews. Numerous questions remain unanswered, and many issues still need to be clarified. Further research is essential if those goals are to be accomplished. (McGuire 2002b :163)

There are far fewer methodologically well-founded treatment studies on specific types of programs, offenders and settings than the general 'what works' discussion would suggest. (Lösel 2001: 70)

Most importantly, a review of the evidence against traditional one-to-one work as an intervention is not sufficiently compelling for this approach to be consigned to the rubbish heap of useless methods (Burnett 2002). The nature of one-to-one work being referred to in meta-analytical reviews is generally described as 'non-directive, psycho-dynamic therapy' (e.g. see Lösel 2001). However, by the 1970s the psychodynamic approach was dying out as the dominant model for practice. Probation officers, who spent much of their time on 'home visits', were too regularly confronted with the adverse circumstances of their probationers to be purist in applying psychodynamic models in their practice. Far from being rooted in their offices like psychoanalysts, they always had an eye to what McIvor (1990) described as 'concrete services relevant to social need'. They applied task-centred and problem-solving casework and they provided copious amounts of family-based work. Indeed, though it was not labelled as such, their approach was more like 'multi-systemic therapy', which has recently been associated with substantial reductions in reoffending rates (Henggeler et al. 1998).

Criticisms against the non-directive style of standard work are arguably based on a misapplication of the description. A 'non-directive' counselling approach should not be confused with loose, unstructured approaches in which there is no focus for the work and the offender is passive. Used appropriately, a non-directive manner facilitates the equivalent of the 'quiet, eliciting style' of motivational work, as advocated by Miller and Rollnick (2002). Non-directive methods aim to draw out service-users' self-determination and capacity to make responsible choices. The criticisms of traditional practice would be more appropriately directed at the lack of standardisation and accountability. Prior to the reforms of probation practice outlined in Chapters 1 and 2, officers were encouraged to draw on different theories and to develop their practice based on personal strengths and whatever felt appropriate. It was, as Raynor, Smith and Vanstone commented, 'a very individual approach to practice in which it was assumed that only the individual practitioner was entitled to take decisions about his or her work' (Raynor et al. 1994: 92). This leaves scope for both sloppy practice and brilliant practice, but without a sufficient framework to determine the difference.

But an examination of what *is* effective reveals that elements of traditional work, when at its best, are part of the 'effective' package after all. Consider, for example, the conclusion that 'multi-modal, cognitive-behavioural and skills-oriented programs that address the offenders' risk, needs and responsivity [result in] larger effects' (Lösel 2001). This stipulation for programmes can equally apply to work carried out on a one-to-one basis, which can meet each of these conditions. Also, the 'what works' literature promotes a 'multi-modal' approach – in other words, an array of methods and resources to meet diverse offending-related needs. For example, Lipton et al. (2002), suggest that, in addition to cognitive-behavioural work, programmes should provide pro-social modelling with positive reinforcement of non-criminal behaviour and attitudes, self-efficacy and social support and motivational interviewing – all elements in common with traditional practice. Indeed, *individual counselling* is sometimes mentioned as part of the multi-modal cognitive behavioural approach (e.g. Wells-Parker et al. 1995).

We have seen that rejections of traditional practice were partly based on overgeneralised representations of the nature of one-to-one work and ignore what, at its best, it had in common with the now praised multi-modal programmes. Another basis for questioning the dismissal of standard practice arises from an examination of key studies that have been read as discrediting counselling as a method for working with offenders. With so many good reviews of effective practice now at our disposal it is too easy to 'take their word for it' that some methods work and others do not rather than to revisit the studies from which such overviews and meta-analyses are derived.

One such study, respected for its 'scientifically credible design', is the Cambridge-Somerville Study. Not only has this study raised questions about whether counselling might be beneficial in work with offenders, far worse, it is given as an example of methods that 'do harm' (McCord 2003). The original study was carried out in the 1940s. The participants (boys aged nine or ten when the study started) were randomly allocated to the 'treatment group' and to the 'control group'. Both the original study, and a thirty-year follow-up study carried out by Joan McCord, showed that the treatment group went on to commit more offences and also fared worse, in various other ways, than did the control group.

The recipients of the treatment received a whole package of interventions including 'counselling'. We are told that 'The counselling element was variable in quantity, but averaged out at two home visits a month'. As well as being counselled the boys were: 'referred … to specialists when it seemed advisable. Boys were tutored, taken to a variety of sports events, encouraged to participate in the woodwork shop … encouraged to join community youth groups … helped to get jobs … sent to summer camps (McCord 2003: 19). As for the control group, we are informed that they also received 'whatever services were provided by other organizations' (2003: 19).

Apparently, McCord received threatening letters and insults when she delivered the finding that the 'treatment' had done more harm than good. Such extreme reactions say more about the insecurity of the protesters than about the quality of the research, but perhaps a milder form of disapprobation could be justified. The slack definition of counselling applied and the number of uncontrolled variables do not seem to be a good basis for concluding that counselling does not work.

Indeed, McCord carried out an odds-ratio analysis which revealed that the most 'harmful' element was multiple attendance at a summer camp. In one of her papers that looks at this in more detail, McCord (2001: 190) explains:

> A good part of the harm appears to have come through something that happened at summer camp when the boys returned for at least a second stay. We are a long way from understanding how this result came about. I strongly suspect that the boys from the Youth Study tended to bond together, encouraging one another's deviant values in much the style that deviant parents encourage their sons' deviance when they ask for reports about fights in school or other types of misbehavior ... the encouragement is effective because peer responses among misbehaving children provide potentiating reasons for additional misbehavior.

It is also worth revisiting another well-regarded study: the Intensive Matched Probation and After-Care Treatment (IMPACT) study (Folkard et al. 1974, 1976), which was instrumental in sealing doubts about the effectiveness of probation work (Raynor and Vanstone 2002). The study was carried out by Home Office researchers across four probation services and applied experimental conditions. Cases were randomly allocated to 'experimental' and 'control' officers. The former had reduced caseloads of around 20 probationers and were relieved of other duties. In comparison the 'control' officers provided 'normal probation' and carried a typical caseload of 40 to 45. The researchers distinguished two types of officer involvement with offenders (Folkard et al. 1974: 18):

> 'Individual treatment' can be used to describe anything which is said or done to the offender, within the context of the relations between him and his probation officer, most often in the form of discussions in office interviews.

> 'Situational treatment' can be used to describe anything which is said or done, not directly to the offender, but in relation to people or circumstances in his social environment, with special reference to situations of family, work, and leisure. It will be concerned with practical intervention in these situations, and seek to make active use of the offender's relationships with other people.

It was the second type of treatment that the officers in the 'experimental' group were encouraged to apply, and they were also prompted to make use of ancillary staff, voluntary workers and other agencies: arguably an approach that is more similar to case management than counselling. Indeed, the second volume of the research report specified that: 'One of the prime aims of IMPACT was to divert the major emphasis of probation casework away from the office interview between client and officer, towards greater situational involvement in the areas of family, work and leisure' (1976: 13).

The analysis of outcomes showed that there was no significant difference in the one-year reconviction rates between the experimental and control cases. The study was therefore not helpful in boosting the prestige of probation work at a time when the idea that 'nothing works' was taking hold. Some differences did emerge though when the researchers distinguished between offenders on the basis of their risk of reoffending and the extent of their problems. Of some interest to the present discussion, offenders with moderate or high criminal tendencies and average or few personal problems who were referred to 'experimental' officers had significantly higher reconviction rates than those who received 'normal' probation supervision. 'Individual treatment' was more typical of what the study referred to as 'normal probation' and is closer to the interpersonal one-to-one work that is the subject of this chapter.

Supportive evidence

Some investigations (e.g. Bailey 1995; Brown 1998; Rex 1999) have begun to look inside the 'black box' of work with offenders on a one-to-one basis, exploring practitioners' and offenders' perceptions of what influences them in the change process. Generally, such qualitative studies have revealed that standard probation practice can be pivotal in assisting desistance from crime (though there are exceptions, for example see Farrall 2002, discussed below). Probationers in Sue Rex's study of community sentences and desistance identified the discussions with their supervisors as helping to foster and sustain a decision to desist from crime. Rex's analysis underscores the relevance of continuity and reciprocity in offenders' contacts during supervision – characteristics that require interpersonal relationship rather than one-off contacts. Probationers made more effort out of a sense of obligation and loyalty in response to the support they have been given and the commitment and efforts of the officer. Officers, for their part, were able to capitalise on the relationship that had been built up to encourage socially responsible behaviour.

Studies by Chris Trotter have provided some quantitative evidence of the effectiveness of 'one-to-one work' outside of accredited programmes. Some officers were trained in the use of a pro-social modelling (PSM) approach, which included counselling techniques such as reflective listening and building a caring staff–offender relationship, as well as a focus on solving social problems. The supervision by officers who were PSM-trained was associated with higher rates of compliance, lower recidivism and lower rates of subsequent imprisonment over a four-year period (Trotter 1996, 2000).

Beyond such investigations of assisted desistance, the large body of research on desistance from crime is of relevance to an understanding of effective practice and there is scope for a better integration of the 'what works' and the 'desistance' literatures, as has been convincingly argued by Maruna (2000) and McNeill (2003). Desistance research is helping us to unpick the nature of the interplay between agency variables and social variables (e.g. Maruna 2001; Farrall 2002; Burnett 2004).

The most large-scale of recent empirical studies on the role of probation practice in promoting desistance was carried out by Stephen Farrall (2002). In a longitudinal study over a period of two years, he investigated the effects of probation supervision on the criminal careers of 199 probationers in six services. Disappointingly for the Probation Service, Farrall (2004: 201) concluded that 'probation supervision would appear to have had little impact upon the resolution of obstacles [against desistance from crime]', but, qualifying this, he added that 'it may be important in building and encouraging motivation'. This is reminiscent of the half empty and half full glass: we could reverse the conclusion and argue that a highly effective and important way in which probation staff and youth justice staff have an impact on desistance is by eliciting motivation from the people with whom they work – though they may need to improve their skills and procedures in carrying out such work. Based on his findings, Farrall argued that there is no problem with the thinking skills of most offenders and that attention should be focused instead on addressing their need for employment or for decent housing. No doubt his argument is applicable in some cases.

Summarising the desistance literature, McNeill presents a triangle of desistance with three planes, explaining that 'desistance resides somewhere in the interfaces between developing personal maturity, forming new or stronger social bonds associated with certain life transitions, and individual subjective narrative constructions which offenders build around these key events and changes' (McNeill 2003: 151). The work needed in each case on each of these dimensions will depend on assessment and the supervision plan, but for some cases 'part of the worker's task [will be] to build individual capacities or 'human capital' (McNeill 2003: 159). Desistance research by Maruna (2001) and Burnett (2004) points to the potential value of opportunities for ex-offenders to reflect on their past and future, and to reinvent themselves.

Towards an evidence base for interpersonal work

The emphasis on case management and group programmes in recent years has brought supervisory practice in the UK much closer to the USA model of supervision in which the offender has merely to 'check in' on a regular basis. Ironically, commentators in the USA are now advocating the adoption of methods that follow the principles of motivational interviewing (Taxman 2002). There is also a growing band of researchers and policy managers (too many to mention all by name, but see, for example, Christine Knott's references to 'casework' in this volume) who have argued that one-to-one work should be valued as an important component of structured programmes and, in appropriate cases, should be regarded as an intervention in its own right.

However, more research is needed to enrich our theoretical understanding of such interpersonal work and to build up an empirical evidence base. The complete absence of an evidence base until relatively recently, and the variety of techniques and methods that loosely fit into the 'one-to-one' category, make it suspiciously likely that those elements of traditional practice that were effective were never uncovered, never distinguished from work that was mediocre or adverse. The remarkable lack of monitoring and systematic evaluation within the probation service until very recently resulted in a 'demonstrability gap' (Raynor et al. 1994: 31). Quite simply, there has never been a rigorous evaluation of standard one-to-one supervision in the community and what it involves when we open the package.

We can draw support for this argument from points made in the 2002/03 Annual Report of the Probation Inspectorate (HMIP 2003: 49):

> It is not yet clear that the factors so far being measured regarding the delivery of accredited programmes are those that are significant for effectively reducing re-offending ... the Service needs a more finely grained picture of which aspects of practice produce the desired outcomes that are essential to get it right.

Research into one-to-one practice – call it 'relationship-based work', 'motivational interviewing', 'casework' or whatever – should be part of this 'finely grained picture'. The evidence so far on this category of work with offenders (and the interpersonal processes therein) is conflicting because different approaches are being lumped together. What has been evaluated (in so far as there have been decent, relevant evaluations) has been all manner of one-to-one interactions, informed by different theories and aimed at varying categories of offenders, and performed according to differing levels of skill and expertise. Effective work has been buried under this pot-pourri of personal counselling. We need to dig under all the conceptual confusion to get at the mechanisms and micro-mechanisms that many of these approaches have in common, and at others which distinguish them.

A way forward would be to undertake a study of three contrasting methods at different points across the spectrum: (1) mentoring by volunteer members of the community; (2) standard one-to-one supervision of Community Rehabilitation Orders; and (3) even though somewhat removed from the criminal justice system, counselling or psychotherapy carried out by accredited counsellors aimed at promoting desistance from problematic behaviour (such as drug or alcohol abuse). Indeed, Worrall (1997: 109) has noted that: 'The role of counselling in probation has always been ambiguous. Historically, the exhortation to "advise, assist and befriend" was more closely associated with the duties of citizenship than with professional skills and knowledge'.

It is time to draw a clearer line between that which can be carried out by a volunteer member of society or less qualified support staff and the kind of professional intervention appropriate for the most persistent and challenging offenders. Again, this is in keeping with conclusions in the Inspectorate's Report that the Probation Service needs to 'target its resources on higher risk offenders and, in particular, supervise persistent offenders more intensively' (HMIP 2003: 6) and that 'the voluntary sector has much to contribute by way of services to offenders' (HMIP 2003: 8).

One of the first steps, if we are to build up this evidence base for differentiated individual work, will be to carry out a survey of what one-to-one work is still being undertaken in the service, by whom and for what purpose. What supportive work is being done, including preparatory work, reinforcement work and relapse prevention? To what extent are services using 'motivational interviewing'? Kemshall and Canton et al. in their study of programme attrition found that 'Motivational interviewing is commonly identified by Areas as the mechanism by which they are combating attrition' but they commented that 'It is less clear, however, that staff are trained, or when trained, actually competent in this method' (2002: 7). And to what extent is one-to-one work, in addition to the Priestley programme, being applied as a intervention in its own right as well as being a part of case management? How much and in what ways are volunteers, mentors and support staff being engaged for such roles?

As part of an examination of individual work with offenders, we will also need to investigate skills and styles used by practitioners and effective helpers. Research in the mental health field shows that individual counsellors have different drop-out rates and different success rates and that counsellor style and techniques make a difference (e.g. several relevant studies cited in López-Viets et al. 2002). In the criminal justice field, Trotter (1996, 2000) has identified practitioner style and techniques as critical. Further, our 'finely grained picture' should look at how all the aspects just mentioned interact with the character-istics and 'responsivity' of the individuals they are working with. 'The facets of responsivity are under-explored, and there is considerable work to be done to examine what styles of intervention suit which clients' (McMurran 2002: 254). Groupwork is more appropriate for some but is not suitable for everyone: the adoption of the Priestley One-to-One Programme shows clear recognition of this. But research is needed to explore which clients will fare better in groups and which in individual sessions, and the stages in criminal careers when individual inter-ventions might be usefully employed.

Conclusions

I have no illusions about the nature of traditional probation practice. My own time in the service was during the 1970s and 1980s when practice was highly individualised according to the home-grown philosophies and idiosyncratic working styles of officers, and when 'personal integrity' and genuine concern for individuals were valued in officers at least as much as their theoretical knowledge and professional training. The nature and quality of supervision was a lucky draw for probationers and ex-prisoners coming out to voluntary after-care or on licence. Moreover, the extent to which officers focused on offending behaviour was variable, probably with important consequences for effectiveness (see Willis 1983).

A survey in ten probation services in the mid-1990s (Burnett 1996) revealed that little had changed. Officers were clinging to an auton-omous mode of working and were resistant against approaches requir-ing them to spend more time on case management and monitoring and to be more systematic in referring cases to programmes and specialist projects. The content of a supervision plan was still too dependent on the arbitrary decisions of individual members of staff. I therefore welcome the overhaul of the probation service in recent years. It would be a great pity though if, in striving to update and toughen its image, and to introduce rigour into its practices, the Probation Service relinquishes an essential ingredient of effective practice. The cliché about 'throwing out the baby with the bathwater' has been over-used but seems to perfectly fit the argument – and to replace the need for further words.

References

Bailey, R. (1995) 'Helping offenders as an element in justice', in D. Ward and M. Lacey (eds), *Probation: Working for Justice*, 1st edn. London: Whiting & Birch.

Bandura, A. (2001) 'Social cognitive theory: an agentic perspective', *Annual Review of Psychology*, 52, 1–26.

Biestek, F.P. (1961) *The Casework Relationship*. London: Unwin University Books.

Brown, I. (1998) 'Successful probation practice', in D. Faulkner and A. Gibbs (eds), *New Politics, New Probation?* Probation Studies Unit Report 6. Oxford: Centre for Criminological Research, University of Oxford.

Burnett, R. (1996) *Fitting Supervision to Offenders: Assessment and Allocation in the Probation Service*, Home Office Research Study 153. London: Home Office.

Burnett, R. (2002) 'The case for counselling as a method for working with offenders', *Vista*, 7 (3), 216–26.

Burnett, R. (2004) 'To re-offend or not to re-offend? the ambivalence of convicted property offenders', in S. Maruna and R. Immarigeon (eds), *After Crime and Punishment: Pathways to Offender Reintegration*. Cullompton: Willan.

Burnett, R. and Appleton, C. (2004) 'Joined-up services to tackle youth crime: a case-study in England', *British Journal of Criminology*, 44, 34–54.

Farrall, S. (2002) *Rethinking What Works with Offenders: Probation, Social Context and Desistance from Crime*. Cullompton: Willan.

Farrall, S. (2004) 'Supervision, motivation and social context: what matters most when probationers desist?', in G. Mair (ed.), *What Matters in Probation*. Cullompton: Willan.

Folkard, M.S., Smith, D.E. and Smith, D.D. (1976) *IMPACT Intensive Matched Probation and After-Care Treatment. Volume II. The Results of the Experiment*, Home Office Research Study 36. London: HMSO.

Folkard, M.S., Fowles, A.J., McWilliams, B.C., McWilliams, W., Smith, D.E., Smith, D.D. and Walmsley, G.R. (1974) *IMPACT Intensive Matched Probation and After-Care Treatment. Volume I. The Design of the Probation Experiment and an Evaluation*, Home Office Research Study 24. London: HMSO.

Henggeler, S.W., Schoenwald, S., Borduin, C., Rowland, M. and Cunningham, P. (1998) *Multi-Systemic Treatment of Anti-social Behavior*. New York: Guildford Press.

Her Majesty's Inspectorate of Probation (2003) *Annual Report 2002/2003*. London: Home Office.

Home Office (1999) *What Works: Reducing Re-offending*. London: Home Office Communication Directorate.

Kelly, E.W. (1997) 'Relationship-centered counseling: a humanistic model of integration'. *Journal of Counseling and Development*, 75, 337–45.

Kemshall, H. and Canton, R. with Bailey, R., Dominey, J., Simpkin, B. and Yates, S. (2002) *The Effective Management of Programme Attrition: A Report for the National Probation Service (Welsh Region)*. Leicester: De Montfort University Community and Criminal Justice Unit.

Leibrich, J. (1991) *A Study of the Probation Division's Perception of Its Role in Reducing Re-offending*. Wellington: Department of Justice, New Zealand.

Leibrich, J. (1993) *Straight to the Point: Angles on Giving up Crime*. Otago, New Zealand: University of Otago Press.

Lipsey, M.W. and Wilson, D.B. (1998) 'Effective interventions for serious juvenile offenders', in R. Loeber and D.P. Farrington (eds), *Serious and Violent Juvenile Offenders: Risk Factors and Successful Interventions*. Thousand Oaks, CA: Sage.

Lipton, D.S., Pearson, F.S., Cleland, C.M. and Yee, D. (2002) 'The effectiveness of cognitive-behavioural treatment methods on offender recidivism', in J. McGuire (ed.), *Offender Rehabilitation and Treatment: Effective Programmes and Policies to Reduce Re-offending*. Chichester: Wiley & Sons.

López-Viets, V., Walker, D.D. and Miller, W.R. (2002) 'What is motivation to change? A scientific analysis', in M. McMurran (ed.), *Motivating Offenders to Change: A Guide to Enhancing Engagement in Therapy*. Chichester: Wiley.

Lösel, F. (2001) 'Evaluating the effectiveness of correctional treatment: a review and synthesis of meta-evaluations', in G.A. Bernfeld, D.P. Farrington and A.W. Leschied (eds), *Offender Rehabilitation in Practice: Implementing and Evaluating Effective Programs*. Chichester: John Wiley & Sons.

Mann, R.E., Ginsburg, J.I.D. and Weekes, J.R. (2002), 'Motivational interviewing with offenders', in M. McMurran (ed.), *Motivating Offenders to Change: A Guide to Enhancing Engagement in Therapy*. Chichester: Wiley.

McCord, J. (2001) 'Crime prevention: a cautionary tale', *Third International Interdisciplinary Evidence-Based Policies and Indicator Systems Conference*, July.

McCord, J. (2003) 'Cures that harm: unanticipated outcomes of crime prevention programs', *Annals of the American Academy of Political and Social Science*, 587, 16–30.

McGuire, J. (2002a) 'Integrating findings from research reviews', in J. McGuire (ed.), *Offender Rehabilitation and Treatment: Effective programmes and Policies to Reduce Re-offending*. Chichester: Wiley & Sons.

McGuire, J. (2002b) 'Motivation for what? Effective programmes for motivated offenders', in M. McMurran (ed.), *Motivating Offenders to Change: A Guide to Enhancing Engagement in Therapy*. Chichester: Wiley & Sons.

McIvor, G. (1990) *Sanctions for Serious or Persistent Offender: A Review of the Literature*. Stirling: University of Stirling Social Research Centre.

McMurran, M. (2002) 'Future directions', in M. McMurran (ed.), *Motivating Offenders to Change: A Guide to Enhancing Engagement in Therapy*. Chichester: Wiley.

McNeill, F. (2003) 'Desistance-focused probation practice', in W. Hong Chui and M. Nellis (eds.), *Moving Probation Forward: Evidence, Arguments and Practice*. Harlow: Pearson Longman.

Maruna, S. (2000) 'Desistance from crime and offender rehabilitation: a tale of two research literatures', *Offender Programs Report*, 4, 1–13.

Maruna, S. (2001) *Making Good: How Ex-convicts Reform and Rebuild their Lives*. Washington, DC: American Psychological Association.

Mead, G.H. (1934) *Mind, Self and Society*. Chicago: University of Chicago Press.

Miller, W.R. and Rollnick, S. (eds) (1995) *Motivational Interviewing*, 2nd edn. New York: Guilford.

Monger, M. (1964) *Casework in Probation*. London: Butterworth.

Morgan, R. (2003) 'Foreword', in HMIP, *Annual Report 2002/2003*. London: Home Office.

Priestley, P. (2003) Personal communication.

Raynor, P. (1985) *Social Work, Justice and Control*. Oxford: Blackwell.

Raynor, P. and Vanstone, M. (2002) *Understanding Community Penalties: Probation, Policy and Social Change*. Buckingham: Open University.

Raynor, P., Smith, D. and Vanstone. M. (1994) *Effective Probation Practice*. London: Macmillan.

Rex, S. (1999) 'Desistance from offending: experiences of probation', *Howard Journal*, 38 (4), 366–83.

Rex, S. (2002) 'Re-inventing community penalties: the role of communication', in S.A. Rex and M. Tonry (eds), *Reform and Punishment: The Future of Sentencing*. Cullompton: Willan.

Rollnick, S. and Miller, W.R. (1995) 'What is motivational interviewing?', *Behavioural and Cognitive Psychotherapy*, 23, 325–34.

Taxman, F.S. (2002) 'Supervision – exploring the dimensions of effectiveness', *Federal Probation, Special Issue: What Works in Corrections*, September, 14–27.

Trotter, C. (1996) 'The impact of different supervision practices on community corrections', *Australian and New Zealand Journal of Criminology*, 28 (2), 29–46.

Trotter, C. (2000) 'Social work education, pro-social modelling and effective probation practice', *Probation Journal*, 47, 256–61.

Vennard, J. and Hedderman, C. (1998) 'Effective interventions with offenders', in P. Goldblatt and C. Lewis (eds), *Reducing Offending: An Assessment of Research Evidence on Ways of Dealing with Offending Behaviour*. Home Office Research Study 187. London: Home Office.

Vennard, J., Sugg., D. and Hedderman, C. (1997) *Changing Offenders' Attitudes and Behaviour: What Works?*, Home Office Research Study 171. London: Home Office.

Wells-Parker, E., Bangert-Drowns, R., McMillen, R. and Williams, M. (1995) 'Final results from a meta-analysis of drink/drive offenders', *Addiction*, 90, 907–26.

Williams, B. (1995) 'Introduction', in B. Williams (ed.), *Probation Values.* Birmingham: Venture Press.

Willis, A. (1983) 'The balance between care and control in probation: a research note', *British Journal of Social Work*, 13, 339–46.

Worrall, A. (1997) *Punishment in the Community: the Future of Criminal Justice.* London: Longman.

Chapter 11

Using community service to encourage inclusive citizenship: evidence from the CS pathfinder

Sue Rex and Loraine Gelsthorpe

This chapter reflects on what offenders might be able to gain in terms of 'citizenship' from performing unpaid work for the community. It reports on various initiatives that began with practitioners during the mid-1990s with the aim of capitalising upon the practical setting within which community service occurs and the nature of the contacts with supervisors and beneficiaries into which it brings offenders. The thinking behind such initiatives was that community service can offer powerful opportunities for offenders to become more active and responsible citizens by learning more socially responsible behaviour, acquiring skills that can be used in employment and developing a greater belief in their capacity to make a valued contribution to society. The Community Service Pathfinder projects funded by the Home Office under the Crime Reduction Programme reflect a concerted effort to apply this thinking and to evaluate the results, representing a move towards evidence-based practice in community service.

Key elements of the Community Service (CS) Pathfinder projects involved supervisors acting as pro-social models and offenders working towards certification for employment-related skills while undertaking community service.[1] Focusing on pro-social modelling, below we trace its origins and development in community service work through a pilot project between the Institute of Criminology and Cambridgeshire Probation Service leading to its inclusion as a strand in the CS Pathfinder projects. We consider what might be learnt from the experience of these initiatives for the future development of pro-social modelling as a component in the Enhanced Community Punishment scheme, now 'Recognised' by the Correctional Services Accreditation Panel. One particular question in which we are interested is how offenders, through their experiences of performing community service, can gain access to the social capital that will help them move away from offending towards active participation as citizens. In our view, it is intrinsic to the meaning and spirit of pro-social modelling that attempts are made to accommodate social diversity and to treat offenders as full human beings, who are socially and culturally differentiated (Gelsthorpe 2001).

Citizenship

The term 'citizenship' has been bandied around in very recent years in a wide range of educational and social policy contexts. It is a concept with a long history, of course, notably in some of the writings of Aristotle, but it came into its own perhaps in Marshall's seminal writings in the 1960s. These drew attention to the idea of the foundations of consensus not so much resting in the pursuit of particular policies or the formation of particular political structures, but in the establishment of wider and deeper social rights for citizens (Marshall 1963). Marshall's account of citizenship was one of evolutionary development of the defined rights of individuals expressed in terms of their progressively acquiring judicial, political and social rights. Modern meanings of citizenship may take us away from 'rights' as such, although Marshall's intended emphasis on participation in social life has endured. Indeed, in educational circles we learn that since 2000 there have been programmes for the study of citizenship in secondary schools (McLaughlin 2000).

While there is ongoing debate about the purposes of citizenship education, the essence of citizenship is such that programmes go far beyond 'civics' as such and emphasise social responsibilities as well as political rights. Indeed, good neighbourliness, social and moral responsibility, political literacy and community involvement (volunteering) have all been mentioned as key ingredients of citizenship (Faulkner 2001, 2003; see also Office for National Statistics 2001); abstinence from crime is taken for granted. In some ways, citizenship may be described as a 'politics of attachment' (Kraemer and Roberts 1996), in other words, the 'social bonds' (Sampson and Laub 1993) that bind people to communities. However, it should be acknowledged that there has been relatively little attention to notions of attachment or social bonding through community activities and relationships (Gelsthorpe 2001), which arguably have a symbolic as well as a grounded existence (Rustin 1996). Most of the work done in this area relates to the quality of parenting and delinquency (see Utting 1996, for instance).

One area of thought that is of relevance to our purposes here, however, concerns the notion of 'capital'. In the last decade there has been international debate about the role of civil society (Blunkett 2003), and specifically about civic associations, in sustaining the horizontal relationships of cooperation and trust that are perceived to be at the root of a healthy democracy. The discussion has been particularly vibrant in the USA, prompted by Putnam's (1995) argument that there is a close connection between effective governance and high levels of civic participation. His original research referred to Italian regional government institutions, which looked similar at one level but which performed very differently. As he put it:

> You tell me how many choral societies there are in an Italian region, and I will tell you plus or minus three days how long it will take you to get your health bills reimbursed by its regional government. (Putnam 1993)

Robert Putnam's thesis was that civic associational life, as measured by membership of voluntary civic organisations, was a critical factor not only in promoting individual well-being and localised goodwill, but in building pools of social capital which in turn contribute to social cohesion and political and economic development. Thus citizens' forums, swimming clubs and a variety of voluntary groups may all serve to promote community support, networks of communication and community defences (against social adversity, including crime). Hagan and McCarthy (1997: 229) helpfully set out that social capital:

> ... originates in socially structured relations between individuals, in families and in aggregations of individuals in neighbourhoods, churches, schools and so on. These relations facilitate social action by generating a knowledge and sense of obligation, expectations, trustworthiness, information channel norms and sanctions.

There are links here with 'human capital', which broadly relates to the personal skills and knowledge that individuals possess and which facilitates access to education, work and other resources, and enhances their ability to hold down jobs and achieve in them. Coleman suggests that 'It ... is created by changes in persons that bring about skills and capabilities that make them able to act in new ways' (1988: 100). Thus we can see that social capital might stimulate personal skills and resources (human capital) and vice versa. Probation services frequently try to improve the human capital of the offenders they supervise by opening access to employment schemes and partnerships or by offering programmes in thinking skills, safe drug use, anger management and so on. The results of such efforts appear to be disappointing to date since there have been few convincing studies regarding a demonstrable effect of links between employment and levels of crime; moreover, the exigencies of the labour market are beyond the control of probation officers (Crow 2000). However, employment opportunity is but one element of human and social capital. We want to suggest that there might be other elements of community service that can facilitate the development of human and social capital – and thus enhance citizenship.

Realising the potential in community service to promote citizenship

The late 1990s brought together several quite separate developments relating to community service practice, which coalesced in important and perhaps unforeseeable ways to bring community service on to the rehabilitative agenda (see Rex 2001). This was especially surprising given the nature of the interest in community service before that time: predominantly in its effectiveness as an alternative to custodial sentencing (see: Pease 1985; Bottoms 1987; McIvor 1990). Indeed, the concern to ensure that community service was effective as a punishment had found expression in the application of National Standards to community service in 1989. This was *before* Standards were applied to all aspects of community supervision as part of the implementation of the Criminal Justice Act 1991 (Home Office et al. 1992).

One of these developments, training offenders in employment-related skills, came in the form of practitioner initiatives starting in the mid-1990s. Seeing that there might be benefits in enabling offenders to achieve tangible gains from undertaking community service work, CS units in various parts of the country pioneered schemes to enable offenders performing community service to gain qualifications, for example in vocational training or key skills. Their involvement in such schemes improved job satisfaction for CS supervisors; it was also seen to make their task easier in providing an incentive for offenders to turn up and to comply with instructions. An added motivation was the additional funding that such educational activities generated from the FEFC (Further Education Funding Council) as well as other bodies which could be used to enhance CS practice. Northumbria Probation Service was an early pioneer of this kind of work, running skills accreditation models – with European funding – from 1995. Pre-NVQ training and accreditation was introduced within CS in Norfolk and Cambridgeshire in 1997 as part of a five-county collaboration with the College of West Anglia. In Gloucestershire, too, during 1997 a small group of CS supervisors and CS officers started to work with ETE (education, training and employment) staff to offer Open College Network (OCN) units of competence in vocational and employability skills in partnership with Gloucestershire County Council. Further details of such schemes are provided in the appendices to Rex et al. (2003).

Some of these practitioner initiatives were likely to have been influenced by Gill McIvor's (1992) study of community service in Scotland, which looked beyond CS as an alternative to custody to investigate the nature of offenders' experiences in performing the work and their subsequent reconviction. Starting in 1986, the aim of the various evaluations reported by McIvor was to examine the extent to which the order had met a range of policy objectives. The research was prompted by the concerns of managers and practitioners about the impact of perceived inconsistencies in the way in which community service schemes were being run in Scotland.

Given the extent of these Scottish studies across 12 schemes in four local authority areas and the importance of the findings, it is worth setting out the latter in some detail. In essence, it was found that the quality of their experiences in undertaking community service appeared to have a positive impact on offenders. Specifically, McIvor (1992) reported that certain features of that experience were associated with finding community service very worthwhile: having a great deal of opportunity to acquire practical and interpersonal skills; regarding the work as very useful; and having a great deal of contact with the beneficiaries of the work. An association was also found between seeing the work as very worthwhile and higher rates of compliance and lower rates of recidivism, which was particularly strong in the case of offenders who were unemployed or had a history of statutory social work supervision. As McIvor acknowledges, offenders who most valued their experiences of community service may have been different from others in important respects that accounted for their lower rates of reconviction. However, the background variables available to the researchers did not seem to explain the differences.

In England, the interest prompted by McIvor's work in Scotland was intensified in the light of the findings of various unrelated research studies (Lloyd et al. 1995; Raynor and Vanstone 1997; May 1999). These all showed that in comparisons of reconviction community service had a slight advantage over other sanctions, a difference for which there was no obvious explanation. Indeed, according to Prime (2002), Community Punishment Orders (CPOs) seem to have maintained an advantage over combined orders and straight Community Rehabilitation Orders (CROs, previously probation orders) but not over CROs with additional conditions to attend programmes. For persons commencing supervision in the first quarter of 1999, two-year reconviction rates were 1.7 per cent below the predicted rate for CPOs, but only 1.2 per cent and 0.7 per cent below in the case of combined orders and straight CROs respectively (for CROs with conditions, the figure was 2.6 per cent).

As such results are based on a comparison of actual reconviction rates with the rates predicted on the basis of offenders' criminal justice characteristics, there is always a possibility that they can be explained by some factor that the prediction model failed to measure. However, May (1999), having taken account of some social factors, concluded that the sentence itself may have had a positive impact on reconviction. Coupled with McIvor's (1992) work, these kinds of findings at least suggest that community service may have something to offer that is worthy of closer investigation.[2]

In any event, by the late 1990s, interest had rekindled sufficiently in the rehabilitative potential of community service to lead to its inclusion as one of the Pathfinder projects sponsored by the Home Office under the Crime Reduction Programme (see Probation Circular 35/1999). We will say more about the CS Pathfinder projects below. They did not in fact represent a new departure, but brought community service back to the original vision of the Wootton Committee. They provided an opportunity finally to test that Committee's hope that undertaking constructive work for the community might bring about a changed outlook on the part of the offender (Advisory Council on the Penal System 1970).

Using pro-social modelling to encourage social responsibility

In an apparently unrelated development, the late 1990s also saw a growing interest among both practitioners and researchers in an approach to supervision known as pro-social modelling, which had been developed in Australia by Chris Trotter (1993, 1996, 1999). Trotter's approach was to train Community Corrections Officers (CCOs, equivalent to probation officers) in workshops on how they might incorporate pro-social modelling into their supervisory practices. He then conducted an evaluation on the use of pro-social modelling by trained CCOs and comparison groups, based on case file analysis and questionnaires completed by probationers. He found that the breach and reconviction rates of offenders supervised by CCOs assessed as using 'pro-social' methods (more common among the trained group) were significantly lower than other groups of offenders, a difference that was sustained over a four-year follow-up period. The difference was striking: where some evidence of pro-social modelling was found, reconviction rates after four years were 49 per cent compared with 73 per cent where no evidence was found (Trotter 1996). Although Trotter found a slight tendency for CCOs to use pro-social modelling with lower-risk offenders, pro-social modelling remained a significant factor taking offender risk levels and the level of training, education and experience of the supervisor into account. However, in Trotter's model, pro-social modelling was combined with problem-solving and reflective listening and it is not clear how he disentangled these various elements for the purposes of evaluation (Raynor 1998).

So what is pro-social modelling and why might it be promising? According to Trotter, it is 'the practice of offering praise and rewards for ... pro-social expressions and actions ... The supervisor becomes a positive role model acting to reinforce pro-social or non-criminal behaviour' (Trotter 1993: 4). Two strands can be discerned in this definition: reinforcement through encouragement and reward; and modelling through the supervisor's demonstrating the behaviour that is desirable. In essence, the supervised person is given a definite lead and this is done in a positive and constructive way. This has resonance with the findings of studies on British probation practice summarised in Rex (1999), which suggest that probationers want supervision to be a 'purposeful' experience and are prepared to take a certain amount of direction from probation officers who show respect and concern for them. Findings such as these may explain why pro-social modelling warranted mention in HM Inspectorate of Probation's Effective Practice Guide as 'a necessary input for effective programme delivery' (HMIP 1998: 49–50) despite the lack of direct British evidence about its effectiveness. Parallels can be drawn between pro-social modelling and other techniques, such as mentoring and motivational interviewing, used in probation practice to motivate and prepare offenders, for example, to attend offending behaviour programmes (Burnett 2002). Beyond that, it seems possible that pro-social modelling might help to promote the developmental processes – the changes in an individual's sense of maturity and responsibility – associated with desistance from offending (Rex 2001).

It is in community service rather than probation practice that pro-social modelling has been most systematically developed in the UK, initially through pilot work between the Institute of Criminology and

Cambridgeshire Probation Service and then through the CS Pathfinder projects. We will say more about both initiatives below. They came about largely because community service was seen as a natural environment in which to model pro-social behaviour and to offer encouragement and reward for pro-social statements and actions. In showing offenders how to perform tasks, to work as a team and to improve their performance, CS supervisors can act as pro-social models. In exhibiting a positive stance towards training and employment, they can help offenders to perceive opportunities to engage in further training or more rewarding employment. As McIvor's (1992) study suggested, the work itself can offer tangible reward in the form of a sense of achievement in completing a task and doing something useful for the community. These rewarding experiences can be reinforced through direct contact with beneficiaries to enable offenders to see at first hand what people have gained from the work undertaken for them. Considering how the framework of pro-social modelling might be applied to her findings, McIvor has characterised the most 'rewarding' community service placements as reintegrative and entailing some reciprocity and exchange in which the offender both offers service to others and is given the opportunity to acquire skills:

> In many instances, it seems, contact with the beneficiaries gave offenders an insight into other people, and an increased insight into themselves; the acquisition of skills had instilled in them greater confidence and self-esteem; and the experience of completing their community service orders placed them in a position where they could enjoy reciprocal relationships – gaining the trust, confidence and appreciation of other people and having the opportunity to give something back to them. (McIvor 1998a: 55–6)

The above implies a need to foster more direct contact between offenders performing community service and the beneficiaries of that work, which might be negotiated by CS managers when they are organising CS placements (Johnson and Rex 2002). Such efforts may have wider implications in helping to develop the 'direct exchange relationship' between communities and criminal justice agencies identified by Dickey and Smith (1999) as an important constituent of community justice. Here, the authors see community service as providing an opportunity simultaneously to punish and restore and as providing 'openings for more complex co-operation between community corrections agencies and the public they depend on for authority and resources' (Dickey and Smith 1999: 24).

What we find particularly interesting about the application of pro-social modelling in the community service setting is the fact that, unlike general offending programmes, the focus is not directly on 'offending behaviour'. The evidence referred to above indicates that the practical setting in which CS occurs, and the nature of the contacts into which it brings offenders, might well offer learning experiences at least as powerful as an approach that tackles offending in a more didactic fashion. The theory is that the performance of community service may engage offenders in the kind of altruistic activity that produces 'teaching points' similar to those in cognitive skills training, which 'emerge, however, from experience rather than academic training' (Toch 2000: 275). Moreover, the offender may gain 'grounded increments' in self-esteem, which promotes the development of self-efficacy as theorised by Bandura (1997). All in all, these seem to create important opportunities for offenders to develop their capacity for active participation as citizens and to gain greater access to social capital as outlined by Coleman (1988, 1990) among others.

This is not to suggest that community service should be reinvented through the application of a new set of techniques. The idea of applying pro-social modelling systematically to community service is to reinforce its apparent potential to have a positive impact on offenders' behaviour. It seems very likely that 'pro-social models' already exist among community service supervisors, although they may not have fully realised particular aspects such as the use of rewards or be fully aware of the possible impact of their behaviour on the people they supervise. In evaluating the impact of pro-social modelling, a further aim is to provide evidence on the basis of which to take forward community service practice.

Piloting pro-social modelling

An opportunity to investigate how principles of pro-social modelling might be applied to community service practice and to evaluate the impact arose through a partnership between the Institute of Criminology and Cambridgeshire Probation Service dating back to the early 1990s. In 1997, it was agreed that the Institute and Cambridgeshire Probation Service would mount a joint research project as part of their collaboration. The Institute was interested in the contribution that pro-social modelling, coupled with principles of legitimacy, might make to efforts to turn offenders away from crime (see Bottoms and Rex 1998). For their part, Cambridgeshire Probation Service was interested in developing these practices in community service as well as in probation supervision, seeing an opportunity to build upon pre-existing initiatives such as pre-NVQ training to further enhance the work undertaken with offenders under CS supervision. In agreeing to pilot pro-social modelling in community service, what appealed to practitioners was that, rather than an 'off-the-shelf' manual, they were being given a set of principles to incorporate in their practice (Lowe and Rex 1998).

Effectively, the pilot work was undertaken over a period of two years – from autumn 1997 to autumn 1999 – and provided some interesting challenges (as reported by Rex and Crosland 1999). The decision to develop pro-social modelling and legitimacy in community service and probation practice followed briefings for staff in Cambridgeshire towards the end of 1997, and volunteers were then sought to train as pro-social models. The project was launched at a Day Conference in December 1997 (Rex and Matravers 1998) and a workshop was held in February 1998 to enable participating CS supervisors and managers to develop ideas about how they might use pro-social modelling in their practice. Following a testing-out period over the summer of 1998 and a review day in September, the project and associated evaluation went live in October 1998. Data collection was undertaken for a year, with the aim of comparing offenders supervised by project supervisors with those supervised elsewhere in Cambridgeshire Probation Service.

Unfortunately, various factors associated with the implementation of a small local project with limited resources imposed limitations on the findings. Data collection proved difficult in a dispersed CS unit in which individual offices had developed slightly different practices. For instance, the plan to use 'before' and 'after' Crime Pics II scores to measure changes in attitudes and self-perceived problems was foiled by the failure to secure sufficient valid 'after' administrations for analysis. Another limitation was imposed by a lack of continuity that seemed, to some extent, an inevitable aspect of the CS operation. Some of the CS supervisors who had originally volunteered as pro-social models were lost to the project due to staff moves following the training; new recruits were found but had not been able to participate in the workshop with their colleagues (although they were given individual training). Furthermore, the practicalities of delivering CS in the face of offenders' employment and childcare commitments, the need for them to get to the work site and the unpredictability of the weather usually ruled out an offender's being supervised by the same supervisor throughout his or her CS hours. Despite these constraints, efforts were made to maintain continuity of supervision during the pilot, sufficient to enable us to look at the experiences of offenders who had spent at least 60 per cent of their order supervised by a project supervisor.

The findings of what was a small pilot involving seven CS supervisors and 56 offenders are inevitably inconclusive, but there were positive indications. Offenders supervised predominantly by project CS supervisors were more likely than offenders supervised predominantly outside the project to report experiences consistent with pro-social modelling and legitimacy (on a questionnaire designed to assess exposure to pro-social modelling). They were also far more likely to select positive statements about their experience of community service (i.e. that they were pleased with a job well done, were glad to have done something for the community and were pleased with what they had learnt). As well as gaining better work ratings (possibly as a 'reward' by their 'pro-social' CS supervisors), offenders supervised within the project were less likely than other offenders to have unacceptable absences or to have been breached. Interviews with offenders supervised within the project provided illustrations of rewarding experiences, such as the following in which appreciation from the beneficiary and praise from the CS supervisor appear to reinforce each other:

> On our last job, we got a letter from the people where we actually did the work and they thanked us – the whole group not just individually. [The supervisor] told everybody. Well, I saw the letter, but he came out and said 'well done, thank you very much for doing it'. (Offender – Cambridgeshire CS pilot)

Evaluating pro-social modelling as a CS Pathfinder strand

These findings were sufficiently promising for pro-social modelling to be included as one of the key strands in the CS Pathfinder projects selected by the Home Office and announced in Probation Circular 35/1999, making the investigation of an evidence base for community service official. The projects were implemented in ten probation areas in spring 2000 (including Bedfordshire and Cambridgeshire as a result of a joint bid building on Cambridgeshire's pilot work) and evaluated by the Institute of Criminology in conjunction with the Probation Studies Unit based at Oxford (reported in Rex et al. 2003). Altogether, pro-social modelling featured in five of the seven projects involving seven probation areas, but they all took somewhat different approaches. In Bedfordshire and Cambridgeshire, pro-social modelling was implemented as a single strand; elsewhere it was combined with other initiatives. Thus in Northumbria and Durham, it was brought together with key skills training and accreditation; in Hampshire, Somerset and Leicestershire (all separate projects) it was an element in a package intended to 'tackle offending-related needs'. Two other projects implemented skills training and accreditation as a single strand.

Combining various strands in this way clearly offered opportunities to develop CS practice in a variety of ways to maximise its effectiveness. The rationale was, for example, for pro-social modelling and skills accreditation to reinforce each other in that gaining skills, putting together a portfolio and achieving the relevant award would all offer powerful 'rewarding' experiences. Putting it in terms of citizenship, pro-social modelling and obtaining recognised qualifications might interact with each other to assist offenders in gaining access to 'social capital' (Coleman 1988, 1990). However, from the point of view of the evaluation, measuring multiple strands implemented differently in different projects created complexities.

For the purposes of the evaluation, we have been able to use findings from the different projects to compare the respective strands, looking at pro-social modelling and skills accreditation both on their own and in combination. It also proved possible to negotiate both in-county and external comparison groups.[3] In addition to using information from probation area databases, we developed various research tools with a view to measuring pro-social modelling and its impact (as well as other strands in the project). Offenders' exposure to pro-social modelling was examined by adapting the questionnaire used in the Cambridgeshire pilot and devising a scoring mechanism comprising four scales: treatment (T); value to offender (O); motivation (M); and value to beneficiary (B). Interviews with staff explored their understanding and use of pro-social modelling as well as the implementation of the various projects and the level of preparation and training provided for staff. We also have a range of output and intermediate outcome measures, such as 'before' and 'after' Crime Pics II scores and completion of accredited skills awards. Unfortunately, we were unable to conduct a comparative analysis of the impact of particular CS placements and supervisors due to a combination of an unavoidable lack of continuity in CS supervision and the sheer complexity of collecting and analysing the relevant data.

Findings from the pathfinder evaluation are necessarily inconclusive at this stage in the absence of reconviction findings. Two-year reconviction rates will not be available until autumn 2004, at which point we hope to examine the relationship between reconviction rates and other outcome measures and questionnaire scores to assess whether there is an association between greater exposure to pro-social modelling (as reported by offenders) and better outcomes.[4] Unfortunately, even then, the profile of project offenders seems likely to impose limitations on the scope for positive change or for assessing the impact of the projects on different groups. These could be characterised as a fairly 'settled' white male group of offenders with a low–medium risk profile and few women or members of ethnic minority communities. Over half were in employment or education; only 3 per cent were in accommodation that we would categorise as 'unstable' (bed and breakfast, hostel or no fixed abode). Furthermore, only 8 per cent were female and 11 per cent were recorded as from an ethnic minority.

Despite these limitations, our analysis of intermediate outcomes has produced promising indications, on the basis of which the delay before reconviction data become available allows a period of optimism. Second administrations of Crime Pics II showed statistically significant reductions both in pro-criminal attitudes and in self-perceived problems. According to ratings provided on termination summaries, staff thought that around 60 per cent of the offenders had undergone positive change and had good prospects for future change. Asked whether undertaking community service had made a difference to them, around three-quarters of offenders completing the offender questionnaire said that the experience had made them less likely to offend. When we have data on two-year reconviction rates, we will be able to offer judgement about the strength of such predictions. We also hope to be able to compare the effectiveness of the different pathfinder strands. Provisionally, however, we can report that projects focusing on skills accreditation produced the best intermediate outcomes although the cost of pro-social modelling was considerably lower (and it too produced positive outcomes in some areas). A combination of the two strands appeared effective.

One point that strikes us here is the fact that any positive potential is likely to be realised only if the projects are sensitive to social and cultural issues (race and gender differences for instance). In other words, the projects should be conceived and delivered in such a way as to accommodate social diversity. While there have been long-standing complaints about sentencers' apparent reluctance to impose community service on women (Barker 1993; McIvor 1998b; Howard League 1999), preliminary indications from the pathfinder findings on community service are that women may well gain from the experience according to their own perceptions of improvement in skills. Looking at self-reports of the impact of community service, just over two-thirds of the women in our sample reported that community service had helped them change the way they saw things (compared with nearly 60 per cent of the men). In both cases, offenders thought that community service would make them less likely to offend. Not only is it possible that these findings will encourage sentencers to use community service more (particularly for women), but it is arguable that the choice and delivery of projects for women (as for men) may be critical to their potential impact overall. Indeed, rather than treating offenders as composite offenders with a risk/need score, recognition of race and gender and social and cultural differentiation carries the possibility of engendering reciprocal 'respect' (Gelsthorpe 2001). A lack of responsiveness to such differences runs the risk of diminishing potential effectiveness by casting a shadow over the legitimacy of the community service requirement in the offender's eyes and therefore limiting the promotion of good citizenship. Sensitivity to the offender as an individual, conceived as part of pro-social modelling, thus symbolises inclusive citizenship, for it promotes respect and mutual obligation (Gelsthorpe 2001).

Similar points may be made in relation to people who are excluded from mainstream opportunities for education and employment because they lack access, training or qualifications. Sensitivity to their distinctive needs in the conception and delivery of community service may enhance the legitimacy of the criminal justice system in their view (see Paternoster et al. 1997) and thus promote inclusive citizenship as a by-product of the mutual respect engendered.

Looking forward to Enhanced Community Punishment

In the meantime, policy and practice has been moving forward apace. Building on the CS Pathfinder projects, an 'integrated system' of Enhanced Community Punishment (ECP) has been developed for accreditation by the Correctional Services Accreditation Panel. It was given 'Recognised' status by the Panel in September 2002 and preparations are now underway for its national implementation from October 2003 (plans are described in Probation Circulars 71/2002, 4/2003 and 40/2003). Without wishing to sound churlish, we harbour some doubts as to whether 'enhanced punishment' conjures up the reintegrative aspirations underlying the practice initiatives leading to the CS Pathfinder projects. Like the community punishment order from which it takes its name, such a title seems to emphasise the punitive rather than the reintegrative aspect of performing work for the community.

The ECP scheme incorporates the key strands implemented in the pathfinder projects, the intention being to allocate offenders to different levels on the basis of their assessed 'risk' (see National Probation Service

Briefing Issue 8, December 2002). In addition to a 'baseline' level comprising pro-social modelling, further levels involve placement quality standards and guided skills learning.[5] The speed of implementation, before reconviction data is available from the evaluation of the pathfinder projects, is driven by policy imperatives: the SDA (Service Delivery Agreement) Targets to achieve 25,000 commencements of ECP by 31 March 2004 and 30,000 completions during 2004/5 (referred to in Probation Circular 71/2002). Ultimately, the aim is to contribute to the Home Office PSA (Public Service Agreement) Target 10 of reducing the rate of reconviction of all offenders under community supervision by 5 per cent compared with predicted rates (see National Probation Service 2001).

Conclusions – towards evidence-based practice

The inclusion of community service within the Home Office's crime reduction agenda carries major implications for how community service fits into the sentencing framework and its role as a punishment. It underlines its value as a constructive and quite possibly a rehabilitative sanction in its own right and not just as an alternative to a prison sentence. We would suggest that developing its reintegrative potential enhances rather than diminishes the capacity of CS to offer reparation through the development of closer links with beneficiaries and the kinds of placements that enable offenders to gain skills while undertaking demonstrably useful work for the community. In view of the imminent implementation of the ECP scheme, and in the spirit of furthering evidence-based practice, it might be useful to conclude with some questions for practice and policy raised by the evaluation of the CS Pathfinder projects.

For the future development of practice, one important question is how to ensure that pro-social modelling is practised consistently by CS supervisors and reinforced at every level in the organisation – as was found necessary during the Cambridgeshire pilot and the CS Pathfinder projects. This raises a number of issues; one is how to ensure that potential pro-social 'models' are recruited and appropriately trained. Another is how to assure quality in a setting where the use of a video camera may well not be feasible. Equally important is the need to develop appropriate CS placements that provide offenders with 'pro-social' opportunities and to allocate offenders to those placements from which they are likely to benefit within the constraints imposed by transport, employment and childcare.

Among the questions for policy is how to ensure that offenders likely to benefit from the accredited scheme have that opportunity by being sentenced to the relevant orders, especially given the numbers of low-risk non-serious offenders now being sentenced to community service (Morgan 2003). This requires an engagement with sentencers that has begun with the recent release of an ECP video for sentencers (according to National Probation Service Bulletin 12, May 2003). The Chief Inspector of Probation has offered the challenge that, failing the resuscitation of financial penalties, consideration might be given to 'contracting out the supervision of community punishment' (HMIP 2003: 7). Here, the introduction of the customised community sentence in the Criminal Justice Act 2003 (of which 'compulsory work' will be just one component) creates the opportunity to ensure that the different interventions which the community sentence can comprise are appropriately targeted at offenders with varying levels of risk and offending-related needs.

Notes

1 The Criminal Justice and Court Services Act 2000 came into force in April 2001 and renamed the community service order as the community punishment order (CPO) and the combination order as the community punishment and rehabilitation (the 'combined') order. For consistency, we use 'community service' throughout this chapter to refer to the work undertaken by offenders under a CPO or a combined order.
2 For a different view, see Killias and Ribeaud (2000), who suggest that lower rearrest and reconviction rates following community service compared with short sentences of imprisonment may result from offenders' seeing their conviction and sentence as fair rather than because of improvements in jobs and life prospects.
3 In-county comparison groups were available in Norfolk and Leicestershire which did not implement the pathfinder project across the entire county. External comparison groups were provided in Lancashire and Warwickshire. In total, these provide nearly 1,000 offenders to compare with the 1,851 included in the project evaluation.
4 Like the main study, the reconviction study is being undertaken in collaboration with the Probation Studies Unit, Centre for Criminological Research, Oxford University.
5 Placement quality standards are based on the audit of CS placements used by some of the pathfinder projects to support pro-social modelling. The aim of the audit was to assess how far placements incorporated features identified by McIvor (1992, 1998) as 'rewarding' – contact with beneficiaries, work obviously useful to the beneficiary, opportunities to acquire practical and interpersonal skills.

References

Advisory Council on the Penal System (1970) *Non-Custodial and Semi-Custodial Penalties*. London: HMSO.

Bandura, A. (1997) *Self-Efficacy: The Exercise of Control*. New York: Freeman.

Barker, M. (1993) *Community Service and Women Offenders*. London: Association of Chief Officers of Probation.

Blunkett, D. (2003) *Civic Renewal: A New Agenda*. London: Home Office.

Bottoms, A.E. (1987) 'Limiting prison use in England and Wales', *Howard Journal*, 26, 177–202.

Bottoms, A.E. and Rex, S.A. (1998) 'Pro-social modelling and legitimacy: their potential contribution to effective practice', in S.A. Rex and A. Matravers (eds), *Proceedings of the Clarke Hall Day Conference*. Cambridge: Institute of Criminology.

Burnett, R. (2002) 'The case for counselling as a method for working with offenders', *Vista*, 7 (3), 216–226.

Coleman, J. (1988) 'Social capital in the creation of human capital', *American Journal of Sociology*, 94 (Suppl.), s95–s120.

Coleman, J. (1990) *The Foundations of Social Theory*. London: Belknap Press.

Crow, I. (2000) 'Evaluating initiatives in the community', in V. Jupp et al. (eds), *Doing Criminological Research*. London: Sage.

Dickey, W.J. and Smith, M.E. (1999) *Rethinking Probation: Community Supervision, Community Safety*. Washington, DC: Office of Justice.

Farrell, S. (2002) *Rethinking What Works with Offenders. Probation, Social Context and Desistance from Crime*. Cullompton: Willan.

Faulkner, D. (2001) *Crime, State and Citizen*. Winchester: Waterside Press.

Faulkner, D. (2003) 'Taking citizenship seriously: social capital and criminal justice in a changing world', *Criminal Justice*, 3 (3), 287–315.

Gelsthorpe, L.R. (2001) 'Accountability: difference and diversity in the delivery of community penalties', in A.E. Bottoms, L. Gelsthorpe and S. Rex (eds), *Community Penalties: Change and Challenges*. Cullompton: Willan.

Gelsthorpe, L.R. and Rex, S.A. (2004) 'Community Service as reintegration: exploring the potential', in G. Mair (ed.), *What Matters in Probation*. Cullompton: Willan.

Hagan, J. and McCarthy, B. (1997) *Mean Streets*. Cambridge: Cambridge University Press.

Her Majesty's Inspectorate of Probation (HMIP) (1998) *Evidence-Based Practice: A Guide to Effective Practice*. London: Home Office.

Her Majesty's Inspectorate of Probation (HMIP) (2003) *2002/3 Annual Report*. London: Home Office.

Home Office, Welsh Office and Department of Health (1992) *National Standards for the Supervision of Offenders in the Community*. London: Home Office.

Howard League (1999) *Do Women Paint Fences Too? Women's Experiences of Community Service*, Briefing Paper. London: Howard League for Penal Reform.

Johnson, C. and Rex, S.A. (2002) 'Community service: rediscovering reintegration', in D. Ward and J. Scott (eds), *Probation – Working for Justice*, 2nd edn. Oxford: Oxford University Press.

Killias, A.M. and Ribeaud, D. (2000) 'Does community service rehabilitate better than short-term imprisonment? Results of a controlled experiment', *Howard Journal*, 39 (1), 40–57.

Kraemer, S. and Roberts, J. (1996) *The Politics of Attachment. Towards a Secure Society*. London: Free Association Books.

Lloyd, C., Mair, G. and Hough, M. (1995) *Explaining Reconviction Rates: A Critical Analysis*, Home Office Research Study 136. London: Home Office.

Lowe, M. and Rex, S.A. (1998) 'Pro-social modelling in Cambridgeshire: the next steps', in S.A. Rex and A. Matravers (eds), *Proceedings of the Clarke Hall Day Conference*. Cambridge: Institute of Criminology.

McIvor, G. (1990) 'Community service and custody in Scotland', *Howard Journal*, 29, 101–13.

McIvor, G. (1992) *Sentenced to Serve*. Aldershot: Avebury.

McIvor, G. (1998a) 'Pro-social modelling and legitimacy: lessons from a study of community service', in S. Rex and A. Matravers (eds), *Pro-Social Modelling and Legitimacy: The Clarke Hall Day Conference*. Cambridge: Institute of Criminology, University of Cambridge.

McIvor, G. (1998b) 'Jobs for the boys? Gender differences in referral to community service', *Howard Journal of Criminal Justice*, 37 (3), 280–90.

McLaughlin, T. (2000) 'Citizenship education in England: the Crick Report and beyond', *Journal of Philosophy of Education*, 34 (4), 541–70.

Marshall, T.H. (1963) *Sociology at the Crossroads*. London: Heinemann.

May, C. (1999) *Explaining Reconviction Following a Community Sentence: The Role of Social Factors*, Home Office Research Study 192. London: Home Office.

Morgan, R. (2003) 'Correctional services: not waving but drowning', *Prison Service Journal*, 145, 6–8.

National Probation Service (2001) *A New Choreography: Strategic Framework 2001–2004*. London: Home Office and National Probation Service for England and Wales.

Office for National Statistics (2001) *Social Capital. A Review of the Literature*. London: Office for National Statistics, Social Analysis and Reporting Division.

Paternoster, R., Bachman, R., Brame, R. and Sherman, L. (1997) 'Do fair procedures matter? The effect of procedural justice on spouse assault', *Law and Society Review*, 31, 163–204.

Pease, K. (1985) 'Community service orders', in M. Tonry and N. Morris (eds), *Crime and Justice*, 6, Chicago: University of Chicago Press.

Prime, J. (2002) *Progress Made Against Home Office Public Service Agreement Target 10*, Home Office Online Report 16/02. Available at: www.homeoffice.gov.uk/rds/pdfs2/rdsolr1602.pdf.

Putnam, R. (1993) *Making Democracy Work: Civic Traditions in Modern Italy*. Princeton, NJ: Princeton University Press.

Putnam, R. (1995) 'Bowling alone: America's declining social capital', *Journal of Democracy*, 6 (1), 65–78.

Raynor, P. (1998) 'Pro-social approaches and legitimacy: implications from research in Mid-Glamorgan and elsewhere', in S. Rex and A. Matravers (eds), *Pro-Social Modelling and Legitimacy: The Clarke Hall Day Conference*. Cambridge: Institute of Criminology, University of Cambridge.

Raynor, P. and Vanstone, M. (1997) *Straight Thinking on Probation (STOP): The Mid Glamorgan Experiment*, Probation Studies Unit Report 4. Oxford: University of Oxford Centre for Criminological Research.

Rex, S.A. (1999) 'Desistance from offending: experiences of probation', *The Howard Journal*, 38, 366–83.

Rex, S.A. (2001) 'Beyond cognitive-behaviouralism? Reflections on the effectiveness literature, in A.E. Bottoms, L. Gelsthorpe and S. Rex (eds), *Community Penalties: Change and Challenges*. Cullompton: Willan.

Rex, S.A. and Crosland, P.E. (1999) *Project on Pro-social Modelling and Legitimacy: Findings from Community Service, Report to Cambridgeshire Probation Service*. Cambridge: University of Criminology.

Rex, S.A. and Matravers, A. (eds) (1998) *Proceedings of the Clarke Hall Day Conference*. Cambridge: Institute of Criminology.

Rex, S.A., Gelsthorpe, L.R., Roberts, C. and Jordan, P. (2004) *Crime Reduction Programme: An Evaluation of Community Service Pathfinder Projects*, Final Report Home Office Research Finding and Occasional Paper 87. London: Home Office.

Rustin, M. (1996) 'Attachment in context', in S. Kraemer and J. Roberts (eds), *The Politics of Attachment*. London: Free Association Books.

Sampson, R. and Laub, J. (1993) *Crime in the Making: Pathways and Turning Points through Life*. Boston: Harvard University Press.

Toch, H. (2000) 'Altruistic activity as correctional treatment', *International Journal of Offender Therapy and Comparative Criminology*, 44, 270–78.

Trotter, C. (1993) *The Supervision of Offenders: What Works*. Sydney: Victorian Office of Corrections.

Trotter, C. (1996) 'The impact of different supervision practices in community corrections: causes for optimism', *Australian and New Zealand Journal of Criminology*, 29, 29–46.

Trotter, C. (1999) *Working with Involuntary Clients: A Guide to Practice*. London: Sage.

Utting, D. (1996) 'Tough on the causes of crime? Social bonding and delinquency prevention', in S. Kraemer and J. Roberts (eds), *The Politics of Attachment*. London: Free Association Books.

Chapter 12

Opportunity, motivation and change: some findings from research on resettlement

Peter Raynor

The context and background of the 'resettlement' research

As most readers of this chapter will already know, the government's recent Crime Reduction Programme consisted of a number of evaluated initiatives intended to lay the foundations for an evidence-based approach to crime reduction, as advocated in an influential collection of research reviews published not long after the 1997 General Election (Goldblatt and Lewis 1998). Among these were a number of projects designed to evaluate promising new approaches to the work of the Probation Service. These were the 'Pathfinder' projects, and included evaluations of cognitive-behavioural programmes, basic employment-related skills training, new approaches to Community Service (which we are now supposed to call Community Punishment) and new resettlement services for short-term prisoners. The first three have already been mentioned in other contributions to this collection, and this chapter draws on the experiences of the team which carried out the fourth study. Although the views expressed in it are the author's own, it obviously depends on and owes a great deal to the efforts of the whole team (the other members were Julie Vennard, Mike Maguire, Sam Lewis, Maurice Vanstone, Andrew Rix and Steve Raybould). The full report of the study is published by the Home Office (Lewis et al. 2003a) and a summary is available in Research Findings 200 (Lewis et al. 2003b).

Our study differed from the other Pathfinders in a number of respects. One of the most important of these was that the services to be evaluated were voluntary rather than provided as part of a process of statutory supervision. This was because the projects were targeted on short-sentence prisoners, sentenced to less than 12 months, who were not included in the arrangements for Automatic Conditional Release (ACR) or Discretionary Conditional Release (DCR) created by the 1991 Criminal Justice Act. A previous study by several members of the research team (Maguire et al. 1998) had shown that the help traditionally provided for this group by probation services under the heading of 'voluntary after-care' had virtually ceased to exist by the early 1990s: little was being done for short-term prisoners, although this group included a high proportion of persistent offenders with many personal and social difficulties and a high reconviction rate. Later reports by NACRO (2000) and the Social Exclusion Unit (2002) expressed similar concerns. The Probation Service was aware of these problems: as one probation manager memorably put it, 'the revolving door can be a downward spiral' (personal communication, 2001). One result of this awareness was the inclusion in the Crime Reduction Programme of a substantial project targeting this group. In essence this aimed to improve the availability and take-up of appropriate post-release services for short-term prisoners, and to help them to make a better transition back into the community on release, with eventual reductions in their future offending.

One other important feature of the resettlement 'pathfinder' was that it was deliberately designed to test and compare a number of different approaches to providing resettlement services. Although the scheme as a whole was initiated by the Probation Service, the Prison Service and the voluntary sector were to play major roles, and eventually there were seven separate 'pathfinder' projects. This created the opportunity for a comparative research design. The most obvious difference was that three of the projects were based on partnerships between particular prisons and voluntary sector organisations, and four were based on partnerships between prisons and the Probation Service. The original plan, which was to some extent realised in practice, was that the voluntary sector projects would concentrate on 'welfare needs' while the probation-led projects would concentrate more on addressing offending behaviour. For example, by the end of the project all four of the probation-led projects were using a group programme as part of their pre-release provision, and in three cases this was a short cognitive-behavioural programme designed specifically to improve motivation and planning for release. The purpose of this chapter is to discuss a fairly small part of the findings of this study (primarily those which resulted from comparing the outcomes of the projects) and to consider, with the help of other studies, whether these may have wider implications for probation practice. The full range of findings from the study can be found in the report.

The meanings of resettlement

One of the first tasks facing the research team was to try to understand this relatively new term 'resettlement'. The traditional terms used in this field were 'after-care' and 'through-care', the former being favoured by those who were mainly interested in what should be done after release (for example, Haines 1990) and the latter by those who wanted to emphasise a continuous process starting with sentence planning soon after reception into the prison, and aiming to integrate pre-release and post-release into a single rehabilitative process (for example, Maguire and Raynor 1997). (This is of course the 'seamless approach' promoted by the 1991 Criminal Justice Act, though it has always been questionable how far offenders themselves perceive it as 'seamless' when they are well aware of the difference between being in prison and being out.) Historically the term 'after-care' was more widely used in the days when probation services saw it as their job to rescue people from prison rather than to collaborate with prisons in a joint rehabilitative effort. 'Resettlement', however, had a different history, and was launched into official language by the 1998 report *Joining Forces to Protect the Public* which announced the results of the Prisons and Probation Review. It is worth looking at what this report said (Home Office 1998: 9):

> 'Throughcare' is the term which lies at the heart of the two services' joint work. It is unlikely to be properly understood outside of the prison and probation worlds … We think that public and sentencer confidence would be enhanced if the focus was on the ultimate goals of 'throughcare' – high quality sentence planning and successful resettlement in the community. Our preference is for this work to be called simply 'Resettlement' …

Was there really evidence that sentencers did not understand what 'throughcare' meant but would understand 'resettlement'? We do not know. Another speculation has been that the new term was preferred because it did not include the word 'care' at a time when it was believed to be important to appear tough on crime. 'Resettlement in the community' sounds good (like 'care in the community') but does it refer to a real community or simply to the state of not being in prison?

In short, the term 'resettlement' was not defined when it was introduced, though one of its aims was presumably crime reduction. There also seem to be overlaps with other concepts in current social policy such as integration, reintegration, re-entry, inclusion/exclusion, pro-social behaviour and no doubt others. Some possible concepts of 'resettlement' are contradictory: for example, does it mean:

- restoration to a condition and social environment roughly corresponding to that existing before imprisonment (which might have been socially excluded or actively criminogenic);

- attempted establishment of a basic adequate standard of living and opportunity which may not have been experienced before (raising problems of feasibility, of measurement and of fairness in relation to non-offenders for whom similar assistance might not be provided);

- re-establishment of social contacts, links or relationships (e.g. family and/or peers, who are important for psychological well-being and a sense of belonging, but may also be part of a crime-prone subculture);

- establishment of new links and connections with pro-social influences and resources (Hirschi's (1969) control theory would suggest this, but perhaps does not distinguish sufficiently between social 'bonds' which are pro-social and reduce offending, and other social connections which may be important for identity but do not constitute reasons not to offend);

- action to identify and address defined needs (criminogenic needs only, or any needs claimed by the offender as criminogenic, or simply any 'welfare' needs? Who defines the needs? Are they expressed, normative or ascribed?).

'Resettlement' rather implies that people were settled before, which they might not have been; 'reintegration' implies that they are not properly 'integrated' at the moment, when some offenders seem to be very well integrated with social groups or environments which do not prevent offending and may encourage it. On the other hand, reintegration for Braithwaite (1989) is a positive term implying not just social bonds but shared values and pro-social influence, and this may be closer to the real aims of 'resettlement'.

One other way to think about purpose is to ask 'why is it the state's job to resettle prisoners?' One answer is that it will help to reduce crime (this is also the main reason given by the Advisory Council on the Treatment of Offenders (ACTO) in 1963) but suppose it turned out to make not much difference to crime levels (which may also be true of imprisonment in general), would that be a reason for abandoning it? Is crime reduction its only purpose? Some other possible reasons for doing it might be as follows:

- Pure 'welfare': ex-prisoners may be suffering various kinds of distress and should be helped on a basis of common humanity. This might have been a sufficient justification for charitable involvement by the early Discharged Prisoners' Aid Societies, set up when prisons were seen by educated elites as scandalously badly run and as inflicting pointless suffering (as distinct from educative suffering, which the elites did not oppose). The charitable transaction allows the receiver to benefit from relief of suffering while the donor benefits from the opportunity to do good. However, even some of the charity was not unconditional: beneficiaries were expected to behave better, at least where drink was concerned, and less drinking was assumed to lead to less crime (Maguire et al. 2000). It is unfortunately doubtful if the pure relief of suffering without any further purpose or general benefit to society would be perceived as a sufficient justification for significant state investment in the resettlement of offenders.

- The purpose of after-care might be to continue rehabilitative or retraining work begun in prison through further supervision, group-work, training opportunities, referral to other agencies, etc. This is the 'throughcare' model favoured by the ACTO report of 1963 and implicit in current approaches to joint prison-and-probation programme accreditation. It also involves a rather optimistic view of what prisons typically provide for the short-term prisoner. However, it does constitute one clear view of what resettlement is: continuation and reinforcement of the rehabilitative impact of the prison sentence.

- Another view, hinted at by various writers on after-care (e.g. Stone 1985), is almost the opposite. After-care is about giving ex-prisoners the resources and opportunities to relaunch themselves in the community, not because prison has done them good but because it has done them harm (institutionalised them, exposed them to a more criminal subculture, deskilled them socially for life in the open, maybe exposed them to abuse, etc.). This harm should be limited on 'justice' grounds because the punishment should be limited to the term of imprisonment, not continue indefinitely afterwards. This argument, if accepted, could actually justify some positive discrimination in favour of ex-prisoners, but it raises questions about the rationality of a policy which sets out to inflict harm on people as a punishment and then to undo it, both at public expense.

- A fourth rationale might be based on the idea of state-obligated rehabilitation (Carlen 1989; Rotman 1990). Briefly, this doctrine would hold that citizens are obliged to obey the law and refrain from crime, but governments are obliged to seek to maintain a social and moral order such that the opportunities to develop a satisfactory life and to refrain from crime are not so unevenly distributed as to make society's demands on citizens unfair. Offenders deserve rehabilitation as well as penalties if they have been unfairly restricted in their opportunities to build a crime-free life (or have lacked the resources, material or social, for a pro-social lifestyle). Rehabilitation may reduce future crime, but perhaps more importantly it seeks to recreate conditions where pro-social demands have moral force (in other words it reinforces the social contract). This also suggests the establishment or re-establishment of pro-social bonds. There remain issues about compulsion and voluntarism (compulsion for the risky, voluntarism for the needy?) but of the various rationales for 'resettlement', this one seems the most consistent with familiar assumptions about justice.

Implicit criminologies of resettlement

In addition to these different possible meanings of resettlement there are also different models of how to provide a resettlement service. These carry embedded within them different assumptions about why people offend, why they stop offending and how the service provided is intended to influence offending. These ideas are not necessarily made explicit by practitioners, but they constitute in effect an implicit criminology or a set of implicit criminologies corresponding to each model of service provision. For the purposes of this chapter I concentrate on what I take to be the two most influential variants, which might be described as an 'opportunity deficit' model and an 'offender's responsibility' model. Table 12.1 illustrates the differences schematically.

Both these models are ideal types which are not necessarily found in a pure form in the real world, but they do bear some relation to the different approaches and assumptions actually encountered when studying resettlement practice. The first, the opportunity deficit model, sees offenders as offending because they have been deprived of resources and opportunities, and concentrates on putting them into contact with agencies which it is hoped will supply these. This type of service basically responds to offenders' own statements about their needs and reflects the accounts many offenders give of how they got into trouble through lack of some resource or blockage of some opportunity. Such accounts can contain a good deal of truth but tend to allow offenders to present themselves as victims of circumstances who had

Table 12.1 Contrasting models of resettlement

	Opportunity deficit model	Offender responsibility model
Methods	Advice, support, sympathy, advocacy, referral	As left-hand column plus cognitive challenge, motivational and pro-social input
Assumptions about offending	Offenders are victims of circumstances	Offenders can choose how they respond to circumstances
Offender's responsibility for offending and change	Low	High

little alternative but to offend. In such cases they can have a neutralising or exculpatory effect, presenting the offending as an unavoidable (and therefore less blameworthy) consequence of social or personal misfortune or deprivation. Sykes and Matza in their classic paper on neutralisation techniques (Sykes and Matza 1957) discuss a number of variants of this type of process which all have the effect of making offending more acceptable to the offender.

The alternative 'offender's responsibility' approach recognises that social, environmental and personal problems are real, but tends to treat them as challenges or obstacles which confront offenders with choices about how to respond. This is the model implied by phrases such as 'confronting offending' and 'challenging offenders' thinking', and it tends to place an emphasis on helping offenders to develop clear goals for the future and the problem-solving resources and motivation to overcome some of the obstacles they will inevitably face. Such approaches may sometimes run the risk of underestimating the extreme difficulties many offenders face, but have the merit that they present further offending as avoidable and offenders as capable of stopping.

These contrasting approaches bear some similarity to the differences built into the pathfinder projects between those which were intended to concentrate on 'welfare' problems, and those which were intended to take a more proactive approach to challenging offending behaviour and the associated thinking. We were therefore interested to discover, during the course of the research, what differences in assessment, practice and particularly outcomes might emerge between the different projects, and how far these might reflect the adoption of different implicit assumptions about how the resettlement process should work.

The short-term outcomes of the seven projects

Like all the Crime Reduction Programme projects the resettlement Pathfinders were intended to reduce crime and will eventually be followed by a reconviction study. In the meantime a number of interim measures of effectiveness were chosen to provide an early evaluation of the impact of each project. These measures were chosen as plausible indicators of effective practice on the grounds of their use in other reputable studies and the opportunities they offered for comparison. This section is therefore based mainly on three measures which we were able to apply to a reasonable proportion of the prisoners in the projects.

The first is *continuity of service*, or the proportion of prisoners who remained in significant contact with the projects after release. This reflects a general consensus in previous studies of resettlement work with prisoners that contact which continues 'through the gate' is most likely to be helpful (see, for example, HMIPP 2001) and that poor services in custody lead to low levels of voluntary continued contact (Maguire et al. 1998, 2000). Although there has been little attention in past reconviction studies to the rehabilitative effect of continuity in resettlement services, the professional consensus in favour of its importance is so strong that all projects aimed to achieve high levels of post-release contact. Specifically, 'continuity' in this chapter means significant post-release contact and excludes contact which did not continue beyond the day of release as well as excluding a few contacts which were clearly casual or accidental.

The second and third outcome measures used concern changes in prisoners' *attitudes favourable to offending* and *levels of perceived life problems*, both based on the Crime Pics II questionnaire (Frude et al. 1994). This instrument, although not designed specifically as a reconviction predictor, is known to be related to reconviction (Raynor 1998) and has been successfully used in other Pathfinder evaluations as a measure of change (see, for example, Hatcher and McGuire 2001; Institute of Criminology and Probation Studies Unit 2001). Crime Pics II was also easy to use and suitable for repeat administration to measure change. It was therefore adopted as an appropriate offending-related interim measure. In this chapter the figures provided are based on comparisons between Crime Pics II questionnaires completed on entry to the pathfinder projects and those completed by the same offenders at the end of the prison-based part of each project.

The full report of the study contains information on many other characteristics of prisoners, projects and services provided, and the data were explored thoroughly in a search for characteristics which were linked to the main interim change measures. Readers interested in the statistical detail are advised to consult the full report, but for the purposes of this chapter it is sufficient to note that both interim measures of effectiveness appeared to be strongly and significantly influenced by the nature of the project (i.e. whether it was probation-led or voluntary-organisation-led) and by whether prisoners undertook a short motivational programme before release (which was done by many of the prisoners in the probation-led projects). In most cases (i.e. in the case of all male prisoners who undertook programmes) the programme was a specially designed short cognitive-behavioural programme which concentrated on motivation, self-management and some problem-solving skills. It was known as 'FOR-a-Change' ('FOR' stands for 'Focus on Resettlement') and included an emphasis on linking prisoners to appropriate resources outside the prison as well as a focus on thinking and motivation.

Tables 12.2 and 12.3 summarise the interim outcomes for the seven projects. For the purposes of this chapter it is not necessary to name individual prisons or voluntary organisations, so the probation-led projects are designated P1, P2, P3, P4 and the voluntary-organisation-led projects are V1, V2 and V3. All the probation projects ran programmes for all or part of the duration of the projects: P1 was a women's prison and ran a modular programme of which most project members undertook at least a part; P2 and P4 involved some prisoners in the FOR programme during the later stages of the project; and P3, which joined

Table 12.2 Continuity 'Through the Gate': proportions of project starters in significant contact after the day of release (N = 1081)

Project	Number of initial joiners	Proportion with continuity of contact
P1	131	47%
P2	156	42%
P3	49	33%
P4	225	32%
V1	180	22%
V2	189	21%
V3	151	16%

Table 12.3 Changes in crime-prone attitudes and self-reported problems (N = 454)

Attitudes	
P3	−3.52
P2	−2.88
P1	−2.68
P4	−2.31
V3	−0.99
V1	−0.31
V2	+0.63
Problems	
P3	−3.35
P4	−3.33
P1	−3.32
V3	−2.58
P2	−2.42
V1	−1.43
V2	−1.35

the study after the others, offered all project members the FOR programme from the start.

All projects achieved a level of 'continuity' much greater than that observed in an earlier study of voluntary after-care before the Pathfinders were set up (Maguire et al. 2000) but differences between the two types of project are also apparent (see table 12.2). Table 12.3 shows, again in rank order, the average differences in before-and-after Crime Pics II scores for crime-prone attitudes and self-reported problems in each project.

These scores were both available for a total of 454 prisoners, but there is no evidence that those who completed both were significantly different from those who did not. (The uneven coverage was due to the way services were organised rather than to the characteristics of prisoners.) For both attitudes and problems a minus figure represents a decrease and therefore an improvement.

A clear pattern emerges from these outcome measures. For whatever reasons, the type of service provided by the probation-led projects produced consistently better results than the voluntary-organisation-led projects. How might we try to explain findings of this kind?

Models of recidivism: obstacles, pessimism and recidivist narratives

Short-term prisoners' resettlement problems appear typically to be a combination, in varying proportions, of difficulties in access to opportunities and resources, and difficulties having their roots in the prisoner's attitudes, beliefs and habitual responses to problems. These of course may interact and reinforce each other, but if the findings suggest that services which aim to address only one or the other of these are likely to be less successful than services which are capable of encompassing both, this has implications for the models of resettlement which should inform services for this group. Rather than giving priority simply to resource issues such as accommodation problems, it is suggested that better results may be obtained from projects which also identify and address a need for changes in thinking.

Accounting for such differences in outcome draws our attention back to the different assumptions about crime and recidivism which are implicit in different approaches to resettlement. What follows is not an attempt to claim that this is the *only* way to account for differences in outcome: other factors undoubtedly contributed, and still others may emerge as the evaluation of resettlement projects continues through a second phase (Clancy et al. 2003). However, if resettlement services are indeed more effective when they address thinking and motivation as well as providing opportunities, this will have implications for the choice of an appropriate service model.

It is interesting in this context to consider two recent studies of the process of recidivism which point to rather similar conclusions. One is a highly quantitative study designed within a psychological paradigm, and one is a qualitative study in the tradition of interpretive and ethnographic social research. The first concerns what its authors call the 'criminal recidivism process' (Zamble and Quinsey 1997) and the second is based on offenders' own accounts of recidivism and desistance (Maruna 2000). Both these studies point, in very different ways, to the fact that future offending is likely to be influenced by offenders' thinking as well as their circumstances. Very briefly, Zamble and Quinsey's study of released male prisoners in Ontario found that the process of recidivism often involved practical or situational difficulties leading to negative emotion (depression, anger) and perhaps pessimism about the possibility of dealing with the situation other than by offending. This led people to give up on their attempts to avoid offending. As Zamble and Quinsey (1997: 146–7) put it, 'in the case of criminal behaviour, factors in the social environment seem influential determinants of initial delinquency for a substantial proportion of offenders ... but habitual offending is better predicted by looking at an individual's acquired ways of reacting to common situations'. This suggests that services for released prisoners must address not only the problems they face but also the personal resources, strategies and motivation they have available for dealing with them.

Maruna's (2000) interview-based study of offenders in Liverpool suggested that these personal resources are related to the way offenders understand and account for their situation and behaviour. He describes these understandings and accounts as different kinds of narrative, some of which support continued offending and some of which support desistance. For example, those who were continuing to offend saw themselves as victims of circumstances who had little choice, while those who were desisting from offending saw themselves as having taken control of their lives and determining their own futures. In discussing the latter group Maruna (2000: 147) describes the 'narrator's strong sense that he or she is in control of his or her destiny. Whereas active offenders in the Liverpool Desistance Study ... seemed to have little vision of what the future might hold, desisting interviewees had a plan and were optimistic that they could make it work.' Studies such as this lend some support to the idea that resettlement services should address both opportunities and thinking: they should aim to reinforce and support plausible 'narratives of desistance'. There may even be dangers in an exclusive focus on problems of access to resources and opportunities, as if crime were *nothing more than* a response to environmental difficulties or restricted opportunities: this may run the risk of reinforcing recidivist 'narratives' in which offenders cast themselves as victims of circumstance. The suggestion that different models of resettlement service contain different implicit criminologies implies that they embody different narratives of why people offend and how they stop. One consequence of this could be that when we provide such services, we have a choice between reinforcing narratives which tend to support desistance and reinforcing narratives which tend to support or facilitate reoffending.

Implications for community sentences

One reason for exploring these ideas further is that they may have wider implications for the process of supervising offenders under community sentences as well as in resettlement. For example, there is a long-standing research finding that low-risk probationers tend to have higher recidivism rates than comparable offenders who receive other sentences. Over 20 years ago Walker and his colleagues found, in a large comparative reconviction study, that first offenders put on probation were twice as likely to be reconvicted as first offenders who were fined (Walker et al. 1981). Although this study can be questioned on the grounds that offenders were matched on previous convictions only and this might not allow for the existence of greater needs or higher levels of problems among those offenders selected for probation, the emergence of risk/need assessment techniques now allows, in principle, the matching of offenders on dynamic risk factors ('criminogenic needs') as well as criminal history. A recent example, drawn from a reconviction study in Jersey, shows that even when offenders are matched on the basis of risk and need assessment the results resemble those of Walker's study.

In this case the matching is done using scores on the Level of Service Inventory – Revised, or LSI-R (Andrews and Bonta 1995) which is the most fully researched international risk-needs instrument (Hollin 2002) and has been in routine use in Jersey since 1996 (see Heath et al. 2002). This kind of study cannot yet be undertaken in England and Wales as we are still awaiting full implementation of OASys, the Offender Assessment System. The Jersey figures quoted (see Table 12.4) are drawn from the low–medium risk quartile of LSI-R scores as there were no probation orders made in the very lowest risk group. In higher risk groups probation had much better results: see Raynor and Miles (2001). Although the numbers in the table are not large, the difference in outcomes between the probation orders and the other non-custodial sentences is statistically significant ($p < 0.05$).

How might we account for such seemingly paradoxical findings? One explanation consistent with the arguments reviewed in this chapter is

Table 12.4 Sentencing in Jersey 1997–9: low–medium risk quartile (LSI-R = 10–15)

Sentence	Number	Mean LSI-R	% reconvicted in 12 months
Community Service	69	12.3	13
Fine	57	12.2	12
Probation	70	12.8	24
Prison	28	12.5	18

that the process of supervision for low-risk offenders may run the risk of reinforcing the wrong kind of narrative: in other words, unwittingly exercising the wrong kind of influence on offenders' thinking. Supervision of the low-risk offender is less likely to focus on the need to challenge thinking and 'confront offending' than would be the case with a more serious or persistent offender, and any input is therefore more likely to be in response to welfare problems raised by the offender. In other words, low-risk offenders may receive a sympathetic and understanding response which does not focus much on offending and concentrates, if anywhere, on social and personal welfare problems.

In terms of the models reviewed earlier, this resembles the 'opportunity deficit' model rather than the 'offender responsibility' model. Studies of what actually goes on between probation officers and the offenders they supervise are still surprisingly rare, but the suggestions made here about the style of supervision which low-risk probationers may be receiving closely resembles that documented by Willis in an early study of the content of probation officers' interviews with probationers (Willis 1983): the emphasis was clearly on problems and offending was hardly mentioned. The narrative approach suggests that this style of supervision risks confirming a narrative which portrays offending as a consequence of difficult circumstances outside the offender's control and therefore not particularly culpable. A style of supervision which does not deal with offending may also carry the message that it is not particularly important whether you offend or not. It would not be wholly surprising if some offenders become more likely to reoffend, or at least feel more free to do so, as a result of this kind of supervision. This may also be one of the processes underlying the well-known 'risk principle' (Andrews et al. 1990) which states that rehabilitation is more likely to be effective when it is not targeted on low-risk offenders.

One reason why these possibilities are worrying is that, as Rod Morgan has pointed out several times, the proportion of probationers who are first offenders has been going up steadily since the early 1990s (Morgan 2002, 2003; Raynor 1998). Probation Statistics give the proportion as 27 per cent in 2001 compared to 11 per cent in 1991 (Home Office 2002a). Morgan describes this as the 'silting up' of probation caseloads with offenders who should have been fined, but it may be even more counterproductive than this if it increases the proportion of probationers who risk being made worse rather than better by their supervision. If resettlement works best when it has a focus on thinking and motivation as well as welfare, so probably does a good deal of what is now on offer within community rehabilitation (formerly probation) orders, and it should be concentrated on offenders who actually require this kind of approach. At least this points to a need for more research on the impact of supervision on people who are not particularly criminal and on whether counterproductive effects can be avoided. We also need more research on how offenders themselves receive and understand the messages implied by various attempts to help them and how these impact on their personal narratives of success and failure.

One final point may seem obvious but bears constant repetition. Many of the prisoners in our study, including many of those who received a good service, did not need to be in prison or did not need to be there for so long. Well-integrated services could have been provided before and after an earlier release, and some could probably have been involved in successful rehabilitative or restorative work without any need for a period of custody. Such approaches to the problem of short-term recidivist prisoners have been widely discussed, for example in the Halliday Report (2001) and in the recent White Paper (Home Office 2002b). The resettlement problems resulting from short prison sentences and the counterproductive impact of the low-risk probation order are two sides of the same coin: people in prison who might do better under supervision in the community, and people on probation who might do better if they were fined. Both point to an urgent need to revive the penal reform agenda summed up in the old phrase 'alternatives to custody'. When probation and youth justice services promoted this approach in the 1980s they had considerable success; when they were made to abandon it in the 1990s they unwittingly contributed to the development of a custodial crisis. The time is ripe, or over-ripe, to be more confident and proactive in promoting strategies to reduce custodial sentencing.

References

Advisory Council on the Treatment of Offenders (1963) *The Organisation of After-Care*. London: HMSO.

Andrews, D.A. and Bonta, J. (1995) *The Level of Service Inventory – Revised: Manual*. Toronto: Multi-Health Systems.

Andrews, D.A., Zinger, I., Hoge, R.D., Bonta, J., Gendreau, P. and Cullen, F.T. (1990) 'Does correctional treatment work? A clinically relevant and psychologically informed meta-analysis', *Criminology*, 28, 369–404.

Braithwaite, J. (1989) *Crime, Shame and Reintegration*. Cambridge: Cambridge University Press.

Carlen, P. (1989) 'Crime, inequality and sentencing', in P. Carlen and D. Cook (eds), *Paying for Crime*. Buckingham: Open University Press.

Clancy, A., Hudson, K., Maguire, M., Peake, R., Raynor, P. and Vanstone, M. (2003) 'Evaluation of Resettlement Pathfinders: Interim Report', report to Home Office (unpublished).

Frude, N., Honess, T. and Maguire, M. (1994) *Crime-Pics II Manual*. Cardiff: Michael & Associates.

Goldblatt, P. and Lewis, C. (eds) (1998) *Reducing Offending: An Assessment of Research Evidence on Ways of Dealing with Offending Behaviour*, Home Office Research Study 187. London: Home Office.

Haines, K. (1990) *After-Care Services for Released Prisoners*. Cambridge: Institute of Criminology.

Halliday, J. (2001) *Making Punishments Work: Report of a Review of the Sentencing Framework for England and Wales*. London: Home Office.

Hatcher, R. and McGuire, J. (2001) *Report on the Psychometric Evaluation of the Think-First Programme in Community Settings*. Liverpool: University of Liverpool Department of Clinical Psychology.

Heath, B., Raynor, P. and Miles, H. (2002) 'What Works in Jersey: the first ten years', *Vista*, 7 (3), 202–8.

Her Majesty's Inspectorates of Prison and Probation (2001) *Through the Prison Gate: A Joint Thematic Review*. London: Home Office.

Hirschi, T. (1969) *Causes of Delinquency*. Berkeley: California University Press.

Hollin, C. (2002) 'Risk-needs assessment and allocation to offender programmes', in J. McGuire (ed.), *Offender Rehabilitation and Treatment*. Chichester: Wiley.

Home Office (1998) *Joining Forces to Protect the Public: Prisons-Probation*. London: Home Office.

Home Office (2002a) *Probation Statistics England and Wales 2001*. London: Home Office.

Home Office (2002b) *Justice for All*, CM 5563. London: Stationery Office.

Institute of Criminology and Probation Studies Unit (2001) *CRP-CS Interim Report*, report to the Home Office. Cambridge: Institute of Criminology.

Lewis, S., Vennard, J., Maguire, M., Raynor, P., Vanstone, M., Raybould, S. and Rix, A. (2003a) *The Resettlement of Short-term Prisoners: An Evaluation of Seven Pathfinders*, RDS Occasional Paper 83. London: Home Office.

Lewis, S., Maguire, M., Raynor, P., Vanstone, M. and Vennard, J. (2003b) *The Resettlement of Short-term Prisoners: An Evaluation of Seven Pathfinder Programmes*, Research Findings 200. London: Home Office.

Maguire, M. and Raynor, P. (1997) 'The revival of throughcare: rhetoric and reality in automatic conditional release'. *British Journal of Criminology*, 37, 1–14.

Maguire, M., Raynor, P., Vanstone, M. and Kynch, J. (1998) *Voluntary After-Care*, Research Findings 73. London: Home Office.

Maguire, M., Raynor, P., Vanstone, M. and Kynch, J. (2000) 'Voluntary After-Care and the Probation Service: a case of diminishing responsibility', *Howard Journal of Criminal Justice*, 39, 234–48.

Maruna, S. (2000) *Making Good*. Washington, DC: American Psychological Association.

Morgan, R. (2002) 'Something has got to give', *HLM – the Howard League Magazine*, 20 (4), 7–8.

Morgan, R. (2003) 'Foreword', *Her Majesty's Inspectorate of Probation Annual Report 2002/2003*. London: Home Office.

NACRO (2000) *The Forgotten Majority: The Resettlement of Short Term Prisoners*. London: NACRO.

Raynor, P. (1998) 'Reading probation statistics: a critical comment', *Vista*, 3, 181–5.

Rotman, E. (1990) *Beyond Punishment*. Westport, CT: Greenwood Press.

Raynor, P. and Miles, M. (2001) *Risks, Needs and Reoffending: Evaluating the Impact of Community Sentences in Jersey*. Swansea: University of Wales, Swansea and Cognitive Centre Foundation.

Social Exclusion Unit (2002) *Reducing Re-offending by Ex-Prisoners*. Office of the Deputy Prime Minister.

Stone, N. (1985) 'Prison-based work', in H. Walker and B. Beaumont (eds), *Working with Offenders*. London: Macmillan.

Sykes, G. and Matza, D. (1957) 'Techniques of neutralization: a theory of delinquency', *American Sociological Review*, 22, 664–70.

Walker, N., Farrington, D. and Tucker, G. (1981) 'Reconviction rates of adult males after different sentences', *British Journal of Criminology*, 21, 357–60.

Willis, A. (1983) 'The balance between care and control in probation: a research note', *British Journal of Social Work*, 13, 339–46.

Zamble, E. and Quinsey, V. (1997) *The Criminal Recidivism Process*. Cambridge: Cambridge University Press.

Chapter 13

Pursuing evidence-based inspection

Rod Morgan[1]

Whatever the purposes of inspection, none of them is well served unless inspectors arrive at their findings and recommendations on the basis of the best available, objectively verifiable evidence. This could be taken to be a tenet which scarcely needs to be spelt out. However, for various reasons I think it has to be.

First, the inspectorate functions in a political environment. The government claims to be pursuing 'evidence-based' policy (see Home Office 2001a: para. 1). However, those claims are seriously questioned both by members of the government party and by academic and other critics. It is said by some former Labour Ministers, for example, that the government operates on the basis of 'spin' and that its record and standing has been marred by such practices. Moreover, academic critics argue that the government's crime reduction programme is marketed – through the strategy of 'permanent campaigning' (see Heclo 2000) – in such a fashion that 'it is becoming increasingly difficult to distinguish between 'rhetoric' and 'reality', 'fact' and 'fiction', 'signifier' and 'signified' (McLaughlin 2002). Moreover, as several other contributors to this volume have emphasised, much social policy has a weak evidential basis and given the speed of legislative change in the criminal justice field (there are no fewer than five bills before Parliament in the current session with some bearing on probation-related work) there is seldom made time to test propositions before they are enacted.

Secondly, no inspectorate is fully independent of government. I am *Her Majesty's* Chief Inspector.[2] But, de facto, I was appointed by Home Office Ministers. Further, I am totally dependent for the budget of my unit on my sponsoring department, the Home Office, which, within the

current organisational arrangements, effectively means the recommendations to Ministers of Martin Narey,[3] the Commissioner for
Correctional Services. Moreover, my unit is substantially dependent on
the cooperation of the service I inspect, the National Probation Service
(NPS, also part of the Home Office). Our inspection methodology has for
many years involved probation staff in the process of inspection. The
consequence is that we rely on NPS staff for the practical, logistical
implementation of our inspection programme. Further, my staff are all
civil servants, with aspirations and careers to think of. They require me
to exercise conspicuous leadership regarding what they do. I take
personal responsibility for the reports which we publish, the contents of
which may not universally be popular. Finally, I can be instructed by
Ministers to undertake certain tasks specified in the prevailing statute
governing my office (the Criminal Justice and Court Services Act 2000,
s.7).

Thirdly, there is currently within Whitehall, largely because of pro-
tests from public sector workers, a growing sense that the 'modernising
government' agenda and programme has involved excessive reliance on
top-down managerialist devices (data recording, the application of
standards, the fixing of targets, public service delivery agreements,
statistical returns, league tables and so on) with the practitioners – the
public servants actually engaged in the grassroots delivery of services –
being burdened by a proliferating band of regulatory bodies and processes (auditors, monitors and inspectors) whose value is increasingly
questioned (Local Government Association 2001). The number of
regulators, and their cost, has expanded exponentially (see Hood et al.
1999; IPPR 2000; OPSR 2003a). The result may be that in the course of
slimming down and rationalising this overweening regulatory framework, the operational independence of the inspectorates may be
reduced as a result of the insistence by sponsoring departments that
inspectorates 'drive up' 'delivery' and 'performance' as the government
has defined and measured those terms (see Byatt and Lyons 2001; OPSR
2003b). The first of the principles which the government has said should
govern the work of all inspectorates is:

> The *purpose of improvement*. There should be an explicit concern on
> the part of the inspectors to contribute to the improvement of the
> service being inspected. This should guide the focus, method,
> reporting and follow-up of inspection. In framing recom-
> mendations, an inspector should recognise good performance and
> address any failure appropriately. Inspection should aim to
> generate data and intelligence that enable departments more

235

quickly to calibrate the progress of reform in their sectors and make appropriate adjustments. (OPSR 2003b: 5)

On one level this statement could scarcely be objected to. Who could quarrel with such an aspiration? But the devil, as always, is in the managerial detail. What counts as good performance? What is failure? When it is said, as it almost must, that 'It is for Ministers and their departments responsible for a public service to set standards determining how the service is to be delivered and to make sure effective performance management systems are in place …' and that those same Ministers and departments should also 'consider whether inspection of a service is needed, and should set up, commission or disband an inspectorate as appropriate', the stark juxtaposition of managerialism and independent inspection becomes clear. Because inspectorates are increasingly being required to demonstrate that they 'add value', they may, paradoxically, increasingly be tied, and perceived to be tied, more closely to the managerialist agenda during the period when that agenda is ostensibly being scaled back.

I therefore consider it incumbent on me to spell out in some detail what evidence-based inspection amounts to and why it is vital that it be maintained. There can be no place for spin in my repertoire. However, as I explain below, and as other contributors to this volume emphasise, much practice is informed by weak evidence and this has implications for inspection. True independence is less a status and more a capacity (see Mordaunt 1999). Independence is best demonstrated by being exercised, and transparently so. This should mean fostering honest debate about the strength of evidence for practices. It is possibly re-assuring that Ministers and departments are advised that they should 'not be unduly prescriptive about how inspectors should carry out their work' (OPSR 2003b: 9). But it will likely require vigilance to ensure that it is so.

Inspectorate functions

Let us begin at the beginning. Of what potential value is an independent inspectorate? What performance measures should be applied to my unit if its continued existence is to be defended?

I take the bedrock rationale for my existence to be public account-ability. That is, a public interest function, for which my independence – both my status and exercise of my capacity to report fearlessly what I find – is vital. The public ultimately should have a means of knowing what the effectiveness and quality of services delivered are, and not necessarily just according to the performance measures devised and reported by government. The latter may be inconsistent or inadequate.

Secondly, inspectorates should be valued by Ministers for the independent advice that they are able to offer the government. It is insufficiently recognised that Ministers may find it difficult to penetrate the data sets which their predecessors and operational managers have set up. They want to know, or should want to know, what the 'reality' is and what the trends are. They often come to office with no operational knowledge or experience of the service for which they are made responsible and they often have precious little time in which to get the picture. I have been in post since August 2001. I am already working to my third Minister of Probation and Prisons. Operational managers may shield Ministers from possible bad news and are likely to highlight demonstrable good news. That is how they protect their reputations, career prospects, departments and budgets. Inspectors, if they are truly independent, should have fewer vested interests, at least for as long as the government is committed to the existence of independent inspection. That is where their value to Ministers should lie: they should be in a position to offer independent health checks, taken at all levels.

Thirdly, inspectorates should assist services to improve their performance. They may do this in various ways: by probing the interstices of the recorded data and explaining why the performance pattern varies between areas; by raising the consciousness of practitioners regarding how their practices are perceived by customers or users; by identifying good and bad practices; by proposing new standards for measuring performance. There are difficulties associated with all these objectives, not least because it is the task of management to do these things and also because their operational capacity to undertake them is normally far greater than those of an inspectorate. The phrase 'good practice' trips easily off the tongue. But the test of 'evidence-based' may be difficult to satisfy – an issue to which I wish to return. Further, it may be difficult for an inspectorate to demonstrate that anything it does serves directly to improve the quality of services delivered. This is so because inspectorate interventions comprise only one of many stimuli in the stream of consciousness through which operational policy and practice develops and because inspectors are not managers and have no executive power to see that their findings are accepted or their recommendations acted upon.

But let us put these difficulties on one side. It should be clear that if an inspectorate, either in the general accounts offered, or in advice to Ministers, or through the identification of good practices to practitioners, operates on the basis of rhetoric, spin or purple prose, it will soon cease to have legitimacy with its key stakeholders. I think there is a connection between what some analysts have conceptually distinguished as effectiveness in terms of the *production of knowledge* accepted as truthful and effectiveness in terms of *reform*, that is bringing about change (Liebling and Hancock 2003). Inspectors, I believe, must operate on the basis of the best available evidence, capable of being challenged and sustained. This is easily said, however. Operationalising the doctrine is more difficult. I want to devote the rest of this chapter to identifying and illustrating the dilemmas that have to be confronted and the choices made.

Before I do so, one last general word about the nature of an inspectorate. There is a symbiotic relationship between what an inspectorate does and the performance management capacity of the service it inspects (for a more detailed discussion see Morgan 2003a). The boundaries between research, inspection, audit and performance management are in practice blurred. The degree to which an inspectorate veers from inspection into one or another of these other terrains depends upon the existence of reliable data collected by others, particularly the managers of the service being inspected. If key performance data are not available, the inspectorate may itself have to collect it.

It is partly for the above reasons that the work of Her Majesty's Inspectorate of Probation (HMIP) had significantly to change after the formation of the NPS in April 2001 and the National Probation Directorate (NPD) came into existence and began to get geared up. As we shall see, this transition in the operation of HMIP continues.

Reliable evidence, but which?

HMIP has a staff of around 40 and an annual budget of approximately £2 million for Probation inspection (HMIP also leads the Youth Offending Team inspection programme, for which there is a separate budget). The NPS employs some 17,000 staff, supervises in excess of 200,000 offenders at any one time, is divided into 42 Areas in England and Wales and is directed by an NPD which now has a staff approaching 500. It has a budget of roughly £0.75 billion. In addition to supervising offenders subject to court orders and on licence, the NPS: prepares over a quarter of a million court reports annually; undertakes other criminal inquiries and prepares other reports (bail information inquiries, means inquiries, parole reports, etc.); contacts over 13,000 victims of serious sexual or violent offences a year; has a duty to engage in local Crime and Disorder Reduction Partnerships (CDRPs); seconds staff to the 155 Youth Offender Teams (YOTs) and the 146 prisons and young offender establishments in England and Wales; manages over 2,000 places in approved hostels; secures offenders' access to drugs, housing, vocational training and other services the budgets for which are held by other agencies; and so on (see Home Office 2001b; Home Office 2002).

My point is simple. HMIP is small. The NPS has a variety of increasingly complex duties, not all of which can be inspected closely all of the time. HMIP's first dilemma, therefore, is: what to focus on? What is the core business about which the inspectorate should collect evidence across the 42 Areas which it is our statutory duty to inspect?

During 2002–03 we decided to devise a new inspection programme which acknowledged the existence of the NPS and reflected our decision to transfer to the NPD responsibility for collecting general performance data and routinely monitoring the videos of accredited group offending behaviour programmes. Prior to 2001 HMIP and my predecessor, Sir Graham Smith, had acted in some ways as a sort of surrogate NPD and Director General on behalf of the Home Office. That role was no longer appropriate. We had to change. The new programme we have called Effective Supervision Inspection (ESI). We piloted the methodology in spring 2003 and started applying it in June. The new programme focuses on what we judge to be the three core aspects of NPS performance – *assessment*, *intervention* and *outcome*. That is:

- Is the risk-needs *assessment* of offenders well grounded?

- Are the *interventions* which case managers deliver or arrange appropriate (not least in relation to the *diversity* of offenders) and proportionate to the risk-needs assessment?

- Is the *outcome* of the interventions gauged and recorded, and adjustments made to the assessment and supervision plans accordingly?

- And, most importantly, is the *outcome* positive in pointing towards reduced reoffending and increased public protection?

We might call this the *virtuous triangle* of probation work:

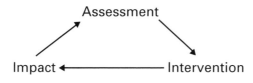

We are reading, with the assistance of local practitioners, an average of 100 files per Area (the number will vary according to the size of the Area). Files are selected randomly from orders and licences that have run for at least six to nine months so that the more intensive phase of supervision will likely have passed. We are also over-representing 'high-risk-of-harm' cases. These file readings then inform interviews with case supervisors, the offenders concerned and other key persons such as programme tutors and agency partner representatives. In these interviews we are probing what priorities are set, why particular decisions are or are not made and what the key participants feel is or is not being achieved. Our ESI criteria are published and Areas are being scored so as to produce separate indices of performance in relation to *assessment*, *intervention* and *outcome*, plus the infrastructure of *management*. These four then generate an overall performance score for the Area. The inspection cycle will last approximately three years.

Our new inspection methodology is different from that which preceded it in several key respects (for a fuller account see Morgan 2003a). It is focused less on *processes* and more on *objectives* and *outcomes*. It involves offenders – what we may term the key *users* of probation services as such – systematically for the first time. It *integrates* within a single programme what we have previously termed Area inspection and audits of accredited programmes (the latter now become just one of the many *interventions* that might be delivered). Our comparisons of performance will from now on be between *families* of like Areas. Follow-up inspections, previously undertaken routinely, will in future be conducted only in the event of our finding some aspect of performance giving rise to serious concern, in which case the follow-up will be on that aspect of performance alone.

It is essential, if meaningful comparisons of performance between Areas and over time are to be made, that an inspection methodology be stable. Thus approximately 75 per cent of the evidence we collect will form a more or less constant core. But we are reserving approximately a quarter of our fieldwork resources so as to be able to look thematically at issues that will change. This will enable us to look at issues for which routinely we have not had time, or which, for various reasons, are of more specialised or transitory concern.

The latter device prompts the first of several questions regarding our objective of evidence-based inspection. What aspects of performance will we *not* be collecting a great deal of evidence about?

There are some obvious omissions from our general data collection plan. We will not be covering the work of staff seconded to prisons and YOTs, though we are now leading a separate inspection programme, involving eight different inspectorates, on the work of YOTs (see HMIP 2003: Chapter Five). Nor will we be collecting any detailed evidence about the contribution which the Probation Service makes to Crime and Disorder Reduction Partnerships (CDRPs), though we shall make general inquiries about this area of work during the course of interviews with senior management. Likewise, an average sample of 100 cases per Area is unlikely to enable us to make detailed judgements about the operation of particular units, partnerships or programmes – for example, the operation of a particular hostel, offending behaviour programme or partnership facility in that Area. Our conclusions will be more broad-brush. They will concern general questions such as: are interventions provided which generally meet the criminogenic needs or risks presented by particular groups of offenders? Are those interventions generally backed up with effective case management? And so on. We will, though, be able to draw some conclusions about the operation of particular interventions – for example an accredited programme – by considering results for a number of Areas in aggregate. By these means we shall also be able to produce occasional thematic reports on, for example, how appropriately and well the Probation Service generally responds to the differential needs of women, minority ethnic offenders and other diverse groups. This we plan to do.

My first obvious point, therefore, is that the evidence we collect is necessarily selective and targeted. We cannot cover all aspects of performance. My second point is that even those processes which fall within the ambit of our core data collection programme will not always be capable of being looked at as comprehensively as we would like. Let me illustrate the point with reference to two vital policy issues – the production by the NPS of reports for the courts (namely pre- or specific sentence reports – PSRs or SSRs) and the management of risk of harm.

The overwhelming majority of the files we read during the course of an inspection involve a PSR. We are concentrating on the quality of assessments made in them and this should enable us, *inter alia*, to note the appropriateness of the recommendations made, though we are not routinely recording the latter. However, our survey does not include court reports resulting in short sentences of imprisonment or fines or discharges because those court reports do not, by definition, generate live probation case files. It follows that our capacity to make judgements about the wisdom of the Probation Service preparing all the reports currently requested of it, or the overall relationship between the conclusions reached in those reports and the recommendations made and sentences passed, will be limited. This is so because we shall not have seen the full range of court report work done. This is one of many important evidential gaps which we regret but cannot, within the resources available to us, routinely fill. The most we can do is ask each Probation Area whether *they* have instituted systems to analyse these relationships and, like everyone else, we can look to the *Probation Statistics* (Home Office 2002a) which show that the expanding NPS caseload is silting up with relatively low-risk offenders who, in past years, would more likely have been fined (see Morgan 2003b; Hough, Jacobson and Millie 2003), a trend which there are strong indications that Probation court report recommendations have encouraged.

Much the same reservations apply to our assessments of risk of harm and public protection issues. We are over-representing high risk of harm cases in our file-reading samples in order to be able to examine this aspect of work. We shall be able to see whether the interventions delivered and the supervision given is proportionate to the risk of harm presented by each case. However, we shall not have time to look in detail at the quality and effectiveness of the partnerships established with the police and other agencies through the Multi-Agency Public Protection Arrangements (MAPPA). These are issues which we will only be able to consider in depth through thematic inspections, three of which we plan to undertake – on domestic violence, on persistent or prolific offenders, and public protection cases – in the near future.

How adequate is our core evidence?

What of the evidence collected as part of our core programme? How adequately does it enable us to come to good quality conclusions about the mainstream issues – *assessment*, *intervention* and *outcome* – which we say are our central concern? Let us take each of those focal issues in turn.

Regarding *assessment* – whether of risk of harm or likelihood of reoffending – we are clearly able to make baseline judgements. Was OASys, or some other or supplementary instrument used, and in a timely manner? Were all parts of the instrument completed? These processual questions we can answer. However, we clearly do not have the time and resources comprehensively to check the accuracy of the work done. We are not able, for example, to compare the original data available to assessors and their completion of the instruments. Our focus is necessarily largely on whether the processes are comprehensively gone through.

Likewise with *interventions*. We are able to make judgements about whether interventions have been delivered appropriate and roughly proportionate to whatever criminogenic factors were identified in the risk needs *assessment*. And we interview as many of the key persons involved in the delivery of *interventions* as we are able. We also interview the offenders themselves, or at least as many as we are able. But we are generally not able to observe the interventions, either directly or on video. We lack the time. We have to rely on evidence from local managers regarding the quality assurance and control processes locally or nationally in place to form a view about the quality of what is being delivered either directly by the Probation Service or its partner agencies. I will return to this issue.

It should also be noted that we shall be able to do no more than relatively superficially answer the question which, in my experience, is most often asked by politicians and those outside the Probation Service: What does it mean to be on probation? How much time do offenders spend under effective supervision? That question can currently with some confidence be answered only in relation to two groups of offenders – those on Community Punishment Orders and those subject to a condition that they participate in a designated programme accredited by the Correctional Services Accreditation Panel (CSAP). The former have stipulated hours of unpaid work to perform and the latter attend sessions the number and duration of which is fixed by the CSAP when they approve the programme syllabus. Probation staff are generally not required currently to record in their case notes how long they spend with offenders and even in those few Areas where they are asked to do so (County Durham, for example) they mostly do not. It follows that we do not yet have any detailed fix on how long supervision sessions are for different categories of offenders at different stages in their orders or licences, what proportion of offenders are merely 'signing in' on those occasions they are required to report, or what type of staff (probation officers (POs) or less qualified probation service officers (PSOs)) are involved with which categories of offenders, etc. Our new inspection programme will enable us to collect some information on all these issues, but we are unlikely to be able to explore them in any depth. Moreover, there is a desperate paucity of good quality data in the Probation Service on how resources are currently used within the NPS and at what cost. HMIP has argued that repairing this gap in our collective knowledge, a gap which hampers work to assess value for money issues, needs urgently to be filled – a task primarily falling to the NPD (HMIP 2003: 18)

Regarding *outcomes* we are not by ourselves able to consider the ultimate outcome – whether or not offenders reoffend and are re-convicted during a follow-up period. That is a task for research not inspection. But we are able to check whether the files show that risk-need *reassessments* have been undertaken and changes in the behaviour and circumstances of offenders recorded. That is, depending on what is recorded in the files, we are able to say whether homeless offenders have been housed or those with accommodation difficulties have become more settled? Likewise, whether the consumption of those with alcohol or drug abuse problems has reportedly been reduced? Or whether offenders lacking basic skills have acquired any? Or the unemployed got into a job? And so on. Further, we are making arrangements with the Home Office Research, Development and Statistics Directorate (RDSD) to follow through the cases in our file-reading samples to the two-year reconviction point to give a more complete picture on outcomes. We are also discussing with them the possibility of additional secondary analysis of our data with a view to considering the frequency and seriousness of any reconvictions.

We do not of course commit the fallacy of purely attributing individual positive changes in any of these factors to the *interventions* of the Probation Service or the skill, energy and commitment of the individual officers involved. Likewise we do not attribute any deterioration in the behaviour or circumstances of individual offenders to the absence of these qualities in staff. We are of course fully aware that desistance is generally a product of life-change circumstances and an associated act of will on the part of the offender (Farrall 2002), though the manner in which offenders see themselves and their situation, and thus their capacity to rise above their circumstances, is open to influence (see Maruna 2000). Our working hypothesis is that a Probation Area that is both undertaking systematic *assessments* and delivering targeted *interventions* focused on identified risks and needs will be associated with improved overall *outcomes*. Indeed, were that not the case then the rationale for having a Probation Service would substantially be undone.

Quality assurance and data reliability

I have already made reference to our reliance on the NPS's quality assurance and control systems. This is a key aspect of what I earlier described as the symbiotic relationship between HMIP and the NPS and needs spelling out in greater detail.

The NPD requires every Probation Area routinely to return performance data for analysis to the NPD. The system now used is in part based on one which HMIP developed and handed over to the NPD in 2001–02. Rather than collect performance data – that task now belongs to management – our task is to explore what lies in their interstices and explain why the performance patterns are as they are. That is what we are attempting to do with ESI. However, if our interviews with Area managers are to be meaningful we have to have confidence in the NPD-published performance data. We need to know that the data are reliable and my ability independently to advise Ministers about NPS performance depends on our doing more than merely consuming, uncritically, the NPD performance tables.

This is why, early last year, we planned and undertook an exercise with the NPD to second read and, where necessary, third read a sample of case files which had first routinely been read by local team supervisors to assess practitioner conformity with the National Standards for supervision. The results were not entirely reassuring. Discrepancies of substance were found between the assessment of the original reader and the second reader in 20 per cent of the items relating to supervisors arranging contact with offenders and 32 per cent of the items relating to breach action (see HMIP 2003: paras 3, 24–27; the full report of this exercise can be found on HMIP's website – see http://www.homeoffice.gov.uk/justice/probation/inspprob).

This result did not surprise me, and not because whenever performance is measured there are always distorting consequences and problems of data reliability. Probation case files are exceedingly complex and they differ in their organisation and composition from one Area to another, a defect that HMIP has recommended be urgently repaired by the introduction of a national IT-integrated case file (HMIP 2002b: para. 12). When inspecting files and deciding whether a particular Standard has or has not been met, a good deal of reading has currently to be done between the lines of what is recorded. That is, guesses and subjective judgements have to be made. This is no recipe for high inter-rater reliability. We shall pursue the issue of performance data reliability in future exercises in cooperation with the NPD.

Equally important to enable us to benchmark NPS performance is the establishment by the NPD of quality assurance and control systems for all the key processes – assessment, case management, the delivery of accredited programmes and partnership provision of other interventions, etc. – involved in probation work. By *quality assurance* I mean the routine defining of standards of performance backed up by day-to-day management systems to ensure that the standards are met. By *quality control* I mean occasional more arm's length checks to ensure that the allegedly embedded *quality assurance* systems are achieving what they are designed to do.

To illustrate this distinction, the manuals for the delivery of accredited offender programmes which are approved by the CSAP constitute a foundation stone for their *quality assurance*. The audits of accredited programmes which during 2001–03 were undertaken as a separate programme by HMIP constituted a *quality control*. The NPD is currently taking over from HMIP the video monitoring system by area assessors which we have devised. When in place this will constitute part of the NPD's *quality assurance* and *control* system for accredited programmes. My point is this. Many of the evidential shortcomings of our ESI methodology will be resolved once the NPD and NPS have in place adequate quality assurance and control systems – systems which we aim to oversee and inspect in cooperation with the NPD. This is an aspect of the symbiotic relationship between us. We look forward to the development of these systems while recognising that their full implementation will take time.

Promoting good practice

Let me conclude by returning to the question that lies at the heart of evidence-based practice *and* inspection. What constitutes good practice in the sense that reduced reoffending and increased public protection, the ultimate tests of all that we do, are achieved?

Aspects of probation practice can reasonably claim to be evidence-based. There is a solid accumulation of research evidence that certain offending behaviour programmes, if delivered well, alongside other practical interventions, can achieve reduced levels of reoffending (Chapman and Hough 1998; Hedderman, Sugg and Vennard 1997; McGuire 1995, 2002). There is of course a world of difference between delivering such programmes in ideal, experimental circumstances and rolling them out for more general consumption (see HMIP 2002b: para. 9; Lipsey 1995; McGuire 2003). But the programmes are nevertheless evidence-based. There is also evidence that enforcement of standards governing probation supervision is associated with reduced reoffending (May and Wadwell 2001). It was perfectly reasonable, therefore, for HMIP in recent years to focus heavily on inspecting the degree to which offending behaviour programmes were delivered well and National Standards for supervision complied with. We did both through our Audit (2001–03 – see HMIP 2003: Chapter Three) and Performance Inspection Programmes (PIP, 1989–2003 – see HMIP 2003: Chapter Two).

However, this is not to say that all probation practice is evidence-based or that the standards being enforced are the most effective that might be devised. Nor is it to say that reduced reoffending is the only test that should be applied or that there are not other intermediary tests –

sentencer and public confidence, for example – which should not be applied more immediately. Let me briefly illustrate some of those propositions.

The NPS National Standards (Home Office 2002b: Section D) stipulate the frequency of contact between supervisors and offenders subject to community penalties. The contacts stipulated are minimal and it is clearly stated that 'they are likely to be exceeded for offenders who pose risks of serious harm to the public, or a higher likelihood of reoffending, or for those who are subject to additional order or licence requirements' (2002b: D2). Probation staff are expected to exercise their discretion as to the nature and intensity of contact. There are good arguments for leaving such matters to the professional judgements of staff (see McWilliams 1990; McWilliams and Pease 1990). Nevertheless the standard simply comprises a 'contact' which may be two, fifty or any other number of minutes, and though the stipulated, tapering, minimum number of contacts for community rehabilitation orders – once a week for the first 12 weeks, then fortnightly, then monthly (2002b: D15) – makes intuitive good sense and no doubt meets the objective that the courts be satisfied 'that a credible level of disciplined supervision is taking place' (2002b: D1), there is, as far as I am aware, no evidence that the levels either *stipulated* or *actually taking place* have been shown to relate to reduced reoffending. What is clear, I think, is that the Probation Service now enjoys a high level of confidence among sentencers (Hough, Jacobson and Millie 2003) and no doubt the introduction of the National Standards and their gradually improved enforcement has contributed to that.

A distinction can also be drawn between the basis on which the early offending behaviour programmes were accredited by the CSAP and that on which, for example, the recently agreed programme for 'Enhanced Community Punishment' was approved. The latter accreditation is provisional on the grounds of a 'promising hypothesis' as opposed to a proven thesis (see Gelsthorpe and Rex, this volume).

In the case of the programme, shortly to be rolled out as a pilot in eleven probation Areas, for Intensive Control and Change (ICCP) of 18–20 year olds as an alternative to short custodial sentences, accreditation has not even been sought and, as far as I am aware, there is, as yet, little evidential basis on which it could be sought (for a detailed discussion, see Robin Moore, this volume). The genesis is more political than social scientific, though it is clearly plausible that persistent or prolific offenders fully engaged or subject to surveillance for a high proportion of their waking hours will reoffend less and/or that sentencers will find the package an acceptable alternative to custody.

The NPS is to an extent following in the wake of the Intensive Supervision and Surveillance Packages (ISSPs) already rolled out by the Youth Justice Board, an initiative which it is suggested is contributing to the reduced resort to youth custody (Youth Justice Board 2003: 21–2).

Most 'good practice' recommendations which HMIP makes are likely to comprise *procedures*, *processes* or *arrangements* which better implement *policies* – standards, targets or programmes – with variable evidential bases in terms of crime reduction. We must take care how we use the term 'good practice'. The evidential basis of our judgements must be sound. But even when we use the term advisedly it will not necessarily follow that the good practices we recommend support policies that are themselves evidentially well supported. That is a higher order issue to which we shall pay strategic attention in our thematic and annual reports and in collaboration with the NPD and RDSD.

Conclusions

It is clear that there are degrees of 'evidence-based policy' and that evidence-based inspection is inevitably caught up in the wake of those degrees. This is a point which several contributors to this volume also make. At one end of the continuum there is what policy-makers, and I think most politicians, yearn for: policies based on carefully devised experiments that have been systematically evaluated and found, when rolled out in less than ideal circumstances, still to achieve an improved outcome at lower than average cost and to enjoy the confidence of the public at large. We might call these *all-singing-and-dancing-evidence-based-policies*, or what has been referred to as the 'gold standard'. In the criminal justice arena they are seldom found. We are much more familiar with what we may term *quick-and-dirty-evidence-based-policies*, variously alluded to in terms of metals substantially baser than gold. Crime continues to be committed. Sentencers have to do something. Politicians want action. The criminal justice agencies, typically struggling with overstretched resources, have quickly to come up with plans which have a degree of prima facie plausibility and are, in the opinions of their political masters, saleable to the electorate. Some of these policies are undoubtedly characterised by what Bottoms (1995; see also Garland 2001) has termed *populist punitiveness*, that is politicians tapping into the widespread feelings of insecurity in contemporary society. However, I do not think such policies are often cynical in the sense that other commentators use the term *penal populism* (see Roberts et al. 2003: 4–5), that is politicians pursuing policies which they believe will prove popular with the public but which they know will achieve nothing, or may even be counter-productive, in terms of reduced reoffending and public safety.

Politicians and policy-makers generally wish to pursue policies that are effective. The evidence suggests that, ultimately, that is what the public at large want also (see Roberts and Hough 2003). The Inspectorate has a role in promoting informed public debate and in ensuring that the best available, objectively verifiable evidence is the touchstone of assessments about the NPS and the criminal justice system as a whole. If we fail in that mission we will lose credibility and the case for our continued existence will rightly be called into question.

Notes

1 This chapter was prepared when Professor Rod Morgan was the Chief Inspector of Probation. He has since been appointed as the Chair of the Youth Justice Board.
2 See Note 1.
3 Martin Narey has since been appointed as the Chief Executive of the National Offender Management Service.

References

Bottoms, A.E. (1995) 'The philosophy and politics of punishment and sentencing', in C.M.V. Clarkson and R. Morgan (eds), *The Politics of Sentencing Reform*. Oxford: Oxford University Press.

Byatt, Sir I. and Lyons, Sir M. (2001) *Role of External Review in Improving Performance*. London: Public Services Productivity Panel, HM Treasury.

Chapman, T. and Hough, M. (1998) *Evidence-Based Practice: A Guide to Effective Practice*. London: Home Office.

Farrall, S. (2002) *Rethinking What Works with Offenders: Probation, Social Context and Desistance from Crime*. Cullompton: Willan.

Garland, D. (2001) *The Culture of Control: Crime and Social Order in Contemporary Society*. Oxford: Oxford University Press.

Heclo, H. (2000) 'Campaigning and governing', in N.J. Ornstein and T. E. Mann (eds), *The Permanent Campaign and Its Future*. Washington, DC: American Enterprise Institute/Brookings Institute.

Hedderman, C., Sugg, D. and Vennard, J. (eds) (1997) *Changing Offenders' Attitudes and Behaviour: What Works?*, Home Office Research Study 171. London: Home Office.

Her Majesty's Inspectorate of Probation (2002a) *Report on National Standards Data Reliability*. London: HMIP.

Her Majesty's Inspectorate of Probation (2002b) *Annual Report 2001–2*. London: HMIP.

Her Majesty's Inspectorate of Probation (2003) *Annual Report 2002–3*. London: HMIP.

Home Office (2001a) *Criminal Justice: The Way Ahead*, Cm 5074. London: Stationery Office.

Home Office (2001b) *A New Choreography: An Integrated Strategy for the National Probation Service for England and Wales – Strategic Framework 2001–4*. London: Home Office.

Home Office (2002a) *Probation Statistics England and Wales 2001*. London: Home Office.

Home Office (2002b) *National Standards for the Supervision of Offenders in the Community 2000: Revised 2000*. London: Home Office, National Probation Service.

Hood, C., Scott, C., James, O., Jones, G. and Travers, T. (1999) *Regulation Inside Government*. Oxford: Oxford University Press.

Hough, M., Jacobson, J. and Millie, A. (2003) *The Decision to Imprison: Sentencing and the Prison Population*. London: Prison Reform Trust.

Institute for Public Policy Research (2000) *Delivery Change, Supporting Change*. London: IPPR.

Liebling, A. and Hancock, N. (2003) 'Truth, Independence and Effectiveness in Prison Inquiries', in G. Gilligan and J. Pratt (eds), *Crime, Truth and Justice: Official Inquiry, Discourse, Knowledge*. Cullompton: Willan.

Lipsey, M.W. (1995) 'What do we learn from 400 studies on the effectiveness of treatment with juvenile delinquents?', in J. McGuire (ed.), *What Works: Reducing Re-offending: Guidelines from Research and Practice*. Chichester: Wiley.

Local Government Association (2001) *An Inspector Calls: LGA Survey on Inspection in Local Government*, LGA Briefing 234. London: Local Government Association.

McGuire, J. (ed.) (1995) *What Works: Reducing Re-offending: Guidelines from Research and Practice*. Chichester: Wiley.

McGuire, J. (ed.) (2002) *Offender Rehabilitation and Treatment: Effective Programmes and Policies to Reduce Re-offending*. Chichester: Wiley.

McGuire, J. (2003) 'The way ahead: learning from experience', in *Promoting the Practitioner's Experience: Report of Proceedings: What Works Conference*, Manchester, March 2003. London: National Probation Service.

McLaughlin, E. (2002) '"Same bed, different dreams": post-modern reflections on crime prevention and community safety', in G. Hughes and A. Edwards (eds), *Crime Control and Community: The New Politics of Public Safety*. Cullompton: Willan.

McWilliams, W. (1990) 'Probation practice and the Management Ideal', *Probation Journal*, 37, 60–7.

McWilliams, W. and Pease, K. (1990) 'Probation practice and an end to punishment', *Howard Journal*, 29, 14–24.

Maruna, S. (2000) *Making Good*. Washington, DC: American Psychological Association.

May, C. and Wadwell, J. (2001) *Enforcing Community Penalties: The Relationship between Enforcement and Reconviction*, Findings 155. London: Home Office, Research, Development and Statistics Directorate.

Mordaunt, E. (1999) 'Independent inspection: a fallacy that some inspectorates like to tell', *British Educational Research Association Annual Conference*, University of Sussex, Brighton.

Morgan, R. (2003a) 'The future of probation inspection', *Howard Journal*, 43 (1), 79–92.

Morgan, R. (2003b) 'Thinking about the demand for probation services', *Probation Journal*, 50 (1), 7–19.

Office of Public Services Reform (2003a) *Inspecting for Improvement: Developing a Customer Focused Approach*. London: Cabinet Office.

Office of Public Services Reform (2003b) *The Government's Policy on Inspection of Public Services*. London: Cabinet Office.

Roberts, J.V. and Hough, M. (eds) (2003) *Changing Attitudes to Punishment – Public Opinion, Crime and Justice*. Cullompton: Willan.

Roberts, J.V., Stalans, L.J., Indermauer, D. and Hough, M. (2003) *Penal Populism and Public Opinion: Lessons from Five Countries*. Oxford: Oxford University Press.

Youth Justice Board (2003) *Annual Review 2002–3: Gaining Ground in the Community*. London: YJB.

Index

ABE (Adult Basic Education)
programme 97, 116
accommodation 20
and accessing basic skills
provision 125
as an issue covered with case
managers 154t
effect on motivation 150
and ISSP 167
risk/need assessment of 53, 54t,
57t
and supervision planning 60
accreditation 15
changes in the basis for 247
channeling of creativity through
26
of ECP 211, 247
of offending behaviour
programmes 18
accreditation of skills through
community service 201–2
project outcomes 210
accredited programmes 243
NPD's quality assurance and
control system 245–6
and OASys 60
and the Prison Service 135
and the YJB 7, 34

see also cognitive behavioural
programmes; ECP
ACE 3, 49–50, 66
adaptation for young offenders 71
and measurement of change 62–3
and need assessment 52–5
depth of coverage 52–3, 55
reliability 53
validity 53–5
and offender self-assessment 61,
62f
as a reconviction predictor 56–8
and risk of serious harm
assessment 58
use for supervision planning and
targeting interventions 55, 59,
60
value for researchers 65–6
value to managers 64–5
Addressing Substance Related
Offending (ASRO) 18–19
Adult Basic Education (ABE)
programme 97, 116
Adult Literacy and Numeracy
Curricula 99
Advanced Modern Apprenticeships
38
'after-care' *see* resettlement

age of offenders, effect on basic skills
needs and unemployment 120
alcohol abuse
and accessing basic skills
provision 126
effect on motivation 150
and ISSP 167
risk/need assessment of 54t, 56,
57t
and supervision planning 60, 127
and unemployment 121
Anti-Social Behaviour Bill 43
approved premises 4, 20
Arts Enrichment strand of the PLUS
strategy 102–3
assessment
inspection of 242
of young offenders 70–85
see also need assessment; risk
assessment; self-assessment
Assessment, Case Management and
Evaluation see ACE
assessment centres for programme
tutors 22
assessment tools 7
in probation 46–67
development 46–51
future 67
validity and value 52–66
see also OASys (Offender
Assessment System)
Asset 7, 34, 37, 65, 70–85
achievement of goals 79–80
completion rates 73–4
components 71–2
design and development 70–1
future 83–5
impact on practice and
performance 80–3
development of knowledge
base 80–1
risk and contextualisation 58,
82–3
routinisation and professional
judgement 81–2

opinions about 72–3
use 73–9
explanation of conclusions 76–7
intervention planning 77–8
measurement of change over
time 76
open and transparent practice
78
predictive accuracy 74–5
reliability 75–6
resource management 78–9
Association of Chief Officers of
Probation (ACOP) 11
attendance at school see school
attendance
attrition rates 24
for the Basic Skills Pathfinder
123–8
for the Employment Pathfinder
123–4
and motivational interviewing
192–3
for Reasoning and Rehabilitation
(R&R) and Enhanced Thinking
Skills (ETS) 141
for the Think First programme
144–5, 148–9
see also completion rates

basic skills 19
and employment 118–22, 129–30
associated offender
characteristics 120–2
interventions 116–18
design 99–100
national strategy 129
and offenders 114–15, 118–19, 129
see also education
Basic Skills Pathfinder 8, 109
attrition 123–8, 130
implications 128
reasons 125–8
evaluation 109–10, 111–12
implementation failure 130
primary objective 111

selection criteria 112, 122–4
behaviour
  as an indicator of motivation 149
  impact of schools on 93–4
  see also criminal behaviour
breaching
  effect of pro-social modelling
    203–4
  of intensive community
    programmes 162–3
'breadth principle' see multi-modal
  approach
burglaries 20, 91, 161

Cambridge-Somerville Study 187–8
'capital' 200
  see also 'human capital'; social
    capital
car thefts 91
Carter Report (2004) 21, 25, 27
case management 8, 16f, 17, 23
  effect on accessing of basic skills
    provision 127
  single model 25
  in the Think First programme
    153–5
Case Recording and Management
  System (CRAMS) 65
casework 8, 23
  evidence against 184
  and IMPACT 189
  see also social casework
'casework relationship' 183
'catch-all' approach to selection
  122–3
  reasons for attrition 124–8
Children and Young Persons Act
  (1933) 30
Childrens Act (1989) 30
citizenship 199–201
  and community service 201–3
civic associational life 200
cognitive behavioural programmes
  3–4, 7–8, 18–19
  evaluation of prison-based 135–42

evaluation of probation-based
  143–55
  see also multi-modal cognitive
    behavioural approach
Cognitive Centre Foundation (CCF)
  49, 65
'cognitive counselling' 185
Combination Orders 160
community interventions 2–3, 9, 30
  see also intensive community
    programmes
community punishment see ECP
  (Enhanced Community
  Punishment)
Community Punishment Orders
  (CPOs) 203, 243
  reconviction rates 26
Community Rehabilitation Orders
  (CROs) 164, 203
community sentences 160
  and desistance 189
  implications of models of
    recidivism 228–31
  use of ISSP 164
community service 9, 198–213
  effect on citizenship 201–3
  and pro-social modelling (PSM)
    204–6
    pilot scheme 206–8
  training offenders in employment-
    related skills 201–2
  women and 210–11
Community Service (CS) Pathfinder
  9, 198
  pro-social modelling (PSM) as a
    strand 208–11
community surveillance 168–9, 170
completion rates 24
  for Asset 73–4
  for ISSP 173–4
  see also attrition rates
compliance, sources of 150
control theory 220
Correctional Services Accreditation
  Panel (CSAP) 134, 243

see also Joint Accreditation Panel
Correctional Services Review 19
counselling *see* individual
    counselling
court orders in the youth justice
    system 30–1
    see also DTOs
CRAMS (Case Recording and
    Management System) 65
crime
    theories of desistance from 9,
        222–3
    see also offending; property crime;
        street crime
Crime and Disorder Act (1998) 4
    reforms to the youth justice
        system 30–1
Crime Pics II questionnaire 173, 224
Crime Reduction Programme 3, 9, 16,
    217
criminal behaviour
    desistance from 156–7, 227–8
    effect of ISSP 167, 168t, 171, 172–3
    and interpersonal processes 182
    see also offending
criminal careers 145, 150
    and risk/need assessment 54t, 57t
criminal damage 91
Criminal Justice Act (1982) 160
Criminal Justice Act (1991) 160, 201,
    218, 219
Criminal Justice Act (2003) 27, 43, 213
Criminal Justice and Court Services
    Act (2000) 213n
Criminal Justice and Police Act
    (2001) 164
'criminal recidivism process' 227–8
criminogenic needs 47, 66
    assessment 52–5
    reconviction and 56–8
    see also need assessment
'criteria-based' approach to selection
    122, 123
custody
    alternatives to 231

impact of ISSP 161–2, 164–5
impact of 172
negative impact on education
    91–2
    countering 95–6
    see also Juvenile Secure Estate;
        prisons
custody-plus sentences 27

DATs (Drug Action Teams) 20
debts *see* financial management
desistance counselling 182
desistance research 190–1
detachment from mainstream
    education 89–91
Detention and Training Orders *see*
    DTOs
development fund of the YJB 32
'direct exchange relationship' 205
Discharged Prisoners' Aid Societies
    221
'disclosure effects' 53, 62–3
drink problems *see* alcohol abuse
'drop-out' rates *see* attrition rates
drug abuse
    and accessing basic skills
        provision 125–6
    effect on motivation 150
    and ISSP 167
    and reconviction 116, 122
    risk/need assessment of 53, 54t,
        56, 57t
    and supervision planning 60, 127
    and unemployment 121, 122
drug testing 167
drug treatment 20
    see also substance misuse
        programmes
Drug Treatment and Testing Orders
    20, 22
DTOs 161, 162
    and educational work 92, 95, 104

ECP 9, 16, 17, 21–2, 211–12
    accreditation 211, 247

education
    and effective practice principles 94
    and employability 115
    and ISSP 167, 168t
    offending and 89–94
    risk/need assessment of 54t, 57t
    see also basic skills; learning
educational interventions 88–106
    design of basic skills interventions
        99–100
    effect of motivation and attitudes
        to learning 100–3
    effect on recidivism 96–7
    features of successful programmes
        97–9
    infrastructure for effective
        delivery 103–5
Effective Practice In-service Training
    (INSET) pack 38
Effective Practice Initiative 3, 6, 14–16,
    110–11
Effective Practice and Quality
    Assurance strategy *see* EPQA
    strategy
effective practice in the youth justice
    system 6–7, 29–44
    comparisons with prison and
        probation services 34
    development 31–5
    implementation 35–9
        guidance 35–7
        quality assurance 38–9, 43
        training 37–8, 43
    research base 39–42, 43
Effective Supervision Inspection
    (ESI) 239–40
EFQM (European Foundation for
    Quality Model) 24
electronic information systems
    and changes to *Asset* 84
    promotion by the YJB 7
    see also eOASys
electronic monitoring 168–9
emotional well-being *see* mental
    health

empathy 184
employment 19–20, 119
    as an issue covered with case
        managers 154t
    and basic skills 118–22, 129–30
        associated offender
            characteristics 120–2
    interventions to improve 116–18
    and levels of crime 201
    and offenders 115–16
    risk/need assessment of 54t, 57t
employment history and offender
    characteristics 121
Employment Pathfinder Phase I 8,
    109
    attrition 123–4
    design failure 130
    evaluation 109–10, 112–13
    primary objective 112–13
    selection criteria 113, 122–4, 130
Employment Pathfinder Phase II 110,
    129
employment, training and education
    (ETE) schemes 8, 115
employment-related skills, training
    offenders in 201–2
enforcement of ISSP schemes
    162–3
Enhanced Community Punishment
    see ECP
Enhanced Thinking Skills (ETS)
    136–41
eOASys 17–18, 51, 65
EPQA strategy 33–4
    implementation 35–9
ESI (Effective Supervision
    Inspection) 239–40
ETE (employment, training and
    education) schemes 8, 115
ethnic minority offenders
    in the Community Service (CS)
        Pathfinder projects 210
    data from *Asset* 74, 80, 81, 84
    and the Employment Pathfinder
        113

European Foundation for Quality
Model (EFQM) 24
evaluation research 10–11, 156
delays in release 6, 24–5
into educational interventions
99–100, 105–6
YJB strategy 32–3, 39–42, 43
see also knowledge base
Evidence Based Practice: A Guide to
Effective Practice 3
evidence boxes in Asset 76–7
evidence-based inspection 10,
234–49
good practice 246–8
evidence-based practice 1–11
challenges and limits 10–11
good practice 246–8
in the NPS 14–27
change programme 22–6
future developments 27
progress 17–22
success 26–7
research see evaluation research
exclusions from school 89–91,
114

families
as an issue covered with case
managers 154t
effect on anti-social behaviour
156–7
engagement with 34
see also Parenting Programmes;
parents
family literacy programmes 102
family work 186
effectiveness 63t
in ISSP 167, 168t, 173
female offenders see women
offenders
final warnings 30
financial management, risk/need
assessment of 53, 54t, 57t
'FOR-a-change' 225
funding by the YJB 32

gender
and the Community Service (CS)
Pathfinder projects 210–11
provision of data through Asset 74,
80, 84
and unemployment 121
group work 16, 185, 191, 193
effectiveness 63

health
inclusion in supervision plans 127
risk/need assessment of 54t, 57t
see also mental health
health care resources, access to 82
high-risk offenders
and public protection 21
targeting by ISSP 164–5, 170
see also risk of reconviction status
'high-tariff' Intermediate Treatment
(IT) projects 160
effect on recidivism 169
and reduction in custody rates 165
Hirschi's (1969) control theory 220
HMIP (Her Majesty's Inspectorate of
Probation) 238, 249
adequacy of core evidence 242–4
inspection methodology 239–40
omissions 240–2
quality assurance and data
reliability 244–6
Home Office Research Development
and Statistics Directorate (RDSD)
40
'human capital' 183, 200–1
Human Resources and Learning
strategy (YJB) 96, 98
human rights 199

ICCP (Intensive Control and Change
Programme) 8, 35, 161, 247
IMPACT 160, 188–9
effect on recidivism 169
outcome criteria 171
implicit theories of crime 9, 222–3
improvement initiatives 25

inclusion *see* social reintegration
individual casework 184
individual counselling 167, 184–5,
    187–8, 192, 193
    effectiveness 63t
    see also 'non-directive' counselling
individual treatment by probation
    officers 188
'individual work' *see* one-to-one
    practice
inspection, evidence-based *see*
    evidence-based inspection
inspectorates
    functions 236–8
    operational independence 234–6
    see also HMIP (Her Majesty's
        Inspectorate of Probation)
integration
    of prison and probation
        programmes 18–19
    of the Prison and the Probation
        Service 4, 5
    of youth justice services and
        probation work 4–5
    see also multi-agency work;
        partnerships; reintegration
intensive community programmes 8,
    174
    elements for success 172–4
    history 159–61
    levels of breach 162–3
    programme content 166
    reductions in recidivism 169–70
    see also IMPACT; Prolific Offender
        Projects
Intensive Control and Change
    Programme (ICCP) 8, 35, 161,
    247
Intensive Matched Probation and
    After-Care Treatment *see* IMPACT
Intensive Supervision Programme
    (US) *see* US Intensive Supervision
    Programme
Intensive Supervision and
    Surveillance Orders (ISSOs) 161–2

Intensive Supervision and
    Surveillance Programmes *see* ISSP
Intermediate Treatment (IT) projects
    see 'high-tariff Intermediate
    Treatment (IT) projects
interpersonal skills training for
    offenders 167, 168t
interpersonal work 8–9, 181, 182–4
    evidence base 191–3
interventions
    attrition and completion rates 24
    incorporation of *Asset* into
        planning 77–8
    inspection of 242–3
    relationship between
        measurement of change and 63
    targeting 59–61
    see also basic skills and
        employment interventions;
        community interventions;
        educational interventions;
        probation interventions;
        programmes
intrinsic motivation 182
ISP (US) *see* US Intensive Supervision
    Programme
ISSOs (Intensive Supervision and
    Surveillance Orders) 161–2
ISSP 8, 31, 159–75, 248
    aims and objectives 34–5, 161–3
    compatibility 162–3
    and custody rates 163–6
    educational component 95
    long-term impact 174
    measurement of outcomes 169–72
    and 'net-widening' 165–6
    personal factors influencing
        completion 172–4
    piloting 35
    programme content 166–9
IT (Intermediate Treatment) projects
    see 'hi-tariff' Intermediate
    Treatment (IT) projects

'jeopardy' 162

Job Centre Plus 19–20
Joining Forces to Protect the Public
    219
Joint Accreditation Panel 15, 18
    see also Correctional Services
        Accreditation Panel (CSAP)
'just deserts' paradigm 1
'justice by geography' 15, 18
Juvenile Secure Estate
    and effective practice 36–7
    targets for education and training
        95–6
    transfer of *Asset* information to 78

Key Elements of Effective Practice 36–7,
    43
    evidence base 40–1, 42
    quality assurance process 38–9
    training for implementation 37–8
knowledge base 1
    and *Asset* 80–1
    for basic skills interventions
        99–100
    for interpersonal work 191–3
    and the YJB 39–42, 43
    see also evaluation research

LASCHs (Local Authority Secure
    Children's Homes) 37
learning
    impact of custody 92
    motivation and attitudes to 100–3
    see also education
Learning and Skills Councils 19
Learning and Skills Strategy (YJB)
    94–6
lifers 21
literacy levels
    of adult offenders 114, 117, 118
        effective instructional
            techniques 100
    of young offenders 93, 95, 114
    see also family literacy
        programmes
Liverpool Desistance Study 228

Local Authority Secure Children's
    Homes (LASCHs) 37
long-term non-attendance at school
    89
low-risk offenders
    recidivism rates 229–30
    see also risk of reconviction status
LSI-R (Level of Service Inventory –
    Revised) 49, 66
    and measurement of change 62, 63
    as a reconviction predictor 56–8
    and risk of serious harm
        assessment 58
    use in risk assessment 55
    use for supervision planning and
        targeting interventions 60
    value for need assessment 52–5
        depth of coverage 52–3
        reliability 53
        validity 53–5
    value for researchers 65–6
    value to managers 64–5
    value to practitioners 64

Managing Offenders – Reducing Crime
    11
MAPPA (Multi-Agency Public
    Protection Panels) 21, 242
mental health
    and counselling 193
    and ISSP 167
    risk/need assessment of 53, 54t,
        56, 57t
    and supervision planning 60, 127
mentoring 181, 193
    and interpersonal processes 9
    in ISSP 167
    parallels with pro-social
        modelling (PSM) 204
meta-analysis 2
minority ethnic offenders *see* ethnic
    minority offenders
Misspent Youth 4, 30–1
Modern Apprenticeships 38
modernisation agenda 2

money problems *see* financial management
motivation of offenders
  as an issue covered by case managers 154t
  and attitudes to learning 100–3
  effect on accessing basic skills provision 126–7
  effect on attrition and completion of the Think First programme 149–50
  effect on ISSP 172–3
  see also intrinsic motivation
motivation of staff and accessing basic skills provision 127–8
motivational interviewing 9, 182, 191, 192–3
Multi-Agency Public Protection Panels (MAPPA) 21, 242
multi-agency work
  and effective practice 43
  in the National Probation Service 22
  with young offenders 31, 43
  see also partnerships
'multi-modal' approach 167, 186–7
  of ISSP 172
  of the YJB 34
multi-modal cognitive behavioural approach 187
'multi-systemic therapy' 186
multiple problems, effective strategies for 130–1, 167

'narratives of desistance' 228
National Offender Management Service (NOMS) 5, 25
National Probation Directorate *see* NPD
National Probation Service *see* NPS
National Qualifications Framework for youth justice services 37–8
National Specification for Learning and Skills for Young People on a Detention and Training Order 95

need assessment
  historical development 46–51
  and supervision planning 60
  value of assessment tools for 52–5
  see also risk/need assessment tools
need principle 47
'net-widening effect' 165–6
A New Choreography 4–5
New Labour government 3
new public management 2
No More Excuses 30
non-attendance at school *see* school attendance
'non-directive' counselling 186
'non-directive, psycho-dynamic therapy' 185–6
non-intervention 30
'non-treatment paradigm' 1–2
'nothing works' 1
NPD 238, 239
  analysis of performance data 244–5
  and effective practice 34
  quality assurance and control systems 245–6
NPS
  creation 6, 14, 17
  duties 238–9
  and evidence-based practice 14–27
    change programme 22–6
    future developments 27
    progress 17–22
    success 26–7
  and integration of services 4–5
numeracy levels
  of adult offenders 118
  of young offenders 93, 95

OASys (Offender Assessment System) 15–16, 17–18, 22, 50–1, 66, 67
  and measurement of change 62, 63
  and offender self-assessment 61
  as a predictor of reconviction 56–8

and risk of serious harm
assessment 58
and targeting interventions 60–1
use for supervision planning and
targeting interventions 59–61
value for need assessment 52–5
depth of coverage 52–3, 55
reliability 53
validity 53–5
value for researchers 65–6
value to practitioners 64
offenders
basic skills and employment
113–18
needs and associations 118–22,
129–30
motivation of *see* motivation of
offenders
self-assessment *see* self-assessment
by offenders
as victims 9, 222–3, 228
see also ethnic minority offenders;
high-risk offenders; low-risk
offenders; sex offenders;
women offenders; young
offenders
offender's responsibility model of
resettlement 9, 223
offending 66
attitudes to 173–4
and drug use 20
link between education and 89–94
and risk/need assessment 54t, 57t
theories of 9, 222–3
see also criminal behaviour
offending behaviour programmes
7–8, 18–19, 134–57
prison-based cognitive
behavioural programmes
135–42
probation-based cognitive
behavioural programmes
143–55
offending history *see* criminal careers
officers *see* probation officers

OGRS2 120
OGRS (Offender Group Reconviction
Scale) 48, 56, 59, 136
one-to-one practice 8–9, 180–94
evidence against 184–9
evidence base 191–3
supportive evidence 189–91
types 181–2
opportunity deficit model of
resettlement 9, 222–3
outcomes, inspection of 243–4
overcrowding in prisons 162

Parenting Programmes 33
parents 31
and *Asset* 83
and the YJB 36, 39, 43
see also families
partnerships and social reintegration
19–20
see also multi-agency work
PASRO (Prison Addressing
Substance Related Offending)
18–19
Pathfinder projects 3, 15, 16, 26
see also Basic Skills Pathfinder;
Community Service (CS)
Pathfinder; Employment
Pathfinder; Resettlement
Pathfinder
penal populism 248–9
performance management
and inspectorates 10, 238
NPS framework 23–5
'permanent campaigning' 234
permanent exclusions from school
89, 90
PLUS strategy 95, 99, 103
Arts Enrichment strand 102–3
community side 104
political agenda
effect on inspectorates 234
influence on the pace of change 26
and intensive community
programmes 162

see also New Labour government
populist punitiveness 248
Post-Release Employment Project (PREP) 97
Priestley One-to-One Programme 193
Principles of Alphabet computer-assisted programme 100–1
Prison Addressing Substance Related Offending (PASRO) 18–19
Prison Service
    induction training for officers 37
    integration with the Probation Service 4, 5
    screening of prisoners for basic needs 114
    see also Juvenile Secure Estate
prison-based cognitive behavioural programmes 135–42
prisoners *see* lifers; short-term prisoners
prisons
    effect on educational programmes 100–2, 103–5
    effects of 221
    overcrowding 162
    reduction in use 231
    running programmes 'through the gate' 18–19, 224, 225t
    see also custody
probation interventions for basic skills and employment needs 109–31
probation officers
    and changing practice 22–3
    types of involvement with offenders 188
probation orders *see* Community Rehabilitation Orders (CROs)
probation service *see* NPS
Probation Studies Unit (PSU) 5, 65, 71
probation-based cognitive behavioural programmes 143–55
probation-led projects 9, 218

comparison with voluntary-organisation-led projects 225–6
Professional Certificate in Effective Practice (Youth Justice) 38, 96
programmes
    assessment centres for tutors 22
    see also cognitive behavioural programmes; family literacy programmes; intensive community programmes; interventions; ISSP; offending behaviour programmes; substance misuse programmes
Prolific Offender Projects 161
    evaluation 170
property crime 161
    see also burglaries
pro-social modelling (PSM) 20, 186–7, 190
    as a Community Service (CS) Pathfinder strand 208–11
    consistency 212
    definition 204
    piloting 206–8
    and social responsibility 203–6
prostitution 29
PSOs (probation service officers) 22–3
public protection 21
punishment 221
    community service as 9, 201, 205, 212
    see also ECP; populist punitiveness
'punishments in the community' 1

qualifications
    effect on basic skills needs and unemployment 120
    for youth justice practitioners 37–8
quality assurance
    and data reliability 244–6
    and the YJB 7, 38–9, 43
    see also EPQA strategy
Quality Assurance Framework 38

random drug testing 167
RDSD (Research Development and Statistics Directorate) 40
reading instruction for adults 100
Reasoning and Rehabilitation (R&R) 136–41
recidivism 1
  effect of ISSP 169–70
  models 227–8
    implications for community sentences 228–31
    and participation in education 96–7, 116
reconviction predictors 56–8
  accuracy of *Asset* 74–5
reconviction rates
  effect of community service 202–3
  effect of ISSP 170
  effect of prison cognitive behavioural programmes 136–41
    reasons 141–2
  effect of pro-social modelling (PSM) 203–4
  effect of the Think First programme 145–9
    post-group sessions 152–3
    pre-group sessions 152
    role of case managers 153, 154
  and evidence-based practice 26–7
  and unemployment 115–16
  see also risk of reconviction status
Regional What Works groups 24
rehabilitation 2, 3
  community service and 9, 203, 212
  as a component of intensive community programmes 170
  effect of continuity in resettlement services 224
  and the 'risk principle' 230
  of young offenders 93
  see also state-obligated rehabilitation
reintegration 16f, 220
  see also social reintegration

relationship-based work *see* interpersonal work
relationships
  and community service 205
  influence on motivation 150
  and risk/need assessment 53, 54t, 57t
  see also families
reoffending rates *see* recidivism
reparation 31, 167
  through Community Service 212
reprimands 30
research base *see* knowledge base
Research Development and Statistics Directorate (RDSD) 40
resettlement 9, 217–31
  continuity 224, 225–6
  implicit criminologies 222–3
  meanings of 219–22
  reasons for 220–2
Resettlement Pathfinder 9, 217–18
  short-term outcomes 224–6
resource management
  and *Asset* 78–9
  matching service levels to risk 59
responsibility *see* offender's responsibility model of resettlement
restitution *see* reparation
restorative justice 5, 21
  evaluation 33
  and ISSP 167, 168t
Restorative Justice Programmes 32–3
rights of individuals 199
risk assessment
  historical development 46–51
  and LSI-R 55
  matching service levels to 59
'risk classification' 170
risk management plans 21
'risk principle' 59, 230
risk of reconviction status
  assessment tools as predictors 55–8
  use of *Asset* 82–3

effect on accessing basic skills provision 126
effect on basic skills needs and unemployment 120–1
effect on recidivism in intensive supervision programs 170
of participants in prison-based cognitive behavioural programmes 141
see also high-risk offenders; low-risk offenders
risk of serious harm
assessment tools as predictors 58–9
use of *Asset* 71, 82–3
risk/need assessment tools 48–67
definition 48
future 67
matching service levels to risk 59
and measurement of change 62–3
and offender engagement 61–2
as predictors of risk of harm 58–9
as reconviction predictors 56–8
types 48–51
value as need assessments 52–5
value for researchers 65–6
value for supervision planning and targeting interventions 59–61
value to managers 64–5
value to practitioners 64
see also Asset
robberies 91, 164

school attendance
effect on basic skills needs and unemployment 120
link with offending 89–91, 114
schools
impact on behaviour 93–4
reintegration of offenders 91, 92
Secure Estate *see* Juvenile Secure Estate
Secure Learning Centres 95
Secure Training Centres (STCs) 37

self-assessment by offenders 61–2
in *Asset* 71, 83
sex offenders, programmes for 15, 16
shoplifting 20
short-term prisoners
and the custody-plus sentence 27
post release services 9, 218
and resettlement problems 227, 231
significant others *see* relationships
'silting up' of probation caseloads 230
situational treatment by probation officers 188
skills accreditation through community service 201–2
project outcomes 210
Skills for Life strategy 95, 99
social capital 19, 183, 200–1
access through community service 199
social casework 183
social cognitive theory 182
social reintegration 17
and partnerships 19–20
social responsibility, effect of pro-social modeling (PSM) 203–6
Springboard probation ETE scheme 115, 117
'stable learning platforms' 104
state-obligated rehabilitation 221–2
Statement of National Operations and Purpose (SNOP) 2
STCs (Secure Training Centres) 37
Straight Thinking on Probation (STOP) 135
street crime 164
substance abuse
as an issue covered with case managers 154t
see also alcohol abuse; drug abuse
substance misuse programmes 16, 18–19
supervision
of low-risk offenders 230

and 'social capital' 19
  see also Effective Supervision
    Inspection (ESI); ISSP
Supervision Orders 160
  and the use of ISSP 164
supervision planning
  and ACE 55
  inclusion of basic skills needs 127
  and risk/need assessment tools
    59–61
surveillance 168–9, 170
symbolic interactionism 182

tagging 168–9
theft 161
  see also burglaries; car theft;
    robberies
theories of crime 9, 222–3
Think First programme 7–8, 15,
  143–55
  attrition and programme
    attendance 144–5, 148–9
  effect of contact with case
    managers 153–4
  indicators of probability of
    non-completion 152
  offender factors 149–50
  core group work programme 150–
    2
  offender satisfaction 151–2
  post-group sessions 152–3
  pre-group sessions and early
    identification 152
  probation factors 154–5
  prospective evaluation 143–4
  reconviction rates 145–9
    effect of completion in different
      risk categories 147–8
  role of case managers 153–5
'through-care' see resettlement
Towards Evidence-Based Practice in
  Probation and Youth Justice 5
training
  and ISSP 167, 168t
  for probation staff 22–3

for youth justice practitioners
  37–8, 43
truancy 89, 90–1, 114

underachievement in education
  92–4
Underdown report (1998) 3, 6, 14–15
unemployment
  offender characteristics associated
    with 120–2
  reconviction and 115–16
  relationship between basic skills
    needs and 119, 129–30
  see also employment
US Intensive Supervision
  Programme 160
  programme content 166, 167
  targeting 163

values 220
victims 21
  offenders as 9, 222–3, 228
  reparation to 31, 167
  and Restorative Justice and
    Parenting Programmes 32–3
violence, prediction by risk/need
  tools 58, 59
violent offender programmes 18
voluntary after-care for short-term
  prisoners 9, 217–18, 226
voluntary befriending 9, 181
voluntary-organisation-led projects 9,
  218
  comparison with probation-led
    projects 225–6
volunteering 192, 193
  and citizenship 199
  and offender motivation 142

'What do YOU think?' (WDYT) self-
  assessment 71, 83
What Works movement 3, 10, 47
What Works strategy 2000 8, 16–17
  see also Regional What Works
    groups

women offenders
    and basic skills instruction 102
    and community service 210–11
    programmes for 15
    provision of data from *Asset* 80
    and unemployment 121

YJB
    effective practice and quality
        assurance 6–7, 33–5
        implementation 35–9, 44
    evaluation strategy 32–3, 40–2, 43
    function 31
    Human Resources and Learning
        strategy 96, 98
    Learning and Skills Strategy
        94–6
    relationship with the NPS 5

research base 39–42, 43
view of *Asset* 72
YOTs (Youth Offending Teams) 7, 31,
    91
    protocols for access to education
        and training provision 95
young offenders
    assessment 70–85
    educational interventions 88–106
    and ISSP 159–76
    and multi-agency work 31, 43
Youth Justice 2004 7
Youth Justice Board *see* YJB
youth justice system
    development 4, 30–1
    effective practice 6–7, 29–44
    integration with services for adult
        offenders 4–5